Recent Research in Psychology

To Christopher and Geoffrey

ACKNOWLEDGEMENTS

My deepest thanks go to the social psychologists who agreed to be interviewed for this project. Their kindness and cooperation is gratefully acknowledged.

I would also like to acknowledge the support of Sigma Xi, The Scientific Research Society for the grant-in-aide of research.

I am very grateful to Barbara Morris, Lorelei Sontag, and M. Brewster Smith for their thoughtful reading of earlier versions of this manuscript. Their comments were of enormous help.

Finally, I would like to thank Elliot Aronson for the enthusiasm he had for this project. He encouraged me to find out what I wanted to know about social psychology. This book is the result. As my friend and advisor, he taught me in the way I learn best and for that I am very grateful.

CONTENTS

INTRODUCTION: CREATIVITY IN A SOCIAL CONTEXT

There is a romantic myth that portrays the creative act as that of a solitary individual in a garret, a studio, or a laboratory, performing mysterious acts which bring about original and decidedly individual accomplishments. While this myth reflects some truth, the reality is that in both the arts and sciences, from the Renaissance guilds to contemporary research teams, people doing creative work have always been part of a complex network of friends, colleagues, peers, and mentors who contribute to the final form of any work.

Science is actually a highly social activity with teams of scientists building on work that has gone before and often in fierce competition with those currently working on similar problems. While science may begin with individual curiosity, its rewards include the recognition by colleagues and peers that mark creative contribution. Some (Kuhn, 1970; Campbell, 1979) argue that what is accepted as scientific knowledge itself is social in nature and that shifts occur when proponents of one theory argue its merits with supporters of an opposing theory. Campbell (1979) even argues that what becomes accepted as theory in science is often mediated by such social factors as recruitment of scientists to that theory. This recruitment takes place through the impersonal vehicle of journals as well as through the personal vehicle of training students.

Partly because of the myth that creation is the act of an isolated individual, there is a vast literature on the psychological study of creativity that is almost wholly concerned with the creative individual. The aptitudes, abilities and personality characteristics of "the creative person" have been studied and documented extensively and it is possible to point to certain clusters of traits that characterize creative people (Crutchfield, 1961; Gough, 1961; Helson, 1961; MacKinnon, 1962).

However, simply because a person *can* be creative doesn't guarantee that he or she *will* be creative. Given the well documented power of situations to shape behavior, it might be useful to investigate environments in which very creative people have been known to develop and to function creatively. One such environment was The Research Center for Group Dynamics established by Kurt Lewin at MIT in 1945.

The Research Center for Group Dynamics:

In the fall of 1945, a group of psychologists assembled in Cambridge, Massachusetts for the purpose of establishing a new research center. This new center, to be devoted to the study of group processes, was a graduate training program affiliated with MIT and under the direction of one of the most influential and creative thinkers in American Psychology - Kurt Lewin.

Kurt Lewin's Research Center for Group Dynamics was at MIT for only three years but it has been called "The crowning glory of his career in the United States (Mandler & Mandler, 1969 p. 403)." The faculty who joined Lewin at MIT, Dorwin Cartwright, Leon Festinger, Ronald Lippitt and Marian Radke, came because they had worked with Lewin at Iowa before the war. The students were young, talented men who came together to study something that had never been studied before scientifically - group dynamics. They came because each of them had somehow encountered Lewin's ideas, or Lewin himself, and had the imagination to be impressed with what he had to offer. All had participated in some way in the war effort and were older and more experienced than traditional graduate students. Indeed, the age gap between faculty and students was remarkably narrow. Many of these students had planned to go on for graduate study at Yale but chose instead to take a chance on this new venture offered by Kurt Lewin.

KURT LEWIN

Kurt Lewin was born in 1890 an area of Prussia that is now part of Poland. He earned his doctorate under Carl Stumpf at the University of Berlin in 1916. After serving in the German Army during World War I, Lewin returned to the academic world. An appointment to the Psychological Institute in 1921 brought him into close association with the Gestalt psychologists Koehler and Wertheimer. He was particularly associated with Koehler, who had succeeded Stumpf as director of the Institute. Lewin's position was that of untenured faculty member at the Institute.

During the twenties Lewin began to attract students from the United States, which was at that time something of a scientific backwater. Thus, according to Mandler (1969), "the groundwork was laid for the influence of the most important immigrant to remodel American psychology in the subsequent thirty years (p. 400)."

In 1929 Lewin presented at the Yale meeting of the International Congress of Psychology, where he made an enormous impression with movies that demonstrated his ideas. In 1932 he was invited by Lewis Terman for a six-month visit to Stanford. While he was returning to Berlin from the stay in California, Hitler came to power in Germany. Once back in Germany, Lewin resigned his position at the Institute and in 1933 emigrated to the United States. In a recently published letter (Lewin, 1986), written in 1933 to Wolfgang Koehler, Lewin set out his reasons for leaving Germany. In this letter, Lewin wrote movingly of his internal conflict about his relationship to Germany. With the same kind of analytical curiosity he brought to scientific questions. Lewin traced his life-long experiences with anti-Semitism in Germany and described his feelings about the growing repression he saw around him. His conclusion was that his love of German science notwithstanding, he must leave. From the time of his emigration until his death in 1947, Lewin continued to raise money in support of a psychological institute at the Hebrew University in Jerusalem. Many attribute the shift of his interest from individual dynamic processes to group processes, to his experiences during this period.

Lewin arrived in the United States during the darkest part of the depression. His first position was in the School of Home Economics at Cornell where he was given a two year appointment supported by a grant from the Emergency Committee on Displaced Scholars. There he worked in the nursery school on a series of studies concerning social pressure on eating habits in children. When this appointment ended in 1935, he visited Palestine and then was offered an appointment at the Iowa Child Welfare Research Station at the University of Iowa.

Lewin moved to Iowa in 1935. His position was funded by a grant from the Rockefeller Fund's General Education Board. The appointment was for three years with the possibility of renewal. He remained at Iowa nine years before establishing the Research Center for Group Dynamics at MIT during the closing months of World War II.

Kurt Lewin never held a tenured academic appointment in any university. Yet, each place he worked, students gathered around him - students who changed the face of psychology. He contributed to all aspects of the field: He was a theoretician, an innovative experimentalist, an early proponent of action research, initiator of the exploration of interpersonal dynamics in small groups - and he trained an enormously successful group of researchers in social psychology.

LEWIN'S THEORY AND METHOD

Kurt Lewin viewed his Field Theory not as a formal theory so much as an approach to conceptualization (Cartwright, 1959; de Rivera, 1976) or a point of view (Jones, 1985). In the theoretical style of the times, Lewin was interested in establishing general laws in psychology. His conceptual formulations were shaped into a system designed to lead to understanding the dynamic laws of behavior. As a gestalt psychologist, Lewin began his career interested in learning and perception. He gradually incorporated motivational factors into his system, making him what Jones (1985) called a "hot gestaltist." This interdependence of motivation with perception and learning is what Lewin first called the life space. This concept includes one most important component - the situational field as it is experienced by the individual. Later, Lewin expanded the concept to incorporate situational factors including objective features of the environment as well as actions of other people. But the meaning for behavior of these features of the environment, was seen as a function of the needs of the individual.

Because Field Theory is basically a motivational theory, the individual is seen as a system under tension. Therefore, according to Lewin psychic tensions operating in a psychological field must be examined, in order to understand behavior. The important concepts in Lewin's motivational system were: need, tension, valence, force and energy. These were represented graphically by using a form of geometry known as Topology.

Lewin used Topology to represent the structure of the psychological field and the forces operating in it. It provided a visual language with which to communicate about Field Theory concepts. The person in a field was represented by a "Jordan curve," which is an oval. Everything inside the curve represents those aspects of the person and the environment that would determine behavior. The area outside the curve represents the nonpsychological world. Lewin's early students referred to these curves as eggs, his later students called them bathtubs.

In an important paper, "The Conflict between Aristotelian and Galilean Modes of Thought in Psychology" (Lewin, 1935), Lewin took a step toward devising some general psychological laws. He described a fundamental change in scientific thinking brought about by Galileo. He noted that in the earlier, Aristotelian mode of thought (represented by associationism in psychology), causes are to be found in the properties of occurrences themselves. Understanding phenomena comes about by classifying cases in some way and then studying great numbers of similar cases. Therefore, one then would predict behavior based on the frequency of such behavior in the past. In contrast, in the Galilean or relational mode of thought, causes are sought in the constellation in which the occurrence takes place. It is enough to understand the single case - if it is understood in its entirety. According to Lewin, behavior can be understood only if all the forces operating at the time are known. That is, in order to understand behavior, it is more useful to know all of the forces operating in a given situation at a specific time than to know the frequency of such behavior in the past.

Since behavior is caused by forces operating in the present, changing contemporaneous forces is an effective way to bring about change in behavior. This ahistorical character of Lewin's position allows for effective intervention in an ongoing system once the dynamics of the immediate situation are understood. This insight paved the way for Action Research in the community, which became the focus of work at The Research Center for Group Dynamics. But there was a second benefit emerging from this position. If behavior can best be understood by understanding the forces operating in a given situation, then the best way to understand those forces, and therefore behavior, is to create that situation under controlled conditions. By carefully changing one aspect of that controlled situation, the dynamics operating can begin to be understood. This conceptualization led to experimentation with complex social phenomena in the laboratory and in the field.

Lewin's distinction between phenotypic and genotypic description allowed construction of appropriate variables for study in the laboratory. Genotypic description refers to the underlying dynamics of a situation and phenotypic description refers to experience expressed in the ordinary language of phenomena. Therefore, a boy wanting a bicycle can be understood genotypically in Lewins terms as: there is a vector toward a goal in the boy's psychological field. A specific boy's desire for a particular object, described in everyday language, has been abstracted and understood as a system in tension toward a goal. Since there are many phenotypic situations that can be understood as a system in tension toward a goal, Lewin and his students were able to construct a variety of phenotypic situations (experiments) to test some of the genotypes (dynamics) in which he was interested. This idea guided research on such phenomena as the power of unfinished tasks (Ovsiankina, 1928; Zeigarnik, 1927), satiation (Karsten, 1928), level of aspiration (Hoppe, 1930; Lewin, Dembo, Festinger & Sears, 1944), substitution (Lissner, 1935; Mahler, 1933), anger (Dembo, 1931), regression (Barker, Dembo & Lewin, 1941) and group decision (Lewin, 1947b).

These concepts, along with his insistence on the importance of attending to what the situation means to the individual, led to a particular style of experimentation which Lewin developed and his student Leon Festinger refined and polished. Lewin was a master at transposing a life problem into experimental form. Great care was taken to retain the essence of a question as it was translated into an experimental variable. It was this ability to link theory with data that Leon Festinger (1980) pointed to as one of Lewin's greatest talents.

Action Research and Group Dynamics:

In addition to the experimental test of his theoretical formulations, Lewin was interested in the development of theory useful for solving social problems. Lewin's statement, "There is nothing so practical as a good theory," is so widely quoted that it is nearly a cliche. It is a statement about the interdependence of theory and practice. He was attempting to extend his field theory to take into account and to influence the broad social determinants of behavior. This interest developed after his emigration to the United States in 1933. Some observers (Cartwright, 1978) believe the situation in

Europe which led to his leaving Germany, and the differences he encountered between the United States and Germany once he arrived here, are responsible for this broadening of his interest. It was at this point that Lewin truly became a social psychologist.

Dorwin Cartwright (1978) has written that for Lewin "there was nothing so theoretical as a good practical problem (p. 178.)" The testing of practical theories was called Action Research. According to Cook (1984), this method was a three-step process consisting of program planning, execution, and program evaluation or factfinding in real-life settings. Results from this process were then used in the next cycle of program planning. One key component in Action Research is participation of the subject - according to Lewin's theory, the situation as it exists for the subject must be taken into account. This approach led to studies in both industry and community affairs conducted by two organizations set up specifically for that purpose immediately following World War II.

The Research Center for Group Dynamics and The Committee for Community Interrelations: Lewin's Theory and Practice:

The Research Center for Group Dynamics at MIT was established with three fundamental objectives (Lewin, 1945). According to Cartwright (1959), these objectives were to develop a scientific understanding of the functioning of groups, to bridge the gap between social science knowledge and practice, and finally to establish a program offering a Ph.D. in group psychology. A flier was printed and circulated in order to recruit students. It said in part:

> The Research Center offers a Ph.D. in Group Psychology. Its training is designed to educate research workers in theoretical and applied fields of group life and to assist in training practitioners. The student will have an opportunity for field work in industry, in the community and in other aspects of group life.

> In research, the main task of the Center is the development of scientific methods of studying and changing group life and the development of concepts and theories of Group Dynamics. Main areas of investigation are to be: industry, minority problems, and the relation between economics and culture.
>
> The Center has associated itself with a number of "field cooperators" in these areas; that is, with organizations of different types which are ready to cooperate in field experiments, and which offer to students occasions for field work. A number of Fellowships and Research Assistantships are available to graduate students. The staff of the Center comprises at present the following persons some of who are, however, still occupied with army or government work: John Arsenian, Dorwin Cartwright, Leon Festinger, Charles Hendry, Ronald Lippitt, Marian Radke and Kurt Lewin (Lewin, 1945, p. 135).

During the three years they were in residence at MIT, research was designed and carried out on such issues as leadership (Lippitt & French, 1948), group cohesiveness (Back, 1951; Thibaut, 1950), group productivity (French, 1950), the effects of group membership on it's members (Schachter, 1951), cooperation and competition (Deutsch, 1949), intergroup relations (Lippitt & Radke, 1946), communication and the spread of influence within groups (Festinger, Schachter & Back, 1950; Festinger & Thibaut, 1951) and social perception (Kelley 1950; Pepitone, 1950). Many of these studies were doctoral dissertations.

Concurrent with the founding of The Research Center for Group Dynamics was the establishment of the Commission for Community Interrelations (CCI) for the American Jewish Congress in New York. According to Marrow (1969), it was Lewin's hope that these two organizations would work together to combine scientific study with Action Research in an effort to answer questions about human affairs - particularly those regarding prejudice. The Research Center for Group Dynamics at MIT was seen as the research component sponsoring laboratory and field experiments designed to answer questions about basic group processes and how to bring about change in group life. CCI was designed to explore the roots of prejudice through Action Research in the community. The origin of Lewin's interest in prejudice is plain. His interest in group dynamics is a level of abstraction removed from the study of prejudice. This research was problem-oriented and cut across disciplinary boundaries. Findings from research carried out by the Group Dynamics people at MIT were to be used by CCI, headed by Stuart Cook, in an Action Research program which was then to feed problems back to the MIT experimenters.

With these two organizations, Lewin was attempting to bring to life his vision of the interdependence of theory and practice. During the last two years of his life, he spent an enormous amount of time and energy raising money for and traveling between these two creations of his. Some believe this intense schedule contributed to his early death in February 1947 - at the age of 56.

What follows on these pages are the stories of some of the men who were The Research Center for Group Dynamics. Two faculty (Dorwin Cartwright and Leon Festinger) and six men who received their graduate training under Lewin at MIT (Kurt Back, Morton Deutsch, Harold Kelley, Albert Pepitone, Stanley Schachter and John Thibaut) describe the development of their interest in Lewin's work, their experiences with him, and how those experiences later affected their own work. These accounts are based on face-to-face in-depth interviews. The choice of whom to include is based solely on the practical consideration of availability for interview. With one exception, the other men who received their training as graduate students at The Research Center for Group Dynamics during the 1945-1948 period have either died or live outside of the United States.

The Development of Experimental Social Psychology:

The men here describe the environment Lewin created that allowed them as students to develop as creative scientists. This remarkable array of talented students went on to shape the field of social psychology for nearly four decades after Lewin's death in

1947. Lewin was legendary for attracting groups of students and stimulating creative work. But this particular group, the one assembled to work together at MIT at the close of the war, was remarkable in its ability to sustain and build on that body of creative work. They not only shaped the field of social psychology but they trained a substantial proportion of the next generation of its most influential practitioners. Taking citations as a measure of influence on a field, in a recent citation analysis of social psychology textbooks (Perlman, 1984), eight of the ten most cited social psychologists are direct descendants of this line of researchers.

Here the Lewin students discuss not only their own training but also describe the methods they use when working with their students. Following these accounts are those of several renowned social psychologists who were trained, or heavily influenced, by members of the original MIT group. They are in a position to comment on the way the second generation of Lewinians refined experimentation in social psychology.

The remaining interviews are organized into two "family groups" of experimental social psychologists. First, students trained by Stanley Schachter and then Schachter himself, discuss Schachter's lab and working style. The second group is comprised of students and "grand-students" of Leon Festinger. First, two students trained by Elliot Aronson discuss their training, followed by Aronson himself. Aronson, along with Judson Mills, whose interview follows Aronson's, was trained by Leon Festinger at Stanford. Leon Festinger has the last say - since, as it will become clear, he influenced profoundly everyone who came before.

Through all this, there is a search for qualities of the social psychological environment during Lewin's MIT years that enabled certain gifted students to develop the skills, enthusiasm and confidence to be creatively productive for many years afterward. Specifically, was there anything passed on from the MIT environment that could account for the success of the next generation of Lewininans or was it simply that those who gathered at the Research Center for Group Dynamics after the War were men with the insight and imagination to take what Lewin offered them and filter it through their own talents? The interviews reported here focus on the process through which these men became psychologists, how they were trained, how they have gone about conducting research, how they train their students, and their views on Kurt Lewin's influence on that process.

THE FIRST GENERATION: THE RESEARCH ENVIRONMENT AT MIT

In the original "manifesto" establishing The Research Center for Group Dynamics, Kurt Lewin (1945) characteristically placed the Center into context. He wrote passionately about the urgency of coming to understand group life. Alluding to the nuclear age just born and to the world war just ended, he pointed out that man had come to control some aspects of nature but was still unable to manage social forces. He made a plea for research aimed at developing a scientific understanding of social dynamics.

The group of students that gathered at The Research Center for Group Dynamics at the close of World War II were almost certainly selected for heterogeneity of interest, yet they shared a profound common experience. They had all spent the previous years in some branch of the armed forces. Several had earned masters degrees before entering the service. Most had spent the war years in some kind of research activity. Therefore, the students who selected themselves into Lewin's environment at MIT were older and more experienced than traditional graduate students. They had developed their own ideas, ideas that resonated with what Lewin was offering.

In his interview, Robert Krauss, characterizes them as "hard-headed idealists." He suggests that what Lewin offered was "a vision of a way of dealing with the things that were perceived as having caused this catastrophe." This was an elite (most had opted out of Yale in favor of MIT) and experienced group of men making an informed choice about their future. In terms of the selection of students into the program, Leon Festinger suggests that it was largely self selection because, he said, "I don't think anybody *knows* how to do selection that is that good."

The Environment at MIT:

These men had elected to enroll in a Ph.D. program in a new discipline, group psychology, at a university known for excellence in engineering and science. They had an arrangement with Harvard which allowed the students access to courses there and this must have somewhat counteracted the perceived risk of entering the unusual graduate program being offered by MIT.

Immediately after the war there was a move to establish interdisciplinary departments in various universities. Notably, Harvard established the Department of Social Relations which included social and clinical psychology, cultural anthropology and sociology. The University of Michigan established a joint sociology-psychology program. These programs were, in time, to fracture along disciplinary lines. There were also a number of interdisciplinary research institutes established, some of them direct descendents of teams put together by the government to solve problems during the war. This organizational fad was presumably due to the success of such wartime problem-centered projects. But MIT had been operating this way for years and had a tradition of establishing ad hoc interdisciplinary laboratories. This experienced tolerance for interdisciplinary activity was a boon to Lewin's group.

In his interview, Dorwin Cartwright describes the institutional environment at MIT as "the most productive institution I have ever experienced." He explains that it was a combination of flexibility and high scientific standards. When he assumed the administrative duties after Lewin's death, Cartwright was astonished at the lack of control exercised by the MIT administration. He experienced instead, an open-mindedness and tolerance for wild ideas. The institutional attitude at MIT was "we hired you because you are an expert in the field and if that's what you want to do, ok." At MIT, scientists collaborated on projects while maintaining their departmental affiliation. Once a particular project was completed, they returned to their home department. Cartwright believes that this institutional attitude made it possible for Lewin to establish a uniquely productive environment. He said this was partly because they were social scientists at MIT, which was an "Institute of Technology," and therefore there were no established disciplinary boundaries for the social sciences. "If we wanted to talk like anthropologists, nobody was going to shoot us down." This allowed them a tremendous flexibility in approaching problems. Kurt Lewin's characteristic working style - really an atmosphere he created - contained features that meshed nicely with MIT's established history of problem-centered projects, flexibility, and lack of social science boundaries.

On the Frontier:

Within the institutional environment, Lewin created his own micro-culture. Even though most of the graduate students report little direct contact with Lewin himself, the inspiring atmosphere he created had a strong impact on them. In his interview, Morton Deutsch describes the enthusiasm and confidence that Lewin imparted. John Thibaut, one of the few students to work directly with Lewin at MIT, speaks eloquently of student's feelings about being part of something important and "in coalition with some powerful, fateful movements that were going to carry us." This feeling of doing *important* work is one that is described repeatedly by Lewin's students. De Rivera (1976) reports that a nearly identical atmosphere surrounded Lewin's group at the Berlin Institute - a different group of people, working on different problems, in different times. The atmosphere there is described as cooperative, enthusiastic, with a sense of verging on the edge of discovery. It appears that Lewin carried this atmosphere with him and created it again and again.

Immersion in Research:

One aspect of Lewin's working atmosphere that nearly all the men mention was the fact that they were immediately and always involved in research. The faculty had no undergraduates to contend with and so their job was to conduct research with the help of the graduate students. There was little course work. The students participated in each other's disseration research using whatever methods were appropriate for the problem - often the methods were invented. These dissertations were integral parts of the larger research effort being conducted at the Center.

Lewin's Interdependent Working Style:

Much has been written about Lewin's style of working. He once wrote that he was incapable of thinking productively as an individual (Lewin, 1936). The way he worked was by talking with other people. He would talk about his work, their work, it didn't matter. He talked with people individually or in groups - he was forever collaborating. John Thibuat describes their walks along the Charles River discussing Lewin's notions of quasi-stationary equilibria. It was Thibaut's job to take notes and write up the discussion. Lewin would then rework it and return it. Cartwright describes regular meetings with Lewin in a tea shop across the street from the university while he was a postdoctoral fellow at Iowa. Together they were planning a Topology workbook. Again, they talked and it was Cartwright's job to formulate these discussions.

This interdependent style of Lewin's gave birth to what was known by all his students as the "Quasselstrippe." These were regular meetings during which research problems were discussed and solved. These meetings were essentially brain storming sessions concerned with solving problems encountered in the research - everything was discussed from problems of theory to problems of data interpretation. All of the discussions were conducted in the language of Topology and focused on the underlying dynamics of situations. Ronald Lippitt (1947, p. 88) once wrote of these meetings:

> Over and over he made clear that the atmosphere of the discussion must be such that no one had any fears of "sticking his neck out" in expressing any idea, no matter how unformulated it might seem. At such meetings a student discussed his research problem at some stage of its development. Never, have I participated in a group process so free of criticism and ego-oriented defenses, and so full of spontaneous "thinking out loud."

Kurt Back seconded this view and explained that if the work under discussion had been completed, those who were responsible would be very defensive about it.

Lewin established these meetings every place he worked - one suspects they formed around him simply by virtue of his working style. Kurt Back speculates that Lewin needed students to pull him back when he went "way off" with his ideas. With Lewin, everything was "in progress." John Thibaut comments that Lewin "did not regard anything he had ever done as a settled matter." The students learned what had happened up to that point but nothing was "regarded sacredly. He was just so open and hence he was never defensive about any criticism and welcomed the sharpest criticism." Thibaut attributes this to Lewin's "enormous confidence." These meetings were a primary organizational facet of Lewin's environment that was adopted and used by some of his students. His students, and their students as we will see, tried to recreate these kinds of meetings when they were heading their own research operations. The key was to use the group interdependently and not as a forum for finished work.

Task Centeredness:

Lewin's personal style included a complete lack of status orientation. The problem, the research, the discussion - all of these were important and anyone who could contribute was welcome. It was one of the things which in his interview, Albert Pepitone says attracted him to Lewin when they first met. The crucial thing was not status but how you related to the task at hand. This characteristic caused problems for Lewin as an administrator. Cartwright compares Lewin with Rensis Likert in this regard. Cartwright worked with Likert during the war. He describes them both as dominant in the sense that "their ideas were persuasive. They were not domineering in an autocratic sense and they weren't status oriented. Neither one gave a darn about rank or hierarchy or position or any of those things. They were both just incredibly open to discussion." He continues by saying that many decisions were made by the people who simply happened to be around when a problem came up and often those who weren't there "would be put out by it." Cartwright feels that this mode of decision making "helped foster creativity in the sense that you were encouraged to come up with ideas. Neither of the two men would be very punishing for mistakes - but they would correct." Cartwright adds that with both Lewin and Likert he felt the need to provide some structure. His role was to be as he put it "the brakes on the machine." Lewin's characteristic lack of status consciousness combined with his intense task centeredness had a liberating effect on his students. It is not surprising then that when the time came Cartwright, and the others who made the decision, opted for the compatible environment that could be provided by working with Likert at Michigan.

Lewin's Theory:

Nearly all the men interviewed are careful to point out that Field Theory is not really a theory in the formal sense. But it was useful nonetheless. According to Jones (1985), Lewin himself described it as "a method: namely a method of analyzing causal relations and building scientific constructs (Lewin 1951, p. 45, orig. 1943)." Cartwright says, "It is a theory about theory...he sparked ideas, concepts, points of view that are reverberating still." Thibaut conceives of it as a conceptual system which then allowed other very creative people to "develop special little theories like Tamara and Sears and Leon did with level of aspiration which *is* a theory or the tension system theory that Zeigarnik, Ovsiankina and later Murray Horwitz applied and was quite exciting." He continues:

> He had these concepts which could be so wonderfully useful, they were very carefully defined, but they enabled one flexibly to work on various situations, to study practical situations or contributed situations. You could invent situations, that is you could use them synthetically, or you could analyze situations. The influence was very different and hence I think more long lasting than when you have a propositional theory that is subject proposition by proposition to be tested. With Lewin's work, you could use it so that it didn't develop the kind of dogmatic loyalty to propositions about substantive matter. It involved a kind of

> loyalty to a style and way of thinking which allowed a lot of very creative people to work together and use what they needed and they were able to communicate through these commonly understood concepts.

This assumptive framework and common language helped to create a culture with which these men identify even today. In his interview, Harold Kelley tells of writing, together with John Thibaut, an epilogue to their 1978 book, in order to clarify "where the real loyalties were." They did this because someone had accused them of being Hullians.

Working within Lewin's theory required a flexibility and tolerance for ambiguity that is not always part of the cognitive style of academic scholars. But to those who were comfortable with it, the vagueness of the theory was an asset. As Cartwright says, "He was very seminal (because) part of this was that you could read anything into it - it was like reading the Bible."

Tension in the Group:

One final aspect of the Research Center environment which everyone comments on was a tension in the group. This tension was a result of Lewin's attempt to bring together both basic research and application. Morton Deutsch says he thought that while Lewin was alive, "his benign presence kept the tension under control." That "the two were fused in him even though in some of his faculty, that fusion didn't hold." Deutsch thinks the tension was stimulating to the group. Cartwright also believes it was a "creative tension."

These tensions were represented in the faculty by Leon Festinger insisting on rigorous science and Ron Lippitt in the field coping with the problems of Action Research. According to Cartwright, problems "would crop up whenever there was a project with both action and research on the same project." Kurt Back illustrates this by contrasting what happened with the two big housing studies - the one at Westgate which was run by Festinger and the later one at Weymouth that was much more ambitious in scope. As Deutsch puts it "the orientation of Leon Festinger was much more of science. The orientation of Lippitt was much more, 'change the world' and trying to do good - with a bow to science." After Lewin's death, it became Cartwright's task to maintain peace but the group eventually factured along the lines of this tension. This split may have been inevitable. Cartwright comments that the staff had been very young when it was formed and it was natural that they would want to go off and establish themselves in their own right.

After the Move to Michigan:

After Lewin's death, the entire Research Center for Group Dynamics moved to the University of Michigan where they joined Likert's Survey Research Center to form the Institute for Social Research. After the move to Michigan, things changed. Over the next few years the two big rooms they initially inhabited at Michigan, again ignoring status distinctions, were replaced by traditional office space. The Quasselstrippe became colloquia with the focus changing to the presentation of completed research. The increased organizational control they encountered at Michigan was pointed out by Kurt Back who illustrates by describing the problems Stanley Schachter encountered when trying to complete his doctoral thesis.

When Kurt Lewin died, Jack French stepped in as a faculty member at MIT. When the group moved to Michigan, Marian Radke remained in the east and they were joined by Alvin Zander, a Lewin associate from the Iowa days. That left, of the original faculty, Cartwright, Lippitt and Festinger. Picking up the theoretical ball, Cartwright and Harary worked to mathematize Field Theory and came up with Graph Theory. Ronald Lippitt nurtured Group Dynamics, part of which grew and evolved into the t-group business (with the research component fading out.) Cartwright and Zander contributed in a major way to the field of organizational development which maintains some Action Research qualities.

Leon Festinger stayed at Michigan for three years and in 1951 joined Stanley Schachter and Ben Willerman at Minnesota. The lab he organized there incorporated some qualities of the MIT environment including intense task-centeredness, collegiality and the Quasselstrippe. To these he added his developing theory of social comparison, a refined style of experimentation, a penchant for scientific rigor and aesthetic taste. In time another Research Center alumnus, Harold Kelley, joined them after spending several years at Yale. Minnesota thus became the breeding ground for experimental social psychology as it was practiced for the next generation.

Kurt Lewin's approach to science was sifted through this group at Minnesota to emerge as a subtle but pervasive influence on the next generation of social psychologists.

Lewin was legendary for attracting groups of students and stimulating creative work. The men here describe the environment he created. Beyond this, as Kurt Back points out, since there were only four faculty members and Lewin was away most of the time, all of the students had the same dissertation committee. As a result, each student had Leon Festinger on his committee and most of the students make statements about being heavily influenced by Festinger. Indeed, it will gradually become clear that Leon Festinger is implicated in the continued creativity of these men. His vision of the way science is conducted and the standards he required of his students - and all of those trained at MIT were his students - had an immeasurable influence on the entire field of social psychology. It was Festinger's theoretical contributions and his style of laboratory experimentation that became the dominant force in social psychology for a generation after Lewins death. As the students of this original group tell their stories, Leon Festinger's scientific aesthetics can be traced clearly.

INTERVIEWS

The MIT Group

Six of the following seven interviews are with men who were associated with Kurt Lewin at the Research Center for Group Dynamics while it was at MIT. The seventh interview is with Alvin Zander, a Lewin associate at Iowa who later went to Michigan where the Research Center for Group Dynamics came to him.

The first interview is with Dorwin Cartwright who was associated with Lewin both at Iowa and at MIT. When Lewin died, Cartwright became director of the Research Center and oversaw its move to Michigan. His long association with Lewin and intimate connection with the workings of the Research Center give him a unique and broad perspective with regard to the environmental conditions fostering this group of creative men.

Next is an interview with Alvin Zander. His association with Lewin at Iowa gave him some perspective on Lewin's methods of working. His interview is placed second because he is able to describe the organizational changes that occurred after Lewin's death when the Research Center moved to Michigan.

Following those two interviews are interviews with five of the men who were graduate students at MIT: John Thibaut*, Harold Kelley, Kurt Back, Albert Pepitone and Morton Deutsch. In these interviews they describe their reasons for becoming psychologists, how they arrived at the decision to attend MIT, how the Research Center operated, and how they were trained. They also discuss any continuing links with Lewin and the group, how they train their own students, and in many cases they discuss their current work.

---

*John Thibaut died on February 19, 1986. He was interviewed in May of 1985.

As a group, these interviews present a picture of Kurt Lewin, his working style and the environment he created at MIT.

DORWIN CARTWRIGHT

While Dorwin Cartwright was an undergraduate psychology major at Swarthmore College in 1935, gestalt psychologist Wolfgang Koehler emigrated from Berlin and joined the faculty. "I worked with Koehler and this was what really hooked me on the idea of psychology." Cartwright recalled. "He was an overwhelming man."

Koehler persuaded Cartwright to go on to graduate school at Harvard, and arranged a fellowship for him. At the end of his first year at Harvard however, Cartwright returned to Koehler expressing disappointment with his year. "I told him it had been a good year, but I hadn't found anything terribly stimulating. I had been disappointed in the sense that I had been looking for something to get me as excited as I had been at Swarthmore. He thought a little bit and said, 'Why don't you go this summer out and visit Kurt Lewin. I think you might find him interesting.'" Koehler contacted Lewin and when Cartwright wrote and asked to visit at Iowa for the summer, he was invited. "So I went out and inside of a week he had me doing an experiment with him," Cartwright laughed.

The research Cartwright worked on that summer involved measuring decision time as a function of the difference between conflicting forces.

> Lewin had a seminar which he ran called the Quasselstrippe. Just about anybody who was a student or a colleague or anybody who was interested in Lewin would attend. Later, many of us had seminars that were like it but couldn't quite recreate it because he was a unique person.
>
> Let me give you an example. There was an article in a journal about judgment time by a man named Johnson. Johnson had tried to make some order out of the psychophysical research on accuracy of judgment as a function of how many categories one

had to judge. It hadn't been conceptualized at all in terms of conflicting forces. Lewin asked me if I would read the paper and report it to the seminar. And so I did. That whole evening after I presented the paper, Lewin started taking over saying, "now lets look at this." He would go to the blackboard and start drawing those pictures on the board and would have conflicting forces. He would draw these forces and then come out with certain conclusions.

The blackboard was crucial for him for these seminars. If you would start talking he would say, "well, come on up." We would all participate, it was very democratic. He was a completely unassuming sort of person. He dominated in the sense that he generated the ideas.

I was constantly amazed, especially that first year or two when I was working with him. He would be propounding some notion on tension systems or something and it would seem to be just sort of off the cuff and I would say, "Why do you do that, couldn't you just as well do it this other way?" And if I would press him hard enough, he would suddenly stop and say, "Well, now..." and would give me a long lecture about the theory of science and what people before had said about this and it was clear that it wasn't just something that had just come to him. So, often things which you might think were just impulsive or out of the blue, came from his knowing a lot.

Cartwright returned to Harvard in the fall following his visit to Iowa and spent the next two years finishing his graduate work. During each of those next two years, Lewin visited at Harvard during the spring semester. "Because I had been with him in the summer at Iowa meant that I was sort of in special relation to him at Harvard. I helped him find an apartment and various things." Cartwright recalled. Although he was not officially a student of Lewin's, they spent a lot of time together during Lewin's Harvard stays.

> At that time, Boring was chairman of the department at Harvard. He had been the dominant person administratively for many years. In fact, when he went there in the twenties, it was the department of philosophy and psychology. Psychology was a branch of philosophy and Boring wanted to make it a separate department and succeeded - and then he ran the department, so it was really his show.
>
> The whole relationship of Boring to the gestalt psychologists was a fascinating one and there has been quite a bit written about it. Boring had a very ambivalent attitude toward Koehler, but he was sort of curious about Lewin. Boring was crucial for having Lewin at Harvard for those two semesters, in a way he was acknowledging his significance. Lewin's place in the academic world at the time - being kind of innovative and stimulating - was disturbing to people like Boring.

During his third year at Harvard, Cartwright was approached by Boring, who asked if he would be finished with his degree by June. Cartwright replied that he hadn't planned to be. "I still thought I was going to write a thesis with Gordon Allport," he said. Boring said there was a job open at Princeton that he would recommend Cartwright for if he were to be finished in June. "I had been his lab assistant and teaching fellow. This was in the midst of the depression and jobs were very scarce," Cartwright recalled.

> I thought maybe the research I had been doing on my own for the fun of it, on judgment and decision time, which I had begun with Lewin at Iowa, would make a thesis. Until then I hadn't thought of it in those terms - just curiosity. Boring said, "Well, show it to me." So I took him the data and showed him what I had and he said, "I don't see why that isn't a thesis." And so I asked him to sponsor it and he said he would but he had some conditions. One of the conditions was that I could write up the thesis in Lewinian language, but I had to have a final chapter in which I put it all in English. I agreed. I

> am not sure if it it was in English, but there was a final chapter.

So Cartwright managed to do a Lewinian thesis at Harvard, sponsored by Boring whose ambivalence toward gestalt psychology was well known and far reaching.

After completing his degree in June of 1940, instead of going to Princeton Cartwright chose to return to Iowa as a postdoctoral fellow at Lewin's invitation. While at Iowa during this period he encountered Leon Festinger, who had recently come as a graduate student. He worked with Festinger on his thesis which was a follow-up of Cartwright's decision time thesis but using a more elaborate mathematical model. Another of his activities during this period was to meet weekly with Lewin over tea in a restaurant across the street from the University. During these meetings, they planned writing a topology workbook.

> I would take notes and we would plan it and then I would work on it as part of my postdoctoral work with him. It never came off but we did that sort of thing all along.

"After Pearl Harbor," Cartwright recalled, "it became clear that things were going to be different and shortly after that I was asked by Rensis Likert to come to Washington. Lewin had introduced Cartwright to Likert the previous summer. Likert had funding for a central survey research operation and needed staff. Cartwright described Likert as much like Lewin in many ways - particularly in their administrative styles. He believes Likert tapped Lewin's staff thinking he would find people who would be compatible with what he wanted to accomplish. So in February, 1942 Cartwright moved to Washington where he spent most of the war doing research on inflation control and the sale of war bonds.

> I started with strictly a Lewinian analysis of goals and paths and saying if you want the person to buy bonds, what do you set up as a path to that goal so there is this link and I used a straight topological analysis. It was very useful in guiding design of interview questions and asking people about things

> that were relevant. I didn't know anything about survey when we started.

Although Likert was not as interested in theory as Lewin was, Cartwright described their similarities. They were both "chaotic," he recalled.

> They were both dominant people in the sense that what they thought and their ideas were persuasive. There was no doubt in either case who was running the show. But they were not domineering in an autocratic sense and they weren't status oriented. Neither one of them gave a darn about rank or hierarchy or position or any of those things. They were both just incredibly open to discussion. Whenever something would come up with Lewin, he would discuss it and make a decision and the people who didn't happen to be there would be put out by it.
>
> Likert was expanding his operation from about an eight or nine person group to running a full national survey every two weeks. He, like Lewin, made decisions together with whoever was in the office when the problem arose. It was a little hairy but it did convey the feeling that you were important and you felt responsible. They were both that way. It helped foster creativity in the sense that you were encouraged to come up with ideas and neither of the two men would be very punishing for mistakes - but they would correct. Lewin was the most extreme in this. There were so many times when I was working with him that someone would come in with an idea for a thesis or whatever and they would have a discussion. Lewin would get very excited, "Oh, that's a great idea," and so on. At the end of the hour, the person would go out with an entirely different thesis topic. Both of them were that way and I think it does create a good environment but I felt, both with Lewin and with Likert, the necessity of getting some structure in that setting.

> In Washington with Likert, Angus Campbell and I viewed ourselves very much as the two brakes on the machine. With Lewin, I did it without a coalition. He used to say, "Doc, I have never known anybody who could say no the way you do." Lewin would start planning some program or something and I would always be the one raising questions about how were they going to finance it, who was going to work on it and things like that. He was appreciative of it and I didn't feel uncomfortable doing it, it is just my natural style. I am convinced that this is a crucial part of a creative environment, you can't have just chaos and freedom.

Another important aspect of the environments created by these two men according to Cartwright, was task orientation. He said both Likert and Lewin, "were involved in what they were doing and they didn't care about who you were in the sense of status, but how you related to the task - and Lewin was just perpetually that way. He would be involved in doing something with somebody and it wasn't just the person. He couldn't just sit down and chat, it was always about some problem."

> There was something about his acceptance and his enthusiastic support of your ideas and in turn giving you ideas which seemed insightful or solved some problem. For example, when I went out to Iowa because I was frustrated with the kind of psychology I was getting at Harvard, he got me all steamed up - that was only a summer. But even just a casual contact had great effect.
>
> He had a knack, somehow of making an impression on a person - changing a person's life in a funny way on just slight contact. I have run across many such stories. One example is an Englishman, Eric Trist who was a graduate student at Cambridge University in 1933 when Lewin dropped off there on his way to the United States for the year he spent before he finally emigrated.

> Trist was asked to show Lewin around the campus and bring him back in time for a meeting. Which he did. And this was his contact with Lewin - a student showing him around. After the war, Trist got in touch with us at the Research Center for Group Dynamics and we jointly sponsored a journal together. He was an ardent Lewinian - and it all came from that contact of two hours or less. Alfred Marrow, who wrote Lewin's biography, went up to see him about his thesis. He planned to spend the afternoon and return home that evening. He stayed all night developing a life-long collaboration. Well, there are just stories after stories of that kind.

Group Dynamics:

In the middle of the 1930's, the year before Cartwright's first summer at Iowa, Ronald Lippitt arrived and enrolled at the Child Welfare Research Station. At the time, he viewed himself as a developmental psychologist having just returned from studying with Piaget in Europe. By chance, Lippitt was assigned to Lewin as an advisee. Questioning Lippitt about his background, Lewin discovered that before studying with Piaget, Lippitt had attended Springfield College in Massachusetts majoring in group work. Lewin had been in the United States only a few years and was at the time intrigued by the differences between German and American culture.

> Lippitt started talking about how kids and teachers interacted and so on, and out of this they cooked up the idea of doing some kind of experiment in which kids would be led in different ways. One way was essentially the German autocrat and the other the American democrat. I think that is about as sophisticated as it started out to be.
>
> So Lippitt ran two groups for a masters thesis and this seemed promising so they decided to go on

> with it. It began to be clear, partly out of training the democratic leaders who were going to run these kids in this style, that they couldn't agree on what democratic leadership was. That forced them to pull out this laissez faire style - no leadership, in a way. So, that was kind of an unexpected discovery in a way which led to the design of the major study with three styles of leadership - Lippitt's doctoral dissertation (Lewin, Lippitt & White, 1939).
>
> I always thought this distinction between democratic leadership and no leadership was the most important finding. Later on as we were involved in the Bethel workshops and training leaders, I found that so many people had the notion that the way to be a democratic leader was not to do anything at all.

According to Cartwright, "This impact of Lippitt's cannot be overemphasized. His role was very important. Lippitt had a tremendous influence on Lewin to get him interested in groups specifically." Previously, research on groups had focused on such topics as group problem-solving and social facilitation. "These were not groups in any sense of looking at organized group properties or leadership or any of that. They were experiments on aggregates of people which was really a collection of individuals," Cartwright said. "The idea of taking a group as an entity had a tremendous impact." Cartwright believes that Lewin's interest in groups was tied up with prejudice, and the kind of groups he was interested in were racial and ethnic groups - particularly Jewish groups. "Lewin was an ardent Zionist," Cartwright recalled. At the time of his death, Lewin was starting to raise funds to create a Research Center for Group Dynamics at the Hebrew University in what was shortly to become Israel.

Another important influence in the evolution of Lewin's thinking which led to the establishment of the Research Center for Group Dynamics, was Alex Bavelas. When Cartwright returned to Iowa in 1940 for his postdoc with Lewin, Bavelas was there as a graduate student. Like Lippitt, he also came to Iowa from Springfield College trained in group work. "He was just a genius at doing group work," Cartwright said.

> Lewin would have Bavelas lead groups - children's groups - behind oneway glass so we could watch him. Lewin would stand there and watch him and get all excited and say, "See what he is doing, see what he is doing." Then Bavelas would come out and Lewin would tell him what he had been doing and Bavelas would say, "I didn't know that."
>
> Bavelas did a study that was fascinating. It was never published and the only documentation was the movies that were made of it. There was a community center for children, with adult leaders who were paid by WPA. These people who were running it were not necessarily professionally well trained and were kind of demoralized. Bavelas made a deal with the center that he could have half the staff be trained in democratic leadership techniques and leave the other half untrained and then they would observe them. It was kind of a field test of Lippitt's study. It was designed to see if you could train democratic leaders. Unfortunately the main data were simply movies and they were lost.

This study was the next step in the evolution leading to the Connecticut and Bethel leadership training workshops.

Lewin often made movies of the work being done. "He was so visual," Cartwright remembered. In Germany he made movies of children to illustrate his force field ideas.

> One was a child trying to get a duck on the beach and the fear of the waves and the attraction of the duck. You see this vacillation back and forth. They were sensational movies. He showed them during the year he visited the United States in the early thirties. He would show this movie and that was all most of the people could understand. This is just an example of his unconventional approach to data and problems - his openmindedness. He would just try anything.

The atmosphere at Iowa was in some ways tense for Lewin. He was in the Child Welfare Research Station - not the psychology department - sponsored by the dean of the graduate school and director of the Child Welfare Research Station, George Stoddard. Stoddard was also a psychologist who, "vibrated to Lewin. He brought him to Iowa and was a strong, loyal supporter of Lewin, but he sort of did it over the wishes of other people who were there," said Cartwright.

> At Iowa, it was just Lewin and Dembo and a few students who came. Some of them came specifically to work with Lewin, as Festinger did. Bavelas was another who came to work with Lewin. Lippitt hadn't come to work with Lewin, he came because he wanted a degree in child psychology. Zander came later. Barker and White had been there before me. But the others were just people who were around, so he didn't have many students. It was more a tentative island.

At MIT:

The Research Center for Group Dynamics was established by Lewin at MIT during the closing months of the war. The original staff consisted of Marian Radke, Leon Festinger, Ronald Lippitt and Cartwright - all of whom had worked with Lewin at Iowa. Cartwright was the last to arrive because as the the war ended, Likert sent him to Europe to help coordinate a survey of the German population about their morale. This developed into a project to help the military deal with problems of compliance and civilian morale immediately after the war ended. By the time he arrived at MIT, the original group of students had already been selected.

> The recruitment of that group is a fascinating thing. I think the creativity of a group is a function of the people who get there, but what attracts them is critical - a very important thing. People came to

MIT not just on the reputation of the institution. That is, you go to Stanford or Harvard or wherever because it is the place to go - that's one basis for choosing. That recruits talent I think, but not necessarily what will be compatible with the particular environment they finally end up in. Like my first year at Harvard, I was getting educated, I didn't have any complaints except - no sparks.

With Lewin, somehow people came because either they had contact with him or they had heard about him or read about him or had a recommendation like Koehler told me, "You will get along with him." That's what Cook did to Kelley. This way, you got recruitment of people who were susceptible *and* would probably interact well with one another. Lewin had this breadth of interests so he recruited a heterogeneous group of people. For example, Gordon Hearn came there as a person with social work background - no training at all in psychology and he came to get a Ph.D.in in group psychology. Lewin spent hours with him. Every week they would talk and so on.

Cartwright commented on the narrow age gap that existed between staff and the students. Cartwright himself was only two or three years older than most of the students. He said, "I thought, what am I doing up here teaching these guys who just had as much training and more experience in one thing or another as I have? It was just kind of a fluke that I was on the faculty instead of being a student."

I think that was facilitative of a kind of give and take or something that is harder to come by in a structured situation. I don't know how it looked to the others, but I think we were so realistically kind of colleagues, of equals; and then with Lewin's style, it made for a kind of collaboration. Seminars were more problem-solving than indoctrination or something. It created an atmosphere you don't find very often.

After Lewin's sudden death, Cartwright was made director of the Research Center. It subsequently became clear to him that they would have to leave MIT. President Compton had pointed out to Cartwright that MIT's annual budget was at that time greater than the endowment and there was concern about depending so heavily on government contracts. If there were going to be cutbacks, the social sciences at MIT were probably going to be at risk.

Cartwright said he thought that MIT, "for a large institution, was the most productive institution I have ever experienced." It combined the "highest scientific standards you could expect with creativity and flexibility." When he first became director he had a difficult time adjusting to the lack of limits and boundaries imposed by MIT. "I would say, 'Well, can I put in a purchase order?' and they would say, 'Well if you really need it, I don't see why not,' he laughed. Technically the Research Center was a unit in the Department of Economics and Social Science. The chairman of the department was an economist, "nice guy, but didn't know anything about what we were doing - didn't understand it at all."

> You couldn't have done that at Harvard. It was an interesting combination of open-mindedness - come up with any idea and you never got the answer that you couldn't do it because it hadn't been done - sounds like a wild idea. They would say, "We hired you because you are an expert in the field and if that's what you want to do, ok." They were constantly doing new things.
>
> They had a flexible structure. They had what they called departments which were the usual things and then they would set up what they called laboratories. A laboratory was something that of necessity would involved people from more than one department. And the laboratories would be staffed primarily by people assigned from departments who kept their department affiliation but would go to work on projects in the lab. They would be completely task oriented and it was temporary until the completion of the task. The

> task could be a contract or it might be set by an individual.

This kind of environment contrasted radically with Cartwright's experience working in the government during the war, where things had to be done by the book.

> When I came in as director, it was clear to me that Compton (the President of MIT) had said to Lewin, "Ok, you are the expert in this field, we buy it, DO IT." And when I stepped in, I said, "can I do it," and they said, 'well, yeah if you need to.' I have always felt that was very very important and am sure it was part of the reason Lewin got there at all. Compton was president of MIT and he responded personally to Lewin.

Cartwright believes that the institutional attitude expressed by MIT made it possible for Lewin to establish an environment which the students appreciated and benefited from.

> Partly it was MIT and partly we were social science. There were no disciplinary boundaries around. If we wanted to talk like anthropologists, nobody was going to shoot us down. That gave a feeling that we could do anything we wanted to do. The other environment was, "ok, we have made a commitment to social science - *do it*." and I never felt from any of these top scientists - and they were *top* scientists - I never felt any constraint.

"The thing I realized about the field of group dynamics as it developed was that it is interdisciplinary - it was a feature Lewin insisted on from the beginning, " Cartwright said. Lewin produced a brochure which was, "a manifesto of what the center was to be," in which he wrote, "The Research Center for Group Dynamics has grown out of two needs or necessities - a scientific and a practical one. Social science needs an integration of psychology, sociology, cultural anthropology into an instrument for studying group life." All of this reflected the problem orientation of the Center. Cartwright said, "Now that never really came off, but it was his image and his theorizing. If you look at the way the field has developed, an awful lot of what we thought we were doing in that early period - this sort of interdisciplinary work *has* been carried on in specialized ways. But it has been carried on in all kinds of other disciplines. If you look at what's going on in business administration around the country, public administration, education, in a way what happened to the group research is that it got spread all over." Cartwright taught the course in Group Dynamics at Michigan. "By the last eight or ten years there, the bulk of my students would not be psychologists," he said.

In addition to the interdisciplinary nature of the Research Center, there was also the attempted wedding of theory and practice. At the time the Research Center for Group Dynamics was being established at MIT, Lewin was also setting up a research center in New York. This was the Committee for Community Interrelations (CCI), funded by the American Jewish Congress and headed by Stuart Cook. According to Cartwright, "CCI was to be practical and MIT was to be theoretical. It was clear that he wanted all of us at MIT to participate in the scientific guidence of CCI We would go down every so often and have meetings. They would report on their projects and we would raise questions." This "wedding" was Lewin's attempt to put into practice his famous maxim, "There is nothing so practical as a good theory." Cartwright commented that this statement is often used by theoreticians to justify what they are doing when in fact the statement in its original context said, according to Cartwright "that theorists shouldn't be so traumatized by practical problems. He was saying that you have to have both."

There were tensions within the group at MIT which reflected the tension created when theory and practice are integrated. Lippitt represented the applied faction and Festinger, the scientific. "The tensions would come whenever we tried to have a project which was both action and research on the same project," Cartwright remembered. "This tension was a part of the MIT environment - there was no doubt about it. And strangely enough, both sides of this conflict were endorsed by Lewin. He didn't want it to be a conflict and he didn't think it *should* be but he was attached to both Festinger and Lippitt and I was sort of in the middle."

During the Weymouth housing study, there was a clash over methods in the field which illustrates the tension in the group.

Lippitt was supervising group workers who were organizing community projects. They were attempting to raise the esteem people felt for their group by having these projects succeed. Festinger, was in charge of research on the project and was supervising the people who were to collect the research data. His interest was in maintaining a tight experimental design by having group workers do certain things or not do certain things according to the research design. Lippitt accused Festinger of not being sensitive to the difficulties of working in the field. According to Cartwright, Lippitt told Festinger he was constraining what they did and that the project wouldn't work if he insisted on his standards. Which Festinger did. Cartwright believes that it was "a creative tension" even though the issues were never resolved.

Beyond MIT:

Even with tension in the group, the decision was made to move as a unit from MIT. Cartwright said, "There was a lot of attachment and commitment to the students, to the idea that we had a good thing going, that it was causing something of a stir and that it was good to be associated with in some way."

Largely because of Cartwright's successful relationship with Likert during the war, the group finally made the move to The University of Michigan. He said, "I knew I could work with Likert and I knew what kind of environment and management philosophy he had and I thought it would be compatible. Michigan came up with the idea. They proposed that we bring the Group Dynamics Center to Michigan to join the Survey Research Center which had been Likert's group. The Survey Research Center had moved from Washington to Michigan right after the war. The two research centers together were to form the Institute for Social Research, headed by Likert. Angus Campbell, Cartwright's colleague during the war, was to direct the Survey Research Center when Likert moved up and Cartwright was to remain as director of Group Dynamics.

It was a new administrative thing that two outfits could come, intact, within a year of each other to form an institute. Michigan was unwilling to make the usual commitments that a department would make so we were not with tenure - it was all very iffy. It had a lot of creative aspects though which appealed to us - both Likert's group and us.

Our senior staff would have joint appointments with departments and it had been worked out that we would have academic rank, although without tenure. The Institute was set up independently of the departments administratively, even outside of the Literary College. Likert reported directly to the Academic Vice President. We were a research institute, attached to the university. They provided space and building facilities but not salary for our research. We had to be self supporting although we were reimbursed by the university for our teaching. I was a half time professor and a half time director.

The other thing that was crucial for the students who came along in the new era was they were no longer coming to our center to be students but they were coming primarily to the social psychology program which was just founded by Newcomb and other people there. This program was interdepartmental - jointly sociology and psychology and students had to take all those subjects.

A Michigan social psychology degree was a sociology-psychology joint thing and that was close enough to our wild ideology that we were willing to go along with that. That was attractive.

The staff members who moved to Michigan were Cartwright, Festinger, Lippitt and Jack French who had joined them after Lewin's death. Marian Radke was the only staff member who didn't make the move. The students finished their degrees and moved on, but the only faculty member to leave was Leon Festinger who left for Minnesota in 1951 where he joined Stanley

Schachter. The rest of the faculty remained at Michigan but things changed.

> One problem was that this staff was pulled together by Lewin when they were very young. It was very shortly after they received their degrees, before they had established any personal reputation. They were willing to go along as a subordinate to Lewin in a sense of sharing things up to a point. But when it came time to be thinking about your *own* career, your *own* students, your *own* program, you wanted to get out of the crowding of these other people.
>
> I wouldn't possibly set myself up in any way over Festinger or Lippitt - we had been colleagues. That meant they had to be independent in some sense. I tried to create a supportive enough and loose enough environment so they could do that, but it was difficult. And I think that would have happened if Lewin had continued to be alive. I just don't think basically he could have kept that same group together. I doubt if I would have been willing to stay that way indefinitely.

Subsequent Work - Links with Lewin and Collaborations:

After Lewin's death, while the group was still at MIT, Cartwright "inherited" Alex Bavelas as a student. Bavelas had been a graduate student at Iowa, had left without finishing his degree, and had gone to MIT. After the war he stayed on at MIT and was finishing his thesis with Lewin when Lewin died.

> Lewin at one time had suggested that it might make sense in talking about the life space to make an analogy of cells in biology - to talk about cells and boundaries and connections of cells. So he started working out that, plus the problem of how you conceptualize paths which he didn't do very well in his topology. He ended up having little cells and lines connecting them and called this hodology.

Bavelas picked up on that and developed some of the concepts. He wrote essentially just a mathematical paper on it which I inherited. I was very uneasy, not knowing if it was a thesis or it wasn't, so I got some of the mathematicians at MIT to look at it to see if it was nonsense from a mathematical point of view. They said, no, it wasn't a mathematical thesis, but it was original and it made sense.

That led to some communication network studies. When we came to Michigan from MIT, I felt that one thing I wanted to make sure was that the Center tried to pursue a little further this topological - mathematical interest of Lewin's to see where it was leading. So Festinger and I drew up a proposal and went to the Rockefeller Foundation to get some money so we could hire a mathematician at least part time from the mathematics department at Michigan to be on the staff and work on this.

So Leon and I recruited a mathematician named Harary and showed him Bavelas' thesis. Harary said, "Well, all you people have independently discovered what mathematics knows as graph theory." And I said, "Well, gee whiz, why didn't the mathematicians at MIT tell me that." It turned out that the first book published in the field had been published in German just before the war and was only recently available in the United States. This was intriguing, that here Lewin and Bavelas had independently discovered or invented a branch of mathematics that was just emerging.

Harary and I then worked on this with another mathematician named Norman. We got out a book on graph theory. We weren't the sole influence but I think our book did much to provide a mathematical basis for network ideas which were being developed more intuitively and even clinically, as it were, by a lot of people.

> The concept of social networks I see as - not exactly a direct descendent of group dynamics but there are links and some of the people who have done a lot with networks were clearly Lewinian - French had a big role in it.

Cartwright said he is "absolutely puzzled by the question of Lewin's present role in the field."

> I keep finding all kinds of extravagant statements that are just not true. I think there is a mindless reverence. But on the other hand I think there is no doubt that he has had more influence on what has happened in the field than any other single individual - but not directly.

Overall, Cartwright believes Lewin's theoretical ideas have become so much a part of the field that he doesn't get credit for them anymore. He said, "In one place I have often quoted, Lewin asked 'What is field theory?' and answered that it is not a theory but an approach - it is a theory about theory. It was this theory, along with his personality, that sparked ideas, concepts, points of view that are reverberating still. He was very seminal. Part of this vagueness was that you could read anything into it - it was like reading the Bible."

ALVIN ZANDER

Alvin Zander was an undergraduate major in general sciences at the University of Michigan and continued on for a masters degree in public health. He came to realize that "many of the contagious diseases at that time, were largely social psychological problems because people didn't do what they ought to do." He said, "There wasn't much social psychology taught in those days," so he took courses in educational psychology. After spending a year at The University of Chicago on a scholarship, he returned to Michigan and earned his Ph.D. in educational psychology.

While he was in graduate school, Zander worked as a community organizer in a program on Adult Community Education at the University.

> I had a job organizing community councils in small towns in the state. This was the special idea of one man there who believed that people could best learn what they wanted to know if they helped their communities prosper.
>
> I helped organize sixty community councils and had a radio program on Saturday afternoons to tell the members about what was going on in the various towns. That is how I came to be interested in groups - how these groups got started and why some succeeded and some failed. In the midst of that work, Ron Lippitt's masters thesis was published and I learned about Kurt Lewin.

Zander was so interested in Lippitt's thesis that he drove down to Iowa to see Lewin. Lewin not only talked with him but invited him home to dinner. Zander said, "I finished my degree in January and Lewin offered me a job at Iowa."

> Kurt had funds from The General Education Board of the Rockefeller Foundation to have one fellow a year. Doc Cartwright had been in that position but

> he had gone off to Washington to work with Ren Likert and Angus Campbell. So Kurt had this opening.

By this time World War II was about to begin and Lewin was working on food habits, which didn't particularly interest Zander, so he stayed only until the following fall. Lippitt had gone to work in the research service of the Boy Scouts of America and asked Zander to come to work with him. So Zander went to work doing research for the Boy Scouts for the next two and a half years.

> Then it became quite obvious that the draft board was going to be taking me, so Ron Lippitt and I signed up with the United States Public Health Service and we became clinical psychologists over night.

He also taught courses in leadership and psychological first aid to petty officers while in that service.

After the war, Zander taught for a time at Springfield College. While at Springfield, he visited the Research Center for Group Dynamics at MIT frequently and was one of the founders of the National Training Laboratories (NTL) at Bethel, Maine in 1947. When he decided he was ready to move on, he wrote to MIT and to Michigan about jobs. He said, "by that time Kurt had died and the group at MIT was clearly going to be leaving there so there was no sense in going to MIT. Instead, I went to Michigan." He went first into the school of education and when the Research Center for Group Dynamics moved to Michigan from MIT, he joined them. They arrived at Michigan in September of 1948.

At Michigan:

The group moved into the basement of a new Business School building. Together with Likert's Survey Research Center, they formed a unit called the Institute for Social Research (ISR). Most of the senior researchers at ISR also had appointments in various departments at the University - Zander taught both in education and in psychology.

> In ISR we had a hierarchy of positions. At the lowest level was a research assistant, a graduate student, then a research associate who also was a graduate student but with more responsibility. Next, was an assistant or associate program director who was told, "We are thinking of making you a program director (which was the most senior post) We will give you two or three years to show whether you can perform as a program director and can do solid research." We wanted to see whether they could get their own funds, hire research assistants, conduct their own research, get their report done on time and do all the things that a program director had to do.

When the group arrived at Michigan they were were housed in two large rooms - approximately 50 by 75 feet, according to Zander, "so we had a bit of distance between desks.

> By the time I arrived, the Center had an Administrative Committee composed of the program directors. Eventually, the graduate students said they wanted to know what was going on in the meetings so they elected two representatives, one a research assistant and the other a research associate.
>
> The research associates were graduate students or recent Ph.D.'s. Some would stay in Ann Arbor for years because they had a good job with us and they liked doing research. It often was hard to get them out of the nest.

Zander shared a work room with Jack French, Ron Lippitt, Stanley Schachter, Kurt Back, Emmy Pepitone, Al Pepitone and a secretary. In the other big room were Dorwin Cartwright, Hal Kelley, John Thibaut, Burt Raven, Leon Festinger and Cartwright's secretary. Zander said, "I always felt the Center group had very high caliber graduate students."

Later, when Group Dynamics moved out of this space into more traditional offices, the program directors and their assistants were housed as a unit. The directors had a single office while the graduate students working on that project were put in one or more four-person offices.

> We had seminars every Tuesday night from the beginning. Kurt Lewin started it. They had this at MIT and at Iowa we had something called a Quasselstrippe. In the early days at Michigan during the Tuesday night meeting we tried to do theory development. There was an effort to make Lewinian topology work for groups. It would be attended by anywhere from 12 to 20 people - practically the full population of Group Dynamics. Each term there would be a different person in charge.

Faculty and students were on a first name basis. Zander pointed out that the first group of students was about the same age as the faculty. In the early days of Group Dynamics, there were meetings held to report on research in progress but later, according to Zander, "The meetings got so big that the students were afraid to speak up, so the older staff did most of the talking. Eventually, we invited speakers from other parts of the campus. The students started to have their own Thursday noon meetings." The faculty was invited to attend this meeting and a few did so. "It was attended by ten to twenty students and they would usually report on their own research - about how far they had gotten and so forth. I think Bob Zajonc instigated that."

As a research organization, the structure in ISR was such that graduate students worked with program directors on the latters' projects. He said, "if they wanted to do something else, they usually had to go somewhere else because they had to be supported. Most of the students who did their dissertations with me were also my research assistants - so they chose a topic they cut out for themselves from my overall program." Discussing graduate students he has worked with, he said "They become close, like your sons." He said although he has lost track of a few, he knows where most of them are.

Zander's favorite part of the research process is planning the research and running the first pilot studies. He said, "I write a long essay on what we are going to do and why we are doing it because otherwise you forget those things." He believes there is a talent to the running of experiments in a laboratory and that not all people can do it successfully. The main component, he said is "enthusiasm - someone who can get the participants interested. Alex Bavelas got results few others could get because he was a charmer. Some experimenters can get subjects more involved in the experimental task and thus get stronger results."

Zander remarked that over the years, almost nobody among the program directors left until retirement age, except for people who got jobs they couldn't *possibly* refuse - "It was a very stable body. I am not sure why that was so because having to support yourself with grants and contracts is very difficult."

> You have to have enough drive and be strongly enough interested in your idea to seek funds. The procedure was that a person wrote a research proposal and I read it. Anybody else who wanted to could also read it. I read it to make sure that the budgetary requirements were met - just like a business firm. Then it went to the administrative committee and the human subjects committee of the university, then over to the office of research administration and back. A person had to be well organized to prepare a proposal - to get it in soon enough to go through all those committees and yet meet the deadline for submission.

JOHN THIBAUT

John Thibaut received his undergraduate degree in philosophy from the University of North Carolina in 1939. "It was still the depression, so I went to work in the steel mills for a year in Ohio and then I knew I didn't want to be a career steel worker so I applied to Ohio State for graduate work in philosophy." He described his early interests as centering in social, moral and political philosophy, especially in Rousseau, Kant, Hegel, and the British empiricists, which led to an interest in religious philosophy. "I also had left wing sentiments. In the thirties a lot of us did, and I thought I wanted to be a kind of worker priest. So I applied to the Berkeley seminary and was accepted."

But the war came along and Thibaut, deaf in one ear, tried to volunteer and was rejected. Later he was drafted. "They didn't find anything wrong with my ear when they drafted me so they put in 1A and sent me to the engineer school to be an engineering officer. That was on the basis of some test scores on mechanical aptitude they had there. I didn't have the *slightest* mechanical aptitude but I did real well on that test." About the time he graduated from engineering school, during an insurance examination it was discovered he could hear only in one ear. The army gave him a waiver and a desk job editing training manuals.

He was stationed near Washington DC and, "One drunken weekend in a bar, I met an old professor of mine from UNC. I had taken a course or two in psychology and this man said, 'They need people in the aviation psychology program and, true, you aren't a psychologist but you could learn that fast.' So I said, 'Fine.' Two weeks later I had my orders to go to Miami Beach to join a medical and psychological examining unit." It was the fall of 1943. "When I arrived, the major in charge, a psychologist, was dismayed to discover that, not only was I not an engineer - he *needed* an engineer, but I wasn't even a psychologist. I was a philosopher which was the *last* thing in the world they needed."

He worked hard and read everything he could on psychology and was eventually transferred to San Francicso for the duration of the war. There he joined a small research unit comprised of several psychology professors. "We weren't busy enough to do very much, so we studied. We organized little seminars and went through some of the basic texts on physiology, experimental psychology, and statistics, and that was enormously helpful. It was a very small group of very talented young people and they taught me psychology. At least as much psychology as I was capable of incorporating at that time."

Thibaut, released from the army early in 1946, was accepted in psychology at Yale for the following fall. "That was about the end of the big golden era at Yale - just magnificent, during the late thirties when Hull was developing the hypothetico-deductive behavior theory. They had the most *illustrious* group, Marquis, Hilgard, Sears, Whiting - so many of the great ones were there," he said.

His plans changed once he returned home to North Carolina. In the fall of 1946, instead of attending Yale, Thibaut entered MIT to study with Kurt Lewin.

> I came back to Chapel Hill just to wait until fall and to take some psychology with my old friend Fred Dashiell who was chairman of the department there. He was really a very great psychologist, a general experimental psychologist but a man with very catholic orientation. And he said, "really you would be better off with this new man Lewin than Hull." And that was a very *curious* thing for Dashiell to say because Dashiell was very heavily an experimentalist of the traditional sort - very behaviorally oriented. But he also had some intuition what my interests were and so, having already heard of Lewin, I listened. I got a few of Lewin's things out of the library and was immediately captivated by him. I applied and was accepted at MIT for that fall - the fall of 1946.

AT MIT:

When Thibaut arrived at MIT, there were 11 or 12 graduate students and five or six faculty. He recalled that, "The faculty had no responsibility to anybody but us. They had no undergraduate teaching duty, so it wasn't like going through any graduate program now." The faculty were all there, except Lewin himself, who was off trying to raise money.

The program was arranged so that in the first year all the students took a rigorous full year course in basic Lewinian concepts taught not by Lewin but by Marian Radke Yarrow who had completed a postdoc with Lewin in Iowa before the war. There were no textbooks, instead they read "all sorts of things that had been put together." Thibaut was impressed with the way Radke handled the group.

> We were all, you see, probably older than she or at least as old and back from four or five years in the army. I think we were kind of experienced people in our late twenties and were aggressive and eager to get back into academic work after that long deprivation. We wanted to know everything. We wanted to know truthfully and we were critical, aggressive and she bore up to it beautifully. I mean, we gave her a *very* hard time.
>
> Marian put us through the basics, the two McGraw Hill volumes (Lewin, 1935, 1936) of the very difficult technical material, and the Duke monograph,"Conceptual Representation and the Measurement of Psychological Forces" (1938). That was his supreme technical work and we were caused to master with fluency these concepts and then to use them to design projects that would analyze situations in these Lewinian terms. It was a kind of enforced discipline that got imposed on us to think of everything in that language and to become fluent in it.

In addition to the common language they learned, there was also a sense of excitement and urgency. There was a feeling of being on the cutting edge.

> Part of what was really great about the program was that, apart from this big course, everything else was one to one. It was partly that, it was partly a conveying to us of the imminence of big discovery. We thought we were always on the verge of a frontier. We were the avant guard of what would be the future of social psychology and it was that kind of conviction and excitement. It was something like the way some revolutionary leaders felt about the inevitability of the Marxist millennium, we had history working as our ally. We were in coalition with some powerful fateful movements that were going to carry us, so that motivation was tremendous. The optimism, the capacity to believe in the future of this, that it was going somewhere, it was that as a second thing.
>
> And I think then, it was also this language that we learned. You know, field theory - contrary to the way it has been presented - is not really a theory. It is a set of concepts that are highly differentiated but interrelated. It is this set of concepts that enables you to deal flexibly in an analytic way with any kind of situation you want to study - virtually any.

Every Wednesday afternoon there was a research meeting - the Quasselstrippe.

> Things would start and God knows when they would end. They would end when people were so exhausted they couldn't stand up to get to the blackboard anymore. There was something that encouraged involvement and participation by the very graphic representation. It was a matter of competing to get to the blackboard.

But it wasn't just the common language. In addition, Lewin's theory was one of great flexibility, allowing others to create useful little theories within it.

> I think these Quasselstrippe were just incredibly exciting and people got involved and participated. Hardly anybody could sit still. Some of the followers of Hull, of Skinner and some others had been passionate partisans - more kind of patriotically loyal to the ideology. The followers were conformists. That wasn't true of Lewin's group - partly because he didn't have a theory in the same sense.
>
> He didn't have a propositional theory, a theory of some axioms, postulates, and propositions derived in some hypothetico-deductive way. It didn't have substantive propositions. He had a conceptual system, and this then enabled people to develop *special* little theories like Tamara and Sears and Leon did with level of aspiration, which *is* a theory, or the tension system theory that Zeigarnik, Ovsiankina and later Murray Horwitz applied and was quite exciting.
>
> Another example was Kurt's notion about interdependence intra-personally, with various kinds of tension systems related as being more central or more peripheral - inner or outer. This then enabled Bavelas to apply that to communication networks among people.
>
> He had these concepts which could be so wonderfully useful, they were very carefully defined, but they enabled one to work flexibly on various situations, to study practical situations, or contrived situations. You could invent situations, that is you could use them synthetically, or you could analyze situations. The influence was very different and hence I think more long lasting than when you have a propositional theory that is subject proposition by proposition to be tested. Given the

> immature state of psychological science, those things are ephemeral because, even if they are confirmed, they tend to be of such narrow relevance that they are superseded by more comprehensive, wider kinds of conceptions.
>
> With Lewin's work, you could use it so that it didn't develop the kind of dogmatic assertiveness and insistence on kind of loyalty to propositions about substantive matter. It involved a kind of loyalty to a style and way of thinking which allowed a lot of very creative people to work together and use what they needed and they were able to communicate through these commonly understood concepts.

Thibaut believed that learning how to work within the discipline of a precise language, this set of concepts, and then to use those concepts analytically was tremendously important.

Working with Lewin:

Thibaut was one of the few graduate students at MIT who worked with Lewin directly. He attributed this to the fact that Lewin valued Thibaut's background in philosophy. The day before Lewin died, he dictated a letter accepting John Thibaut and Ben Willerman as his dissertation students, but Thibaut was his research assistant from the beginning.

Lewin's style of working was one of interdependence and movement.

> Not every day but whenever he felt like it, he and I would go for a walk along the Charles - across the bridge or along the river. This was when he was working on ideas that got published posthumously in the first two issues of Human Relations. (These articles were "The Frontiers of Group Dynamics; Concept, Method and Reality in Social Science; Social Equilibria and Social Change," (Lewin,

> 1947a) and "Frontiers in Group Dynamics: II. Challenge of Group Life; Social Planning and Action Research," (Lewin, 1947b)).
>
> He was thinking of things like his notion of quasi-stationary equilibria and that kind of thing. He would simply talk and I would listen and then of course I couldn't make any notes - we were walking along - as he was chatting. But he was thinking hard about the problem of how really to move into the social domain - the group domain, when he was sort of captured by prior decisions he had made about the language because it was a phenomenological based language and he was struggling with how to modify it so that it comprehends the social domain.
>
> Those were the things he talked about and it was my job then to go back to our little offices there in a converted electronics laboratory and put something on paper and get it to Winnie, the secretary, who would give that draft to him. He would then rework it and give it back to me and I would - I really was helpless to do much with it - so I would just look at it and make little editorial observations.

Another aspect of working with Lewin was that the students were immediately involved in research. Thibaut, along with Ben Willerman, was assigned the task of studying the operation of a small clothing factory - The Columbia Coat Company in Boston. They were to study cohesiveness of small work groups and the effects of this on norms of productivity. A second assignment was to study effects of ethnicity on cohesiveness within the work groups. They reported to Lewin each week.

Leon Festinger taught a two semester course in statistics. This was the second formal course in the graduate program. Thibaut described the course, "not so much textbook material but really Leon's direct tutelage in giving us problems each week." They began with probablility theory and moved from that to analysis of variance with a bit of correlation and regression mixed in.

There was a seminar taught by Lewin himself but not all the students took it. In that seminar, Thibaut remembered Lewin emphasizing "enormously" how to live with the pattern of numbers. He believed that students now learn very sophisticated statistical routines and logic and computer technology, but they don't learn to live with the numbers and ask questions of them the way he was taught by Lewin. "I mean to just kind of get obsessed with them, to really get down. Even now, I take a page of computations and try to keep them in my head and think about them when I am going to sleep and so on. I was taught to get the table of means and not yet worry - to get that pattern and live with it and think about it and speculate about it, about what it means."

Thibaut suggested that, beyond the fact that the group was older and eager to return to academic work, Lewin attracted "people who were the kind of people who could respond."

> He was just never satisfied, he did not regard anything he had ever done as a settled matter. It was all work in progress and so there wasn't any codified thing that you learned. You learned what had happened up until that point but that was not regarded sacredly. He was just so open and hence he was never defensive about any criticism and welcomed the sharpest criticism. He was enormously confident.

Lewin's confidence either attracted confident students, or it was contagious. Thibaut remembered touch football games in which the lineup reads like a who's who of social psychology. "We used to play the Harvard Social Relations people and beat the *hell* out of them...It was that our program was so much more aggressively confident about all sorts of things that even with inferior athletic ability, we beat the hell out of them."

Another confrontation with the Harvard group was a "kind of debate" between Gordon Allport and Kurt Lewin which Thibaut felt was also a victory for their group.

> It was held at Harvard and we all went along - all the graduate students. We were enormously outnumbered by Social Relations. Allport spoke

> first and he spoke very intelligently and beautifully and gracefully. There was an eloquent statement of his theory of personality as related to social behavior. Kurt just dominated. I mean, there was just no question amongst any of the audience. Kurt spoke, of course with a thick accent and not so eloquently but just with incredibly - with *courageous* statements that were really provocative and so much more exciting. One was polished and finished and civilized and the other was not so civilized, not so literate but in a crude way, so much more powerful. That was even a better victory than at football.

He remembered Lewin advising, "Don't read psychology, read philosophy or history or science, poetry, novels, biographies - those were the places where you would get the ideas. Psychology at this point - it will stifle your imagination."

Beyond MIT:

After Lewin's death, Jack French replaced him as Thibaut's thesis director. After the move to Michigan, Thibaut was still working on his dissertation, a study on cohesiveness of underprivileged groups in intergroup settings (Thibaut, 1950). Lewin's other student, Ben Willerman, moved over into the Survey Research Center at that point.

At Michigan, The Research Center for Group Dynamics were housed in two large rooms.

> They were primitive kinds of conditions in the basement. I was in at a desk next to Leon and then there was Hal Kelley and Cartwright and the secretary. In the other big room there were Ron Lippitt and the rest of them - Murray Horwitz, Albert Pepitone and Stanley Schachter.

They were not housed according to who was faculty and who was student; they functioned as colleagues. "We *were* all colleagues.

There was very very easy communication - and we called them Doc and Leon and so on," Thibaut recalled.

Thibaut had collected his data while still at MIT and was awarded his degree from there in January of 1949. He then spent two years at Harvard as a lecturer and research associate. Included in his research group were Henry Reicken, who had played against Group Dynamics on the Social Relations football team and later went on to work with Festinger and Schachter at Minnesota. Also, there was a graduate student named Ned Jones. Jack Brehm, who went on to study with Festinger and later was a colleague of Jones' at Duke, was their undergraduate assistant. Thibaut and Jones established a particularly close relationship - "like brothers," according to Thibaut.

It was during this time, he reported, that, "I was just sort of discovering Heider. Heider hadn't published very much, but there was this little article in the Journal of Social Psychology on phenomenal causality (Heider, 1946)." He in turn interested Jones who became excited by the ideas.

Thibaut left Harvard in the spring of 1953 and returned to The University of North Carolina where remained. A few months later, Jones came to Duke University, just a few miles away. "There wasn't any social psychology either here or at Duke when he came," Thibaut recalled. In order to remedy this, they formed the Organizational Research Group (ORG) at UNC but it included people coming over from Duke to attend. This group was consciously modeled on the Quasselstrippe.

> We *still* have it in our program here. We call it ORG and at the beginning of each year we go through the history of Lewin's work. We restate how it was in Berlin in that you *never* bring in a finished product, you only bring in something that is in progress and you ask for help.

The term Organizational Research Group was chosen originally because at its inception, the group included two sociologists, and a political scientist along with Thibaut and Jones. The idea was to have people who were actively doing research come in when they needed help and use the group to get that help. Occasionally someone would come in with something that was finished but had "turned out in some bizarre way that was inexplicable," and would use the group to help interpret the results. But always the group dealt with "work in progress," rather than results of completed work.

Subsequent work - Links with Lewin and Collaborations:

Thibaut worked in two areas, procedural justice and what he and Harold Kelley have called interdependence theory. He pointed out that fellow MIT student Morton Deutsch "had concentrated on distributive justice (while) I concentrated on procedural justice. We have a nice division of labor there."

> Kelley and I have developed a language that we think Lewin would have liked. It is something we think he would have been moving toward had he lived longer. It has the same kind of properties in the sense that it is not a theory but a set of related concepts that can be then used so that one can relate - or generate one concept out of another couple of them and so on.
>
> I think that learning how to work within the discipline of a set of concepts and then to use those concepts analytically so that you can study situations and begin to develop a taxonomy of situations in order to handle the whole is very useful.
>
> The situation that Lewin had commenced to study in the beginning was an individual psychological one - coming from his developmental orientation. Kelley and I tend to change that in the way he wanted to change to a social situation, an interpersonal situation or even a group situation. But we firmly believe and try to document that in the epilogue to our second book (Kelley & Thibaut, 1978) - that we are in the Lewinian tradition.

Students at UNC are trained in interdependence theory. Thibaut believed this theory is one avenue to "bring back groups," that it is the *truly* social thing. He said, "This is something Kurt saw very clearly and spoke of - The group is not composed out of similarity, out of categorization, but out of interdependence of fate."

> It is just *harder* to do interdependence things. There is no technology ready. There is ready-made technology, standard individual experimental formats for all, practically everything that is called social psychology: dissonance theory, reactance, commitment theory, attribution theory - they are all individual in relation to some fixed social stimuli that are under the experimenter's control. The effect of the subject's response to change that, whatever it is out there, that doesn't get taken into account, that would simply be a bad experiment. I think that people have simply not confronted, until now - I think now we are beginning to confront it -- the overwhelming importance, regardless of the technical difficulty of studying interdependent relations as the purely social ones. The rest of it is not really social psychology, only marginally so. It is individual psychology in a social setting.

There are a number of threads linking Thibaut's subsequent work with his early training. First, he indicated a direct link of interdependence work with his dissertation which was on the cohesiveness of underprivileged groups in intergroup settings. Another link with his training is the importance of a language with which to communicate about the concepts at hand. Third, in the training of his own students he encouraged them to use whatever method seemed best suited to try and answer a question, although he said, "I just personally feel more comfortable with laboratory experiments. Somehow I don't really believe a thing until I produce it in the laboratory, but that's personal."

A final thread woven into his career with it's origin at MIT is the collaboration with Harold Kelley. Although they were graduate students together at MIT, it wasn't until writing a chapter together for the 1954 Handbook of Social Psychology that their working relationship hit its stride. They collaborated for over thirty years.

Thibaut believed that their interdependence matrix is what Lewin might have come up with to solve the problem he was working on at the time of his death, the problem of overlapping lifespace. According to Thibaut, the original work at Bethel was designed as a laboratory for research on this problem, and was "premature."

> I think that really, even for Kurt, it was premature to try to be so effective practically until you really had a theory that guided. And his essentially individual theory didn't really do that. "There is nothing so practical as a good theory," but you have to have a theory that fits some of the practical things you want to do and the lifespace conceptualization was not adequate to handle a lot of the kinds of social things he really was interested in and wanted to handle.

HAROLD KELLEY

Harold Kelley was first exposed to Kurt Lewin's work while in the army during World War II. He recalled, "John Lacy, the eminent psychophysiologist was leader of a group of enlisted men of which I was one. We were supposed to read Lewin's work and think about whether there was anything that could be done in the realm of leadership. We worked on it very briefly but at least I did become familiar with the Iowa work at that point. I had never heard of it before. For me, social psychology really meant attitudes and prejudice and things like that."

While working in the aviation psychology unit during the war, Kelley encountered Stuart Cook. It was Cook who told him about Lewin's Group Dynamics program at MIT and convinced him to apply. Kelley had received a masters degree in psychology from Berkeley before the war and thinks he would have probably returned there if he hadn't met Cook. "I would certainly not have gone to MIT without Cook's urging. I didn't really know what I was getting into. I didn't know what it was going to become," he said.

> I am so impressed with those little choice points in your life and how much difference those make. This was certainly a very key one for me. Another one was getting into the army in the first place. I was drafted and could have just gone into the army somewhere but there was a man, C.W. Brown, I had impressed at Berkeley who got into the aviation program. He wrote some letters someplace so when I went to Monterey to the induction station, I was assigned to Santa Ana to the research unit. Who knows what was controlling *that* choice point.

His job during the war was to construct test items to aid in the selection of pilots, navigators and bombardier. "I made a lot of good friends and probably learned a little bit more about research or methodology. It was heavily testing and factor analytic work," he recalled.

Looking back he said, "At Berkeley, I think those people we identify as social psychologists were basically personality psychologists and that was the focus there. The Authoritarian Personality work is an example of what I mean. And I wanted to go into social psychology."

At MIT:

Kelley was released from the service and arrived at MIT in the spring of 1946. He remembers the group of graduate students who were selected for the program as being very heterogeneous.

> Trying to reconstruct it from what we were like, it seemed to me it was almost deliberately made heterogeneous in terms of interests, in terms of likely interests and *certainly* in terms of background. We all, I think, had pretty good recommendations from people - probably people that Lewin knew and/or respected.

Kelley toyed with the idea that only good people would have applied to "such an offbeat program," but finally rejected that idea in favor of the letter of recommendation theory. He pointed out that one thing which "reduced the riskiness" of the MIT program was its close relationship with Harvard. Graduate students at the two schools were free to attend seminars at either place. Kelley said Cook had made that an important part of his argument when trying to persuade him to apply.

Kelley was the fourth student to arrive - after Morton Deutsch, Gordon Hearn and Dave Emory. He started classes that spring semester. Their courses included a class in nonparametric statistics from Leon Festinger and later, one in Lewinian theory taught by Marian Radke. He remembers her course as being "very well taught."

> We went through all the Berlin work and the need systems and tension systems, the Zeigarnik and Ovsiankina work - the logic of all that finer work. It is an elegant body of work and she presented it elegantly and we went through it in an elegant, systematic way.

"I don't think I *ever* did research there," he laughed. "I remember being sent out to acquire some old theater curtains or something with which to line a big room that we were going to use as an observation room. They didn't have one-way mirrors. In Iowa I gather, they had used some kind of curtains - kind of an inner liner around a wall - that the observers would hide behind and look out through the mesh." He also recalled helping to develop measures which were to be given to the participants at a leadership training workshop in Connecticut - the precursor to the Bethel workshops.

Part of his experience at MIT was to work as a teaching assistant. "It was a funny thing called Econ 40," he said. "It was like an introduction to human relations for engineering students and was designed/invented by Doug McGregor and Irving Knickerbocker and presided over by Mason Haire. It was a marvelous course. Mort (Deutsch) did his thesis on groups which were classes from that course." It was a big course, broken up into sections which were the responsibility of the teaching assistants. "It was kind of the periphery of things but it took a lot of time," he recalled.

Kelley remembers little contact with Kurt Lewin and believes this was typical of most of the students. "We did have regular meetings in which he presided. I don't remember if one of them was a formal course or the Quasselstrippe, but they struck one as disorganized." There was also a separate, "big course" which all the faculty attended. "I remember *very* little about that course. There was nothing to read as far as I can remember," he laughed.

We did read kind of crazy things. We read Bateson and we read Alexander Layton - *The Governing of Man*. These were readings which had to do with social organization. It wasn't all focused on small groups. It seemed to me that it was focused somewhere between community organization and the group level. So were the projects - the Westgate project and the project down at Weymouth were kind of intergroup - community organization studies. They hired social workers as the key figures.What Kelley remembered about Kurt Lewin was:

> I got this very strong sense of how enthusiastic he could become about a problem and how much he could communicate this enthusiasm to people working on it and really kind of make things seem very important and urgent and exciting. But I do remember also, that you couldn't really fully recapture the content of it very much, later on. Part of what he did was to take a problem and translate it into his terms and he had a rich repertoire of terms that he could use. It wasn't just bathtubs, it was spaces and force fields and all that.
>
> It is difficult to imagine a person with all of Lewin's attributes: the charisma, the breadth of interests, the rigor and the *interest* in rigor but not a compulsion about it - and the aspirations for systematization. There were aspirations for applicable, important influential work. There were components there that each one of us could kind of pick out something and use it for ourselves.

Although Kelley believes he was, "vastly more influenced by Festinger than by Lewin," he and his closest collaborator, John Thibaut, have become increasingly aware of the ways in which they are Lewinian. They were both exposed extensively to Lewin's theoretical work during their courses at MIT. They felt strongly enough about this to address the issue explicitly in the epilogue to their last book (Kelley & Thibaut, 1978).

> We wrote a little section called "Historical Notes," and we really were writing to the point of "are we Lewinians?" So we tried to link our ideas to some of the concepts that we felt were from Lewin, some of the aspects of the approach. Partly, we'd been terribly aggravated by a man who wrote a book on exchange theories that gives a detailed summary of Thibaut and Kelley and so on, and compares it with Homans and Blau. He had several points that indicated how behavioristic we were and at some

> point implied we had some ultimate loyalty to a Hullian kind of theory, which couldn't miss the point by a wider margin imaginable. Anyway, just to kind of spite that kind of view or assessment of us, to show where the real loyalties were, we were really writing it to ourselves, and so it may be quite a bit of window dressing; I'm not sure of the validity of these things. But a couple of points I feel moderately comfortable about; one of them is that our whole goal has been the analysis of interdependence among people; and that's certainly a key orientation that came from Lewin. Now that is a vague concept, and he had interdependence operating on many levels and in many particular contexts; but the notion of interdependence among people in moving toward goals - the basic thing that Mort picked up in developing his thesis, and so on. It was that and somehow managing to do it more flexibly than he was able to do with the concepts he was using at the time. That seemed to me to be kind of the essence of what we were trying to do, and to some degree felt we had done.

Kelley said, "I didn't have much one-to-one contact with Lewin at all, but those ideas *did* take. They were kind of visual, topological - those are very clearly reflected in Thibaut's and my book. I am a very visual person, that's how I learned what this was." He believes that within Lewin's field theory, "were aspirations of building a grand, tight, coherent theory" and that Festinger resonated to that aspect of Lewin's work.

His memories of the MIT years are colored by the facts that he and his family were away from home and it was difficult for them to to adjust to the cold and to the, "scrubby living conditions." They finally found an apartment in the Westgate complex and, became good friends with the Willermans there.

Dorwin Cartwright was his thesis director, but Kelley doesn't remember being supervised heavily while working on his thesis. "I must have checked it with him somewhat," he laughed.

> I must have bloomed or I must have impressed them or they must have liked me. I wasn't really so fully aware of it until years later I guess. I was *very* lacking in confidence at that time. Whatever regard they had for me wasn't expressed in ways that would change that particularly. It took a long time to slowly seep in. I would have liked, when I graduated from there to have taken a job at San Diego State and Doc said no. So I *should* have known from that - or the fact that they hired me. Again, I am so impressed with those little points in your life and how much difference those make."

Beyond MIT:

Kelley completed his degree at MIT in 1948, before the group moved to Michigan. He went along to work with Leon Festinger as a postdoc when the group made the move. The research team at that time consisted of Festinger, Stanley Schachter, Kurt Back, John Thibaut and Kelley.

He described the continuing influence of Lewin's ideas when the group reached Michigan:

> All that early work, that first set of concepts that were in the pressures to uniformity work - the Westgate studies (Festinger, Schachter & Back, 1950), Schachter's thesis (Schachter, 1951), Back's thesis (Back, 1951) and some of the work that Thibaut and I did for Festinger - all that work had in it the concepts of cohesiveness and pressures toward uniformity and the processes of dealing with a deviant and so on. That body of work was basic group dynamics. My thesis wasn't on group dynamics at all, it was on social perception (Kelley, 1950). It was still very much individual psychology.

Of Festinger, Kelley said, "He influenced me enormously in the ways to think about problems and plus being a harsh critic, he is one you kind of internalize as somebody you think about when you are writing - you wonder what he would think. You come away with very high standards."

Kelley remembers teaching a methods course with Ronald Lippitt while at Michigan and mentioned the freedom and opportunity afforded those who are the first in the field. "In any area, the early studies are methodologically kind of slap dash - often more to make a point than to find truth." But Kelley said methodology has never figured very prominently in his thinking about his work. "I get bored very quickly with methodological discussions."

> It is something I know is very salient in lots of graduate programs, the core of the program. The one thing you *can* teach is methods. It is the one part that is standardized and then can be taught to some criteria. But what else you do, how you develop ideas, how big they are, whether you try to systematize, build theories or framework or what not, or take something smallish and pursue it out and all of that - there we have a *whole* slew of different models and probably real disagreements, at least in the short run about the principles, about the ways of doing that.

He continued "I was always a lousy experimenter. I love theoretical work. I *love* coming upon somebody else's set of data that I could make sense of. So I love ex post facto interpretations of data."

Subsequent Work - Links with Lewin and Collaborations:

Kelley went to Yale after he left Michigan and was also influenced by Carl Hovland. "I have really had a lot of contact with great people," he laughed, "Leon being one." He indicated that he had been influenced by Dorwin Cartwright as person who also had systematization or theory building goals. "There would be for me another instance of a role model who says, 'It's ok to think just about theoretical ideas.' And I am not sure many people had that as something they feel free to do," he explained.

"John Thibaut has undoubtedly been the most influential person in my life, certainly my intellectual life," Kelley said.

> When I was at Yale, I was asked by Gardner Lindzey to write a chapter on groups for the Handbook. And he suggested asking Irv Janis to write it with me. I asked Irv and fortunately Irv said no and then I asked John. We were good friends and it was just - we just struck sparks. We could generate for ourselves this excitement. "Oh boy, look how this fits together," or, "Now here's an idea," and pursue things out. And that has been an exceedingly rewarding thing. It has been very exciting - with a strong sense that what we are really building cumulatively is not going to wash away.

The collaboration endured for over thirty years - even though they lived on opposite sides of the country. When they would begin a book, "We could almost assign it to either one," he said, "But in the process leading up to that, we did play different roles. I was much more likely to be kind of a systematizer and he was more likely to bring in a big idea - often from his very wide reading and his wide knowledge of philosophy." They would take turns being first author on their books as an acknowledgement of their true interdependence.

Kelley's goal is to spend the next few years before retirement pulling together several bodies of work. He said, "I am trying to make sense out of three domains of things: First is the situations that people find themselves in - a kind of structure of the problem - type of problem. Second is the types of person properties or dispositions that are relevant to those problems. Third is the types of processes that are generated when a pair of people with their respective dispositions get dropped into this problem and interact about that problem. I am trying to make sense out of these three things at once." He hopes through his analysis to make sense of patterns of processes in various literatures such as self disclosure, the regularity of turn taking in conversations and other relevant areas. He believes the interdependence analysis he and Thibaut have been working on forms an underlying structure supporting these processes.

> I am trying to make sense of the regularities in interpersonal process by explaining the regularities as due to the underlying situations that we find ourselves in on the one hand. And on the other hand, the disposition - whatever terms you want to talk about that it - that we bring to play *in* these situations. So it is partly a way of making sense of the person/situation question that is floating around. My interest in attribution plays into that because it is a very important part of these processes - sizing up the situation.
>
> Now all of this is *very* Lewinian, the notion of types of situations - there it's types of conflict, for example approach-approach or approach-avoidance. It is really a taxonomy of situations. Another very important concept for us is the way people reconceptualize or transform or think about the situation, and that's the way their dispositions are expressed.

Kelley feels the theory needs more development before he would be ready to train students and send them out to train other people as a means of influence. It hasn't developed to the point that it is ready to be tested for implications.

Apart from Thibaut, Kelley's intellectual community includes people with whom he works at UCLA. He mentioned Cartwright as, "somebody I would think of to send a paper to or to try to discuss a paper with." He also pointed to others in the "close relationship area" of social psychology such as Ellen Berscheid. "John Thibaut would be one I would think, 'Well now, I am writing something here, what's *new* in it for John.'"

Looking back over his career, he said, "The greenhouse model really worked for me. Partly the relationship with Thibaut has provided a kind of a greenhouse, stimulating things, providing a kind of warmth."

Kelley discussed a reunion of the MIT group held at Columbia in April of 1978. This meeting was held at his instigation. "I was going to be in New York then and it was the thirtieth anniversary of when we left MIT and it just seemed like a nice idea. I wrote Stan and Mort and they agreed quite readily. Then when we sat down at the meeting I just kind of specified that we were going to go around the room and Stan thought it would never work. He didn't think we would be able to sit there and listen to each other," Kelley laughed. "Well we just had a very nice time. I think by and large we have had a lot of good feelings for each other."

He said he thinks for him many of the friendships really developed after leaving the group. The close collaboration with Thibaut began later and, "Leon over the years has done some good things for me - write a letter to somebody or something." He expressed a sense of having been part of an "inner-group."

> I think more important, having been at MIT, the most important thing there was becoming a member of that group...It has meant a number of very good close relationships, cherished over the years. And equally importantly, a kind of intellectual reference group - the people who I think of when I'm writing something, who I have some hope would understand it and would be sympathetic, but yet the ones I really wonder, "What would they think about it?" So, it's a set of people whose opinions and evaluations, even if I never hear them, are very important to me.

KURT BACK

Even though Kurt Back began his graduate studies in law, he said he eventually became a psychologist because he is Viennese, "so that is automatic." He joked that his mother attended some lectures given by Freud while she was expecting him, so that made him "prenatally selected." Following his father into law Back found that by the time he had finished his education he had become more interested in psychology than in law.

> European law study was very strange. You have a lot of lectures that are completely irrelevant and then you take a cramming course before your comprehensive exams. Everything counts. After that you are finished. So there is always one year where you don't do anything and then one term when you cram. So everybody does something during that year. I did psychology.

At that point in the late thirties, "history interfered," he said. By then, "I decided as law wasn't going to give me a career anyway, I might as well do what I want." While he was waiting in Switzerland to emigrate to the United States, he went to the University of Geneva for one term. After he came to the United States, "I just took psychology."

Back entered New York University as a junior, "with the vague idea that psychology wasn't going to make me any money so I had to do applied psychology and I thought about advertising. That is how I thought about social psychology." His first course in social psychology was taught by a man named Douglas Campbell who had worked with Lewin during Lewin's visit at Stanford early in 1932. It had been Campbell's job at Stanford to help Lewin with the language. Back reports Campbell saying, "Lewin - the way he was, he would talk his ideas out loud and was influential in that way." The text used for the course was J.F. Brown's, *Psychology and the Social Order* (1936), which combined Lewin's ideas with marxism and psychoanalysis. It was the only text used and Back remembers thinking, "It was, a lousy book, it was all so political - it gave you Brown's political views." What he learned in the course, however was topology. "There was no other psychology that we learned," he said.

After graduating from NYU, Back went on to graduate school at UCLA. He recalls the department as being, "quite conservative - both in a political and a psychological way." There was also "a kind of Lewinian underground among the graduate students." This furthered his interest in Lewin and he considered going to Iowa to study. One fellow student actually did go to Iowa for a summer term and came back very enthusiastic about his experience.

By this time it was 1942 and Back was called into the army.

> They had this program to save intellectuals during the war. They didn't talk about it that way but they had what they called the Army Specialist Training Program (ASTP). They pulled people with high IQ and also who had some training, back to school - I was pulled out for that. Of course, the normal thing to do would have been to take languages but they had the quota to fill in psychology and so I went into that. It turned out I was sent to Iowa.

At Iowa, Back was assigned to a statistics course taught by Leon Festinger who had recently completed his degree with Lewin. The director of the program was Kenneth Spence who understood that the men assigned to this unit were advanced students and weren't interested in taking the introductory psychology courses. "We were very bored," Back said.

> We wanted to keep busy. We negotiated to get seminars. Spence gave us one. Also Lewin was giving one. He didn't have any students because of the war so four of five of us attended his seminar. Festinger and all the others who were still around, mostly the women, also attended. The unit was there for two terms.

By the time the war ended, Back knew he wanted to continue in social psychology. He was particularly interested in survey research at the time. "In the end it was between Yale and MIT and at that time I didn't know it would have made a big difference in my life," he said. "MIT was very select, but I got in...I don't think Lewin remembered me at all. But when Festinger picked his research assistants, he picked me."

At MIT:

Back entered MIT in the fall of 1946 and immediately went to work with Festinger on the Westgate housing study (Festinger, Schachter & Back, 1950). He was in the group which came in just a few months before Lewin's death and had little direct contact with him. The courses required for that group included the seminars Back had just taken at Iowa. "I took Lewin's seminar instead and so I had that much contact." It was the seminar for the second year students. "He was going to give another one the second term. And we were all assembled for the first class when we found out he died."

He recalled the tension between Leon Festinger and Ron Lippitt and believes that when Lewin died the group was held together by Cartwright, "who was a good administrator." Previously, Lewin had held the group together, "with charm and by being brighter than anyone...Leon was also brighter, but in a different way." Back contrasted Lewin's style with that of Festinger.

> With Lewin, you would give him an idea and if he liked it he would just go way off and he really needed his students to pull him back. The ones who could closely work with him were that way. Festinger was not.
>
> If you look at his theories, a good study of Festinger's, they are about trying to have everything together, rationally well-organized. All ideas have to fit together nicely. Now that is what dissonance theory says - that everybody tries to put all ideas

> into a consistent framework. I don't know whether that it true of everybody, but it is true of Festinger.

The contrast can be seen in the two big housing studies carried out by the Research Center. In the case of the Westgate Housing study (Festinger et al., 1950), they began with interviews and eventually, "stripped it down to a very specific one-to-one theory and we did the experiments," Back recalled.

One result of that study was the realization that the residents of Westgate, all MIT students and family, might have created a unique situation.

> There was a part of the study which was really asking about the social position of living in the development - what prestige other people have. And one thing we never studied was that Westgate worked because they were all in the same boat. They were all upper middle class kids. The women were rebels because you weren't supposed to get married to a student - somebody who clearly couldn't support you. The women came out in the interviews saying that their mothers were all very upset and would look at where they were living and cry and things like that. Having other couples in the same boat - living below their traditional standard and being attacked by their parents - gave the couples in Westgate a common feeling. We would say today: A group attains cohesion by reference to an outside enemy, here the parents and parents' friends. Then the idea was, "all right, we have something where the social position overrides favorably and completely, the lousy housing."

They began a second housing study which was done in a project south of Boston, in Weymouth. This was shortly after the war and housing was very tight and people had difficulty finding places to live. Many of the Weymouth residents were shipyard workers. Back said, "It was a downward sort of mobility and nobody felt socially like a shipyard worker so they hated the place. They tried to make it a whole community-action research study. Community workers come in and it became this big incoate kind of research which might have been great but then Lewin died."

Lewin was very involved in the Weymouth study. It was to have been "the *great* study," Back said. Lewin at that time was interested in the idea of self-hate and saw this as a way to investigate a group which had negative group feeling. According to Back, "The idea was to change them, to make them a cohesive group - to make them believe in the group, to believe, 'Our project is good, we have good people here, we can do things, we can communicate.'" The idea was really to study "what you can do with people - that would have been the Lewin book. It could have been the bible of the community workers in the sixties," he said.

When Lewin died, work on the Weymouth study had been completed but the data had not yet been analyzed. After the move to Michigan, Leon Festinger and Harold Kelley took it over and, Back said, "it went down again into those single variables which didn't change too much."

> The best thing they got out of it was that we were almost kicked out because people thought we were communists. And they wrote one article about rumor.

Back believes that at Iowa, Festinger's role had originally been to introduce Lewin to statistics.

> If you look at the earlier papers, they are done case by case. You do one experiment, you look *exactly* at the data, you find out what it means - what *the whole thing* meant and then you don't repeat it. You then use the ideas which you got from this one experiment and do a different one. You go step by step and that is how they did it - and you did that with him. They discussed each experiment. You do an experiment one day and then would spend a week discussing it - and then do the next one which wasn't the same experiment. But that is not how you get means and standard deviations.

Back recalls that at MIT, "To get a good dissertation done that was scientifically right, in the long run you had to go to Festinger to get his help. There were four people in the department - everyone had the same committee."

Lewin's Style:

Back's memory of the Quasselstrippe involves their work on the Westgate study. The group went into the Quasselstrippe twice, once during the early stages for help and once at the end with data they were having trouble interpreting.

> We went in there twice within one year. The first time we had the idea that a different course and different ideas and different communication and like that. And during the discussions people got the idea that maybe you run a communications experiment and to figure it out that way. That is how we got started - we had a very vague idea that some places people talk to each other and at other places they don't talk to each other. Now how do you prove that? We went in there at the end of the interviews and had no idea - we didn't say, "those data show that people don't talk." And some people had the idea of running a communications experiment.
>
> The second time the study was almost finished and we had everything explained. We had a beautiful hypothesis and everything - except in Westgate West, which was two stories of five apartments. The people who were center were always very popular and this wouldn't fit with any of the theory and we just went and would say, "Well, here are the data, why is it?" Because again, we didn't try to prove the other theory, we really wanted to have an answer.

From this study came research projects on conformity, on deviance and on communication. These projects were carried out as dissertations by the graduate students.

During the Quasselstrippe, Lewin would sit to one side and people would solicit his opinions. But they didn't worry about contradicting him in these work meetings.

> I was not in the Weymouth study, but I was around and talked to students who were involved. The first year students were surprised and even upset by the way other participants were rude to Lewin. For instance, he had an idea that the manager of the project somehow transmitted his negative feeling about the inhabitants to the residents of the project and made them feel hostile toward each other. The other team members, students and staff would attack Lewin for his "magical" thinking until he retracted this idea. Basically he would stick to his general ideas, but gave in on many specific points.

Festinger's Style:

The research group working on the Westgate study would meet once a week to discuss how to plan. Back recalls, "First we just did the work the first year. The second year we met - we were his students and we went to his home once a week. The third year was in Michigan and there the people who were really interested in communication were together - Thibaut, Kelley..." The way Festinger handled the meetings was, "He would say, 'Well, you are that far, have you any problems - or you are that far, do you need any help?' or something like that."

Beyond MIT:

As mentioned earlier, when Lewin died the loss was felt on both the personal and the organizational level. Once Dorwin Cartwright took over he became aware that MIT was attempting to cut back to "hard money." The students then began to hear rumors of the faculty negotiations with other universities. Since they wanted to move the entire Research Center, including students, as a unit, few universities were interested. The indea was too unusual There were rumors that the faculty had offers of full professorship at various places but they were to come without the students. Another rumor had it that the group could come, but they would be assigned to different departments along traditional academic lines. Back recalled, "They made a decision in the spring of how to do it and then to get some guarantees for the students too." There were four faculty at that point: Cartwright, Festinger, Lippitt, and Jack French who came in when Lewin died. Those who didn't make the move were Marian Radke and of the students, Morton Deutsch and Gordon Hearn had both finished their degrees. Harold Kelley had finished but eventually along as a postdoc.

Back thinks the move to Michigan was possible for two reasons. First, Cartwright worked with Rensis Likert during the war and enjoyed a good relationship with him. Likert had moved his survey research group from Washington to Michigan the previous year and this was the second reason Michigan was a likely prospect: there was precedence for an organized unit to move in. When the Research Center for Group Dynamics arrived, they along with the Likert's Survey Research Center formed the Institute for Social Research.

Michigan was not as loose an organization as MIT when it came to the Research Center's activities.

> I remember Stanley Schachter had some trouble. There were some Michigan people on the committee who felt deception was immoral and didn't want to let him do his study. It was the study where he had all those clubs - The "Johnny Rocco" study, Schachter's dissertation (Schachter, 1951). The final compromise was that anybody who wanted to really stay in the club could, and he would have to run the club for a term.
>
> I observed a few times for him and what he did was he used the same group pressure he used in the study. After the debriefing, he announced that he

> was willing to continue the club for those who so desired, but he induced a group norm not to insist on the club, and wanting to stay. And nobody stayed. But still, he had to make that compromise in order to get along with Michigan. That was our relationship with Michigan.

Schachter needed the clubs only for the experimental session but had been given permission to run the study on the condition that he continue to run them if the members wanted to continue. This is an example of the change in institutional environment the students found once they had moved to Michigan. At MIT, they had been "quite autonomous" and had no one looking over their shoulder.

The students who moved to Michigan were given a choice about which school they wanted their degree from. Back took his from MIT. He said, "See, I just didn't trust promises, I wasn't going to risk having to take exams over."

Subsequent Work - Links with Lewin and Collaborations:

Back received his degree in 1949. He saw himself as a researcher and spent most of the next ten years in a series of research positions. "I thought I was a survey research person, so I went to the census bureau," he said. He stayed there for two years. He then went to Germany on an interviewing research study for Columbia University.

> I went to Puerto Rico and Jamaica, and there I became a group dynamics expert; I did a big experimental study, which naively I did exactly the way it was in the textbook for control groups, with a 4 x 4 design and all kinds of different techniques and content. It was very beautiful. It was so complicated that when we wrote it up, it became the standard in this kind of experiment because nobody has the guts to replicate it.

He worked on applied research - on housing and public health. It wasn't until after all this work that he "decided to break down and get into academic life." There were several reasons given for this decision. Among them was the fact that as a researcher there was the strain of having to look for a new job every few years, "And also, if you have some general ideas, you have no students to work closely with," he explained.

Back has been in the Department of Sociology at Duke since 1959. He said he has fewer students now than he has had in the past and points to the "breakdown" of the social psychology program at Duke as part of the reason. He recalled the time when Ned Jones, Jack Brehm and Darwyn Linder all were on the social psychology faculty. Brehm had been a student of Jones' at Harvard when John Thibaut was there. Back said, "Jones thought Brehm was so smart, he should study with Festinger."

Discussing the Organization Research Group which included faculty from both Duke and nearby University of North Carolina, Back said, "Brehm called it The Seekers." This group had been consciously modeled on the Quasselstrippe by it's originators. He continued:

> I think the crucial thing is you find out that it works, that you have competition to talk, to present. When whoever organizes it has to go around and recruit people, then you have lost.
>
> It is people needing the group for their own problem. First of all it means that if you have to tell them how good your research is already, that you have it all done, you would get very defensive if somebody says, "Well, what is..." then forget it.

Back's research activities have been very diverse. He said, "Throughout my career I have worked in the field from a theoretical, methodological, applied and, cultural point of view." He doesn't think he is a very good experimenter, however, because, "a good experimenter is a stage director." He believes his influence on students has been away from experimentation.

> We don't teach them that research is from experiment to experiment and the only thing you get out of it is an idea for another experiment. Part

> of it may be self defense, but part of my objection is that you can only get people to do things if you know how. What you should learn is to do an experiment and then study the way you are doing it.

The way he currently works leaves very little for students to do. He is writing on teenage pregnancy and when this work is completed he plans to write a book on the population control movement in England and the United States. Occasionally when he works with students he will, "write up my ideas, the beginning and the end, and let them find the evidence - let them write the middle part. This way they can learn and this way we can get things together."

Back believes Lewin's influence on his career can be seen in his "openness to all kinds of methods and all kinds of ideas.. It has caused me difficulty to always fight against the trend." One thing he would like to accomplish is to "write a good book on method."

> There are three different ways of looking at human life. One is experimental, one is social which is this intersection of personality and society and one is the actual interaction. Then you need methods which integrate all three - really saying we are looking at human life and we are using all kinds of methods. Mathematics, experiments - even political history.

Looking back at his experience at MIT as a productive environment, he said:

> I was chairman here for a while and I was interested in how you make a graduate program. What we did was divide up the department into two programs. And so we had the structure and each group had seminars and all that. But you still have to hire Lewin to make it work.

ALBERT PEPITONE

Toward the end of the war, Albert Pepitone was transferred into a psychological research unit directed by Stuart Cook at Langley Field, Virginia. Released from the Air Force in early 1946, he intended to return to Yale where he had done graduate work and received an MA before entering the service. During the spring and summer of that year he accepted Stuart Cook's invitation to work at the Commission of Community Interrelations (CCI) in New York City, which Cook directed. CCI was engaged in a variety of research projects that had to do with combatting racial prejudice and antisemitism. It was there, while writing a *Psychology Bulletin* paper on methods of measuring prejudice and discrimination, that he met Kurt Lewin.

Lewin was an organizer and a principal consultant of CCI and would come down from MIT from time to time to hold discussions about the research projects. The year before Lewin had established the Research Center for Group Dynamics at MIT.

> I read sometime that spring, a brochure about the Research Center. I also learned that he would be down for a consulting visit in July. I mentioned to Cook that I would like to talk to Lewin about the MIT Center and my plans to return to graduate school.
>
> He arrived at the office overheated and excited. I was to learn that Lewin was highly energized and in motion most of the time, rushing from meeting to meeting, intown and out of town, on an endless agenda. He approached my desk: "Pettibone" (even after he knew me well he would sometimes slip on my name) "I would like to speak with you, but it is too hot here. Let us find an iced coffee." We went downstairs and stood at Nedick's counter at Broadway and 50th street for two hours talking

> about a variety of subjects. I spoke a little about myself - that I had worked in several Air Force psychological research projects on selection and training of military personnel, that I had been a graduate student in experimental psychology at Yale, and a musician - an arranger and clarinetist - since my high school days. But most of the talk would have been coded as "social relations between members of different groups," "how political opinions are supported and expressed through newspaper reading," and so on.
>
> I was impressed with several things: the range of his interests, his ability to move across domains and levels of discourse, and his warm accessibility. Although he did most of the talking, I felt that I was participating in a sensible way without any of the restraints that are usually associated with differences in status and authority. The general de-emphasis of differences in rank and the concomitant emphasis on the task and its requirements were two characteristic features of the Research Center at MIT.

This meeting with Lewin, along with the experience working at CCI, led Pepitone to reconsider his plans to return to Yale. Lewin had described the Research Center to Pepitone and it became clear to him that, while it was not a graduate department of psychology, the faculty was part of MIT and would be able to award the doctorate. Moreover, "I had known about the work of some of the people there and believed that the Center would be a unique interdisciplinary combination of interests and abilities." The prewar psychology program at Yale had been predominately a program in experimental psychology set within a framework of stimulus-response learning theory. After his Air Force experience at several psychological research units and after the New York experience in intergroup relations, Pepitone had come to believe that behaviorism was severly limited in dealing with the social behavior of people and that only a thorough-going social psychology based on an analysis of the social environment could do so. He remembers, "It was a combination of this new approach, social psychology, and the remarkably accessible and supportive leader that brought me to the decision to try to get into MIT."

Pepitone write to Lewin later in the summer and was invited up to MIT to meet Dorwin Cartwright, Ron Lippitt and Leon Festinger. Lewin was out of town during his visit, but he received the impression from the interviews that he had been accepted.

In addition to Lewin's accessibility and the de-emphasis of status differences, the supportive attitude toward graduate students probably contributed to the high morale and productivity at the Research Center.

> It was as if in the original decision, they decided to take individuals on their strengths and that was it. Yes, there were examinations, but in looking back I don't have any sense of being tested - that my ability was in question, that's the amazing thing.

At MIT:

He entered MIT in the fall of 1946 and roomed with fellow graduate students Morton Deutsch and Stanley Schachter, in an apartment across the Charles River in Boston. He remembers:

> From the first day we began to learn of the human relations workshops and other projects on intergroup relations. We met a number of researchers and field workers involved in these activities, and began to recognize various kinds of data that were funneled into the Research Center, which became the focus of long meetings attended by different sets of people. Yet all of this was outside the basic graduate student program which included seminars and research participation. There were several seminars which almost everone took - one on research methods, one on field theory, which included Lewin's Berlin and Iowa work.

He described the seminars as being small and lively with students talking a good deal and arguing good naturedly with the instructor.

> I think most of us spent hours on the qualifying examinations but as I see it now, there was relatively little anxiety amongst the graduate students that they wouldn't make it.

Pepitone recalls that in addition to the "in-house" seminars, many students regularly attended seminars at Harvard. He remembers Jerome Bruner's comprehensive seminar on Perception. There were also contacts with graduate students and faculty in the Henry Murray Clinic and the Social Relations department including Gordon Allport, R. Freed Bales, Clyde Kluckhohn, and others.

In addition to the seminars, the graduate program consisted of considerable research participation in the field. There was an array of research experience to be gained including both laboratory and field work. Much of it was funded by outside agencies to whom the researchers reported. The Bethel workshops for leadership training were an enormous enterprise which provided paid assistantships and involved most of the students.

He remembers that they participated on each other's dissertation research. For example, Pepitone helped Morton Deutsch determine the reliability of the coding system used in the studies of cooperation and competition. "There was a lot of interchangeability and each person had a lot of different experiences in research and these were talked about." They were discussed during the Quasselstrippe, where, "different people would hold forth and talk about research and Kurt would talk about field theory - more abstract theory."

> A central characteristic of Lewinian style is evident in the Psychologisch Forschung studies of his students in the Berlin years and in his later research at Iowa. He would always have a finding at the center of the analysis which he would represent in topolotical and force field terms or with some other conceptual device. The representation would then be confronted with other findings and informal observations that were brought up. The representations were evaluated by this process, but were never thought to be written in stone. They were useful tools; they were heuristic in making generalizations and suggesting new research.

In addition to the varied research experience, the students also had opportunities to teach. The Department of Economics and Social Sciences at MIT offered a popular course in human relations which was divided up into several sections each semester.

> A number of us taught social psychology for two or more semesters. We had a remarkable amount of autonomy to teach the content of the course in the way we wanted to, limited only by the need to have a sufficiently common basis for grading. Part of the instruction material was feedback on the research in which the students participated. For example, they were subjects in Deutsch's experiment on competition and cooperation, and Kelley's experiment on person impressions.

Later, after the Research Center moved to the University of Michigan, Pepitone taught the sections of Leon Festinger's graduate statistics course.

Pepitone also commented on the different styles developed by different people in the group after Lewin's death. He recalled, "I think Lippitt was more closely related to the phenomena of the Bethel workshops. Festinger was more experimentally oriented."

Pepitone's dissertation was on social perception (Pepitone, 1950). Leon Festinger was his thesis director and it was through discussions with him that the dissertation was developed. About the time the project was shaped up and ready to go, the group made the move from MIT to Michigan. He reports, "I decided to do the final experiment there rather than at MIT on the practical grounds that I would be there and would be using their facilities. We were basically given the choice to take the degree at MIT or Michigan."

At Ann Arbor, he ran his main thesis experiment in a local school.

> There is another feature of the Research Center that may have accounted in part for the productivity by making it easier to try out research ideas, drop them if they didn't work, or carry them through the necessary control groups and large samples of subjects, namely, the availability of funding. For my experiment I needed three highly trained actors to exhibit and verbalize different amounts of power and approval while interviewing high school students. Many hours were required to train them and run them through the large number of subjects. I do not remember having difficulty obtaining the substantial amount of money for this project.

Beyond MIT and Michigan:

After receiving his degree in 1949, Pepitone reamined for two years at Michigan as a Study Director. He became involved in a number of research projects including a study contracted with the United Automobile Workers union on changing prejudiced attitudes through group discussion. He also helped Cartwright edit the collection of Lewin papers that became *Field Theory and Social Science* (1951). In 1951, he moved to the University of Pennsylvania where he has remained. He said, "Much of the research I did in the early fifties derived from theoretical issues that had been discussed and worked on earlier when I was at the Research Center. Toward the end of the fifties and in most of the sixties, I worked in the area of cognitive processes."

Later, in the 70s he began to look to the other social sciences for "both theoretical connections and data connections." This has continued and intensified in recent years. He currently considers himself to be a "cultural social psychologist" and teaches an undergraduate lecture course in what he calls "bio-cultural-social psychology," in which he elaborates both the biological and cultural bases of social behavior. The specific issues that have occupied him during the past few years are questions of social judgment and attribution. He is currently most interested in human belief systems. "We are doing research which checks the hypothesized functions of beliefs in God, fate, evil, spirits, witches, luck and other 'supernatural' agents and powers," he said.

Subsequent Work - Links with Lewin and Collaborations:

Pepitone attributes "the decline of the group in social psychology," to several factors in combination. First, Kurt Lewin's early death - the loss of the intellectual father. Second and related, the shift of some of the faculty and graduate students of the Research Center to a more individualistic perspective. "One problem," he said, "is that the theory of group dynamics didn't keep pace with the research." Also, research on groups is not only expensive but time consuming.

Overall, he said, "The impact of Lewinian style thinking I believe has been profound, yet it is difficult to pinpoint. It is a style, and styles have few principles." One stylistic feature he pointed to is, "this marriage between data and concepts." A second feature of the style is the distinction Lewin made between historical and contemporaneous conceptions of dynamics - one of the distinctions Lewin discussed that exist between Aristotelean and Galilean thinking. Finally, the Lewinian style included an appreciation and sensitivity to context - the interplay of person with environment.

> From the representation of individual as a-person-in-the-environment "life-space", to the analysis of the group as a dynamic whole, to the analysis of the ecology of groups represented by "channels" and "gatekeepers" who make decisions about what conditions and resources affect the group, to the analysis of "quasi-stationary equilibria" representing the forces that affect groups which

originate in the social structure and culture of a community, the Lewinian approach is thoroughly contextualist and radically different from approaches to social psychology in which the individual is theoretically isolated from all other bodies and souls.

MORTON DEUTSCH

Morton Deutsch became interested in Kurt Lewin's work while he was an undergraduate at City College of New York. He was impressed by a course in social psychology he took from Max Hertzman. He was influenced by the text in the course - J.F. Brown's (1936) *Psychology and the Social Order*. This book combined Kurt Lewin's work with some of the most exciting ideas of the times - marxism and psychoanalysis. The motivational aspect of Lewin's theory appealed to Deutsch because he was interested in clinical psychology. "There was a feeling that Lewin was in touch with the richness of common sense psychology and was concerned with trying to transform that into science, and that appealed to me very much," he recalled.

After earning a masters degree in clinical psychology from the University of Pennsylvania, Deutsch entered the Air Force during World War II and completed a tour of duty as a combat navigator. He then worked as a clinical psychologist in a convalescent hospital until his release from the service in May, 1945. At this point Deutsch wanted to continue graduate work and was torn between clinical and social psychology as the direction in which to go.

He had also been impressed by the Lewin, Lippitt & White (1939) studies of group atmosphere and was interested in "the idea of working on groups and the way groups influence individuals."

> When I got out of the Air Force I was fortunate enough to be able to pick where I wanted to go and actually to arrange interviews with very impressive people - Thurstone and Carl Rogers at the University of Pennsylvania, Don Marquis at Yale and also Kurt Lewin, actually in New York. I had the opportunity to pretty much go wherever I wanted. I found Lewin and his new idea - the idea

> of working on groups and the way groups influence individuals - very exciting.
>
> And he was a *very* charismatic and exciting personality. Talking with him - he bubbled with a certain kind of enthusiasm which was very catching and involving - I was taken by him and his vision and so I decided I would go there; I was fortunate enough to not have any problem getting admitted. I was one of the first three students.

At MIT:

The Research Center for Group Dynamics began operating in the Fall of 1945. When Deutsch arrived, the four faculty - Ron Lippitt, Dorwin Cartwright, Leon Festinger and Marion Radke - were already there. Lewin himself would come and go as his fund-raising schedule allowed. There were few students at first - others came as they were released from the service, with the bulk of them entering in the fall of 1946. The two other graduate students at the time Deutsch arrived were Gordon Hearn, a social worker from Canada and Dave Emery who had been a student of Koehler's. Deutsch thinks one important aspect of the MIT environment was that, "We were a more mature group of students for a number of reasons. Most of us had masters degrees, most of us had been through a war experience and we viewed ourselves as adults. And the difference in both age and psychological perspective was not that great between the faculty and the students."

The group was very cohesive. "It was a *small* group and we had a lot to do with one another in many different ways both as students and working on projects and then socially," he remembers. When they arrived, students were given a lot of responsibility right away.

Deutsch described the innovativeness brought about by the Research Center environment with an anecdote:

> People were looking around to find out something about what made for productive physicists and they found out that Reed College had presumably a

> really marvelous record from their undergraduate program in physics. And then they went to investigate and they found out that the faculty - one of them was always on leave, another was an alcoholic and so the students pretty much did their own thing.
>
> Well, the faculty (at MIT) were not alcoholics, but essentially we were given heavy responsibility. We were given, as students, the responsibility for designing the research for Bethel and for doing a lot of the active creating, thinking and planning. It was not a hierarchical structure, but much more of an egalitarian system in terms of the relationships between students and faculty with the students being given a lot of responsibility very quickly.

According to Deutsch, this was part of Lewin's genius, "that he had a lot of enthusiasm and confidence. He had the sense that we were in the pioneering phase of something and his orientation of openness was expressed in the question: *why not*?" This enthusiasm and the pioneering atmosphere was communicated to the students by Lewin, and liberated them to try things out.

Deutsch described the tensions among the faculty at MIT. Lewin had brought together a very diverse group representing the range of his interests and what he saw the task of the Research Center to be - both basic and applied research.

> The orientation of Leon Festinger was much more to science. The orientation of Lippitt was much more to, "change the world" and trying to do good - with a bow to science. Cartwright is called Doc and he has a pipe and a fatherly, somewhat detached orientation. He tried to be a mediator. He has a very gentle, sort of overviewing approach and tended to step back somewhat from the fray.

The orientations to basic and applied research become more clearly divided after Lewin's death.

> When Lewin was alive, his benign presence enabled this to be contained very well because he represented a kind of unifying force representing science and practice. The two were fused in him even though in some of his faculty, that fusion didn't hold. But the tension, while he was alive, was not bad - it was stimulating.

There were many opportunities to present ideas before a group. He describes the Quasselstrippe which he translated as "winding string," as "a very tough intellectual free-for-all."

> One of the things Lewin created was a kind of openness and so there was that freedom, the sense that you could express ideas. They didn't have to fall into any particular rut, though it was clearly a context in which the general approach of Lewin and gestalt psychology and field theory - that kind of language - was part of the assumptive framework within which we worked. It helped because in effect it gave us a common frame and it was very flexible, it wasn't very binding - it was pretty open.

Because of his background in clinical psychology, Deutsch believes he was put in the role of being "the one who knew about personality." For example, at Bethel it was his job to study how the personalities of group leaders affected the way they interacted with others. Ron Lippitt was officially his thesis advisor but Deutsch remembers little direct guidance being given on his dissertation, a study of the effects of cooperation and competition on group process (Deutsch, 1949). He received his degree from MIT in 1948.

Beyond MIT:

After leaving MIT, Deutsch taught at New York University until the mid-fifties. At the time he was interested in the initiating conditions of cooperation and competition. While at NYU he encountered Howard Raiffa who, with Duncan Luce, was writing a book on game theory (Luce & Raiffa, 1957) who introduced him to the Prisoner's Dilemma. He made good use of this tool in his subsequent work on conflict and cooperation.

He left NYU and spent seven years as a member of the technical staff at Bell Labs - continuing his research on cooperation and competition. In 1963 he moved to his current position at Columbia University Teachers College.

Subsequent Work - Links with Lewin and Collaborations:

Deutsch's favorite part of the research process is in working with ideas - both during the beginning stages, developing ideas for research, or at the end, trying to make sense of data which don't quite fit the original idea. His ideas have been influential in social psychology as well as other disciplines such as sociology and political science which address conflict issues. Throughout his career he has maintained an interest in balancing theory with application.

As a direct influence of his MIT years, Deutsch mentioned, in the training of his own students that he tries to stimulate a cohesive environment in which there is a lot of interaction among the students. Currently, the students in his program are selected for "tough minds and tender hearts," he said. "We want them to have an interest in developing social psychology so it has some practical significance for important social issues." They want to train students who will be interested in the implications of their research for a variety of social issues such as war and peace or justice. He says he has always tried to stimulate and encourage students to take a lot of initiative in their work.

Deutsch enjoys working with students in a kind of apprentice-colleague relationship. Typically they work collaboratively within the framework of his research grants. He likes to have students who are not "disciples," but who might be able to find something interesting in his work. "I like to get stimulated by the students. I like *them* to come and contribute their own ideas." He said the best students are those can take an idea and see something in it that he has overlooked and then develop it in an unexpected way. His goal he said is, "to have a warm, cohesive, cooperative working unit."

> Looking back at the group at MIT, "What I see as central to the creativity of that group was, first of all, it had some very high quality people. Secondly, it had this working atmosphere of collegiality and, thirdly, it had a sense of mission, a sense of uniqueness, a sense of being pioneers.There was a sense of being very special and there was a very clear norm of being productive, developing ideas, your own ideas, and then doing something with them. It was a very strong work oriented group. There was a lot of push toward originality. It was part of the essential component of "This is a special group," doing something unique, original - things that had not been done before. We were changing social science.

INTERVIEWS

Associates

The following three interviews are with social psychologists who have been associated with members of the Lewin line and are in a position to comment on the working style of the group. The first interview is with Robert Krauss, who was trained by Morton Deutsch - although not in an academic setting. The remaining two interviews are with Edward E. Jones and Phil Zimbardo. Jones was closely associated with John Thibaut during his years at Harvard and later in North Carolina. Zimbardo had close connections with several members of the Lewin line.

ROBERT KRAUSS

Robert Krauss went to graduate school at New York University to study with Morton Deutsch. He nearly went to Harvard.

> I didn't go to Harvard because I read something by Talcott Parsons and it so turned me off that I decided I didn't want to, - It wasn't interesting, so I went to NYU. Everybody said I was crazy.
>
> Harvard would have ruined me - it wouldn't have been the right place for me. I was lucky. Most kids, given the choice at that age would choose Harvard and everybody would advise them to take Harvard. And they would be right in some sense - it is just that it would have been wrong for me.

Unfortunately, Deutsch left NYU for Bell Labs about the time Krauss arrived. Krauss wound up working with Murray Horwitz, another of Lewin's MIT graduate students. At that time - in the mid-fifties - Horwitz was still working within the Lewinian framework of topological theory. "He was still drawing eggs and bathtubs and I really learned all that - no one else was doing it," Krauss recalled.

Horwitz was attempting to explore the notion of tension systems through the physiological measurement of such things as muscle action potential. "The idea was that we were going to have a physiological measure of tension systems, which is very interesting because in Lewinian theory there is this notion of tension systems in terms of directed motivation. And in electromyography what you are measuring is called the muscle action potential, or muscle tension. They don't have anything to do with one another and Murray was trying to draw an analogy - that somehow by measuring a physiological system, you would get a 'window into the psyche,' but it never works that way," said Krauss. "I spent two years learning electromyography and nothing ever came of it."

There were other sources of dissatisfaction. According to Krauss, "About that time Horwitz just sort of lost interest in the research. He sort of distanced himself from the whole business as though he had no real role in it and he became a t-grouper." It was also Krauss' feeling that there were few first rate students at NYU, which made it difficult to find people with whom to discuss ideas. "There was just no intellectual sustenance for me," he said.

Disgusted, Krauss quit NYU and went to work for Deutsch at Bell Labs. They had met through Horwitz. Once, while Deutsch was in New York for a meeting of the Topological Society, he had visited Horwitz, who proudly showed him a piece of equipment designed by Krauss. Deutsch told Krauss if he ever needed a job, they could use him at Bell Labs. "If it hadn't been for that, I would have gotten out of psychology," Krauss said. "Although I have never actually taken a course from him, I regard him as the person who trained me."

Krauss said, "What I think I learned from Mort was how to think theoretically, how to frame a problem and how to read the literature, to understand it and relate it to other things." Krauss believes he "learned to be a psychologist" from Deutsch.

Krauss described the Labs at the time as being "like an academic department without students. It was a very loose about who worked with whom, so I sort of worked with Mort on conflict resolution and everybody was allowed to rise to his own level." He said if people were good and "understood what was going on," they eventually would become co-author on something, "simply because you had taken a big hand in working on the thing." They were free to pursue their interests with little interference from those higher up in AT&T - even if the research had political implications. Deutsch was involved in the antiwar movement very early in the Vietnam era. Krauss said, "He was going to a lot of conferences and using the research we had done to say that deterrence is not viable," and the people at Bell Labs didn't interfere. "So from that standpoint it was very very good."

> We were doing work that was very exciting and I think the reward system helped. If you did good work, you got more to say about what you did. The funny thing was that there were six of us in one

> large office and some of us were simply on the level of research assistants who were doing what we were told. Others of us were essentially independent investigators - all sitting in the same office, all receiving the same pay.
>
> There was plenty to do but what happened was Mort and I would do a study and get a result. And I would say, "you know, we have got to do *this* because it is not clear." And he would say, "yeah, we better do that." And so pretty soon we were equal partners - it became a collaboration.

Krauss thinks if he had worked with some other kind of collaborator - "some real hard ass, I probably would have quit." He said he quit graduate school because he found it intellectually unstimulating and believes running someone else's studies would have been "equally unstimulating. But that was never a problem."

Krauss finally went to work on his degree because Deutsch threatened to fire him if he didn't start taking courses. When Deutsch left Bell Labs in 1963, Krauss still hadn't finished his degree but he was promoted to Deutsch's position on the condition that he finish. He remained at Bell Labs for two more years.

After Deutsch left, Krauss began following an interest in communication and has been working in that area ever since. "They sort of liked it, not because it was any more applied than what Mort was doing, but it seemed a lot easier to justify to the vice president of AT&T," he laughed.

> In a way it was opportunistic because I took advantage of things they had available. I figured if I have got all this good technological equipment around, I might as well use it.
>
> I think it was a smart thing to have done and it turned out - in the way things often do turn out - that I couldn't have planned things that well. I really did end up where I wanted, studying the things I wanted to study - although it took me a while to get to that point.

> After a while they decided that maybe social psychology wasn't for them, but I was ok because I wasn't really doing social psychology, I was doing communication and that was all right.

After that he found himself surrounded with cognitive psychologists. Krauss described himself as being very "responsive to the environment that I am in." Having someone to bounce his ideas off is very important to him. He said, "I think that the people who can survive without it are either incredibly brilliant or do boring work and I think there are more of the latter than the former." At Bell Labs during this period, he described how in the process of bouncing ideas off his colleagues the ideas would change as they came back. Given the nature of their interests, the ideas came back with a cognitive cast to them. He said, "They were nice guys who I could spend a lot of time talking to, but I discovered my work was starting to look like theirs and I didn't really want to do that."

Training Students:

> There are two things I tell graduate students. One is, I say you should not study history and systems of psychology until you are old enough to recall some of it. And the other is that graduate students should not be allowed to study philosophy of science. It is seriously bad for them. It gives them principles they haven't earned. They should get to the point where they understand what they are doing before somebody tells them what it is.
>
> I think one of the most destructive things that happened in the fifties was the merging of positivism and behaviorism and there are things you can read back then where philosophy was sort of used as a club to flail the nonbelievers.
>
> Students read philosophy of science as though it was prescriptive. In other words, it tells them how you are supposed to do thing and that is not what it

is at all. It is an attempt of philosophers to make sense out of what we have *been* doing. So they look at what we are doing and they say, "Ah, in some abstract way, this is it." Next week somebody does something different and they have to change the explanation.

I mean, who are the creative people in science? The creative people in science are not the guys - and I won't mention any names - who read four studies, each of which manipulates a variable and then designs a study in which all four variables are together - no rhyme or reason. Why? Well each of these has been shown to be interesting. Now you get them and you put them together and you have interaction effects you can't make any sense out of. That's the way a computer would do research.

Doing research is a much more creative thing than that. I don't think there is much difference between art and science. The difference is at the level of discipline - and by the discipline I mean that the rules of the game are different but basically the game is the same. The game is to try to systematically understand something. A painter tries to systematically understand something about the way we see and respond - not the way we see visually but the way the mind sees and the way we respond to things that we see. And the only thing that is different is that the scientist says, "My game says that I have got to have a fact to correspond to." But the same is really true of the painter.

If you know people who are *serious* artists - if you look at the working artist - what they are doing is a lot more like what I do than Kirk Douglas in Lust for Life or something like that. What do I do? I get an idea and then agonize about how to do the experiment that will be the best test of whether the idea makes any sense. And artists do the same thing. They have an idea and the painting is a way of working that idea out although often their idea is

> not articulate - that they can say it. That is the thing you can't teach either. I don't know how. You get students going through and some of them are smart and some of them are less smart and some of them catch on to things real quick and some don't. But the ones who can recognize a good idea when they have it are the ones who are really going to make it.

It is a kind of aesthetic judgment, he thinks.

Krauss said he believes when it comes to working with graduate students, "There is a main effect, but the interaction effect is the important one."

> The worst kind of student to get is the one who already has a professional orientation - who knows that you have got to do two studies a year and publish at least one. I find that I can't do much with that kind of person because they will do anything you tell them. Give them a study, they will run it and they will do it competently but I don't get much out of it.

For Krauss the reason for teaching is to have young excited intellects around, "who have the capacity to be absorbed and be excited by their work." He said this is a difficult thing to maintain over the years and it helps when there is something coming back from the environment.

When he works with graduate students, "we do *our* work," he said. He tries to find an area where his interests overlap with those of the graduate student, if possible. "Once in a while I will have something I really want to get done, but normally we try and work out a project," he said. He contrasted this with Stanley Schachter's lab which he has observed at close range and characterized as a "family business." Krauss said he now believes he had "unrealistic expectations in graduate school. I think I had expectations that people like Stanley and Leon fulfill but very few people do."

Current Work and Collaborations:

Krauss is currently working in the area of cognitive psychology that has bearing on social behavior. He said, "I really sit on the border of social psychology and cognitive psychology. I don't really do cognitive social psychology, I do a sort of psychology of language."

In one experiment, he and a student analyzed the function of gestures. This study was part of a broader question about whether language is an outgrowth of gesture.

> We did an experiment where there was a difference between the conditions that is on the order of 300 milliseconds. Now, it is significant at the .0001 level and somebody says, "Well, what difference..." Well, it's not that the 300 milliseconds makes a difference. It is that it represents the difference in processing time that tells you something about the question. That's why I am doing it - it is a question.

He said he probably talks to more cognitive psychologists than any other kind but he resents it if people question his being a social psychologist. "There is not really a coherent social psychology of language - at least not yet," he said. "What is happening is that the cognitive psychologists are coming to realize that in order to understand language use, they have to understand the social factors that underlie it."

Collaborations:

Krauss discussed the working relationship he has with Sam Glucksberg who is at Princeton. They have worked together over the past twenty years. He said, "Over time, we sort of learned enough about each other's style that these things are kind of worked out. In certain areas if I say something and he disagrees, he will defer to me. It's like a good marriage."

He said that in working with Deutsch, it eventually evolved to that point. They worked together one-on-one.

> I was a very junior figure in the field and so there was never any doubt in either of our minds who the boss was - who would be making the ultimate decision. But he was very democratic about it. I was sort of brash and young and I tended to shoot from the hip very often. In some ways that was good because he was very reflective and sober. So that was a helpful kind of relationship.

Lewin's Contribution:

Krauss's links with Lewin were through Deutsch, through Horwitz and currently through his colleague, Stanley Schachter. Deutsch is a theoretician who is influential outside of psychology. "Mort *did* talk a lot about Lewin and for obvious reasons would have admired that kind of guy. He particularly talked about his ability to take an observation that somebody made, conceptualize it and then relate it to something."

> There is a style of theorizing that became popular during the time I was going to graduate school and has dominated up until now - what Merton used to call theories of the middle range. They are bigger than hypotheses but far less than grand systems. Mort tends to work a little higher than that. It is not like a Hullian system or a Lewinian system, but it is certainly not like attribution theory. It is something at a fairly high level and that is not fashionable.
>
> If you look at his theories, you can criticize them in a number of ways but you can never say they are inconsistent within themselves. His theories are very rigorous within themselves and it is very hard to do - it is not just free association. It is sort of being able to maintain a coherent argument at *that* level of abstraction. But that level of abstraction, I think largely under the pressure of people like Leon and Stanley in social psychology, went out of fashion.

Krauss' exposure to Horwitz had its impact:

> I learned all this Lewinian lore - the one thing Horwitz did was to transmit the tradition. You would say, "So and so is a function of age." And he would say, "Age isn't a psychological variable. What does age mean?" I said, you know, "One year old, two years old..." And he said, "Well, what does that mean? *What* does that mean psychologically?" And of course Lewin talked about precisely that. Age is not a psychological variable. What you have to talk about is, *what is it* that differentiates one year old and two years old?
>
> Status is not a psychological variable. Why? Because it is a label you put on people. The question is, how is that represented in the person? So if, as Lewin said, the only difference between the younger person and the older person is the permeability of the boundaries of the life space, we can create other situations that make the boundaries permeable and that can tell us something about age - so get somebody drunk, which is a way of making them permeable and that is what is meant by regression.
>
> I don't think anybody ever said this but it is logically consistent to say if you want to study age, you don't have to get people of different ages, you get people all the same age and then do something that will change the permeability of the boundaries. Well - if your theory is right, then that's fine.

The problem then is that the test of the variable is not simply a function of the correctness of the theory, it is also a function of the skill with which the theory has been translated into a variable.

> I think the real contribution that Lewin made was to make the thing called experimental social psychology possible. What Lewin said is, if you want to study something, it isn't necessary to create *that* thing. What you have to do is find out what it

is - how that thing is psychologically represented. So, if we are talking about status, you don't have to give somebody ancestors who came over from England, what you do is you find what is *essential* to status and you distill it. You take away the phenotypic variable and look at what is genotypic.

I don't think anybody has ever really looked at this, but if you look at social psychological experiments before and after - I mean, there is really a disjuncture. It is not just a steady evolution. Just look at the dozens of experiments that came out of the Research Center and the kinds of variables that they studied. That was a *dramatic* and radical proposal. The flip side of it was that if you didn't really understand the genotypic variable, you were really going to have a stupid experiment. And a lot of stupid experiments, I think, derived from that very thing.

For example, you are studying interpersonal conflict and you arrange a situation but the situation doesn't contain in it the things that are important in what you are trying to explain. You create a situation that models it in some respects, but of course it is a situation of its own. Subject comes in, subject sits down. He is not thinking of the situation you are thinking about. He is confronting the situation so that in a lot of the two person game situations - experiments - the problem was that we did not give sufficient consideration to the specific situation the subject was confronted with - the way the subject constructed it. Stanley (Schachter) would have been a *incredible* theatrical director because he has such a wonderful sense of that.

Krauss commented on the conditions existing in the United States at the time Lewin established the Research Center for Group Dynamics at MIT.

These guys had just been through a war and that was - I hadn't been in the army, I wasn't old enough, but I *do* remember that there is this big cohort effect and I think it is a really interesting one. I am not sure there *could* be anything like it without there being this - it was the most cohesion producing kind of experience that I can remember. It was a time when everybody kind of had the feeling that we did the *right* thing and the prosocial feeling was to my recollection very very strong - people were voluntarily doing things for the war effort.

They had been through this experience which I think for all of them - somebody like Stanley would say molded their character in significant ways. Then you have Lewin offering this vision. And it really was a vision of a way of dealing with the things that were perceived as having caused this catastrophe. They were hard-headed idealists.

EDWARD E. JONES

Becoming a psychologist was "really somewhat accidental," said Jones. He entered Harvard College as a transfer student in 1947. "It was right after the war and my own military service. I had always wanted to go to Harvard, but I also thought I wanted to be a journalist and they didn't have a school of journalism," he said. Before military service, he been a history major at Swarthmore.

Entering Harvard as a junior, the newly organized Department of Social Relations appeared to him "like a good place to hide. It seemed to somehow fall in between the pure humanities and the natural sciences and I liked that. It seemed like a nice compromise. It also seemed to fit my interests in politics and social issues. I come from a very liberal family," he explained. "My mother was always doing things like picketing the roller rink because they wouldn't let blacks in. She was a perpetual correspondent to the editor, always airing grievances and so forth." His father was a psychologist. Although the father in no way proselytized the son, Jones once admitted that as a child he "took the Stanford-Binet from many a practicing student and ran pet rats through book mazes in his bedroom (Jones, 1978. p. 59)."

Once at Harvard, Jones said he naturally gravitated to "the psychological areas of the social relations department - social and personality and clinical psychology. The other parts of psychology weren't in social relations."

During the summer of 1947, Jones took a course in personality with Leo Postman and a guest lecture was given by Jerome Bruner. "Bruner was a spellbinder. He was talking about the effects of motivation on perception and I thought it was really very exciting. So when I had to find someone to do my undergraduate thesis with, I went to him," he recalled. This was the beginning of a relationship which lasted through his graduate training, also at Harvard, in clinical psychology.

His undergraduate honors thesis, a small study on apparent movement with just 17 subjects, was the only research he conducted until it came time for his dissertation several years later, although he did assist in several research projects of others. "In those days, it was not uncommon for graduate students - especially in psychology - to do no research or at least very little, until the dissertation," he said. During his third year as a graduate student, when it came time for him to design his thesis, Jones again approached Bruner for suggestions, which eventually led to a focus on person perception.

Bruner was formally supervisor of for Jones' dissertation, but he was on leave during the year Jones worked on the project. "He came back in the fall of 1952 and I had designed my experiment, collected all of my data and was trying to figure out what they meant - He really had very little to do with it up to that point. I had a lot of help from those in the research group to which I'd been assigned," he explained.

Jones' dissertation research was a person perception study which combined aspects of Authoritarian Personality (Adorno, Frenkel-Brunswik, Levinson & Sanford, 1950) work with Asch's "warm/cold" study (Asch, 1946). "I measured the authoritarianism of the perceivers beforehand and I manipulated the stimulus persons in ways that I thought were relevant to authoritarianism to see if highs and lows differed. These results actually came out at the .005 level in the opposite direction of my prediction," he laughed.

> Bruner was very important, but in some ways John Thibaut was more directly involved in my dissertation and was a more direct link from what I was doing as a second year graduate student to what I am doing now. He played a central role in my development, since the Social Relations department at the time was quite "anti-Lewinian."
>
> The personality and clinical people had certainly picked up the conflict models, the dynamic theory of personality and so forth and we learned all about that. But we literally did not know about group dynamics. It was considered to be faddish and not

> really very important. There was a sense that Lewin was a person who was insufficiently knowledgeable about and respectful of "mainstream" psychology. I think some of that influenced other people in the department. I had never heard the name Festinger until I met John Thibaut.

John Thibaut, one of Lewin's MIT graduate students, came to Harvard as a research associate. Thibaut brought with him the style of experimentation which had been developed by Lewin and refined by Leon Festinger. Jones was a graduate assistant in a research group that included Hank Reicken, Renato Tagiuri, John Thibaut and Robert Black, who was visiting from Texas. Jones watched and took careful note of diverse research approaches of the group. "Thibaut and Reicken were doing some pretty classy work," he said. "Although I wasn't co-author or anything, I certainly was involved in hearing them discuss the experiments and watching them run them."

> Support of the group came jointly from the Air Force and the Navy. I was the only graduate student and I was treated like a peer. It was a wonderful experience.
>
> I immediately just fell in love with Thibaut. I mean, he was just a fantastic human being. He was himself interested in person perception and phenomenal causality. He put me onto Heider for example - I had never heard of Heider and that was a real eye opener.
>
> In the spring of 1953, Thibaut went to the University of North Carolina - just as I was finishing my thesis. It was not entirely an accident that I went to Duke because he had been to a party where the Duke chairman was talking about hiring someone in clinical psychology and John recommended me.

Jones believes, "It was just a freak series of coincidences that resulted in my ending up at Duke." His first job offer had been at

Wesleyan but he wasn't particularly anxious to accept it. "I had one of those unbelievable days - twenty four hours in your life that changes the course of your own history," he said. He went in to the office to send a telegram accepting the position at Wesleyan on the last possible day. There he ran into Bruner who told him to delay the telegram because he was waiting for a call about a possible position at Swarthmore that might suit Jones better. In the meantime Jones called to turn down a job offer at Pittsburgh Medical School and wasn't able to reach the person he needed to speak with - so he left a message. All of these things served to make him delay sending the telegram to Wesleyan. That afternoon as he was finally about ready to send the telegram, he received a call from Duke inviting him to consider a position there. "If I had sent that telegram, and if I hadn't bumped into Bruner in the hall, I certainly would have felt commited. It would have made an enormous difference," he said, "because of the very demanding teaching load at Wesleyan in those days."

Although his degree is in clinical psychology, Jones said that by the time he received it, he already knew he wanted to be a social psychologist.

At Duke:

Once at Duke, the close relationship with Thibaut was reestablished.

> He got me involved in the Organizational Research Group (ORG) at The University of North Carolina, a group that originally included both psychologists and sociologists but that eventually was winnowed down to myself, Thibaut, Milton Rosenbaum, and the social psychology graduate students. The group met once a week, every Wednesday night and we would talk about research. We would collaborate with graduate students - I collaborated with Dick DeCharms and Lloyd Strickland, both of whom were UNC graduate students. We did several studies together. The ORG was just part of a

> continuing education in large areas of social psychology that I had missed.
>
> That group was very important to me because. There wasn't any social psychology at Duke at the time.

His first few doctoral students at Duke were clinical students, since no one came to Duke in those days explicitly to study social psychology. "Then Ken Gergen and Keith Davis came along as students and Jack Brehm was hired and we began to have a social program of sorts," he said. Brehm got his degree at Minnesota with Leon Festinger and then spent some time at Yale working in attitude change research. "He came in, just bubbling with dissonance theory," Jones recalled and added that their research styles "complemented each other."

> We had enough ideological congruence so that we never had any basic disputes about the way in which you did things - mainly about experimental social psychology - the importance of theory and so forth. On the other hand, our research styles were totally different so that the students had a distinctive choice of role models.
>
> I was more intuitive and clinical - my experiments were in some ways more complicated and and more real life - more mundanely real as Aronson would say. I wanted to tie my research into theory, but often the complexity of my experimental variables made this problematical. Jack was a more tightly reasoning theoretician. He would do an experiment which made a lot of theoretical sense but didn't necessarily make a lot of sense to the subject. He would manipulate a variable which was closely derivable from theory but it was often hard to know how to get from there to the real world because it would be kind of an unusual, perhaps artificial, experience for the subject. And I think both approaches are quite viable.

In time, the social psychology faculty at Duke expanded to include Darwyn Linder, an Aronson Ph.D. This made a group of three with links to Leon Festinger - Jones through his association with Thibaut at Harvard, Brehm through direct training and Linder as the student of Elliot Aronson, a Festinger Ph.D. This linkage with Festinger was important for another reason:

> Festinger had a group - the graduate students would come over to his house at Minnesota and later at Stanford. They would bring beer and they would talk about their research. In about 1965 at Duke, Jack Brehm came to me and he said, "You know, our students don't know how to do research, there is something wrong." And then he talked about these groups that Festinger had. So we said, "Ok, lets start having these groups." And we did. We called it "The Seekers" after the doomsday cult in When Prophecy Fails.
>
> The Seekers were supposed to meet once a week. Sometimes we would postpone it for a week but we met often enough to create an important source of influence. It was modeled after the Festinger groups - we would meet at my house or we would meet at Jack's place or later on, sometimes even at one of the graduate student's and we would drink beer and eat pretzels and somebody would be in charge of talking about his research project. And that thing just took off. It was the smartest thing we ever did.
>
> We do that here at Princeton except it is not at night and it doesn't have beer and again, I think it is very important. Probably the most important part of a student's research training is to have to present an experimental idea or a design, describe their instructions, their recruitment procedures, their manipulation and then have to do this in front of a group of peers and faculty who are going to just tear it apart. I mean, not maliciously, but they are going to raise questions that the presenters never thought of. It happens every week and it is kind of nervous

> making for the student but I really think that is where they learn - not only their own experiments, but they listen to professor B criticize student A and so forth.

Subsequent Work and Collaborations:

John Thibaut introduced Jones to Heider's work while they were at Harvard together. What Jones brought to this meeting, in addition to his interest in person perception, was his clinical experience in graduate school. He had taken a seminar which he described as "actually a group therapy seminar" run by an analyst at Boston State Hospital. The seminar was organized so that "there were only two anchors in reality. One anchor was somebody had to take notes every time and the other was everybody had to write a term paper. nothing else. There wasn't going to be a leader of a discussion, there wasn't necessarily going to be a discussion topic and so we sat there with lots of silence and somebody would get anxious and start talking. That was the seminar, once each week for the entire semester."

> These were all clinical psychology graduate students. We knew each other very well and were sort of competitive and cooperative at the same time - mostly competitive. There was a lot of hostility and funny little issues would come up like, "How can you be hostile with him when you are trying to become a clinical psychologist? You must try and understand his behavior. Therefore, if you understand his behavior, how can you be hostile." And that sort of stuck in my craw. It was a fascinating problem: Under what conditions is hostility legitimate if you really convince yourself that you understand that behavior is multiply determined - is caused by all kinds of things. Given this, what right do you have to get angry at somebody. And so I think that brought to a head my interest in phenomenal causality - at what point do you truncate the causal sequence in order to impose sanctions for example? If somebody

> commits an indiscretion, you can't get away with it totally. You have got to impose some kind of sanctions in order for the social group to function. So all of these concerns got wrapped up in the general theme of Heider's phenomenal causality.

When he made the move to Duke, Jones encountered some cultural differences which contributed to his thinking on person perception and self presentation.

> I had spent all my life in the north, most recently six years in the rather austere social climate of New England and I came down to this culture where everybody greets you in the street even though they have never seen you before and they all say, "come back" and there is this effusiveness, this sort of ritual warmth that is terribly impressive. And you start thinking about subcultural differences and what it all means and the particular difficulty of trying to discern, "Does this guy really mean it when he said that flattering thing?"

Several other things contributed to the development of his ideas. One was the fact that he became the editor of the Journal of Personality. "And being very young and insecure, you sort of desperately wonder whether people think you are doing a good job. And then you begin to realize that you aren't really going to find out," he explained. Another contribution was an experiment he conducted with Keith Davis, a graduate student.

> It was a dissonance experiment and we induce a subject to evaluate negatively somebody in the next room who turns out to be actually a tape recording but the subject doesn't know that. The subject conveys a negative evaluation to this guy either with the illusion of some choice or he was simply told to do it. If he had the illusion of choice, then he ended up disliking the guy. At some later point I asked myself, "Why not turn it around and have the subject say really nice things about the person in the next room Would the subject end up liking him?" And I thought to myself, "Gee, I don't think so."

Jones noted that if he were to organize the evolution of his thinking, it would appear to be more logical than it really was. He said if he were to write about it, he might write something like, "Well naturally if you are going to study person perception you want to study the other side of it, namely what are the stimulus determinants generated by self presentation. And it makes a good story, but I am really not sure that is exactly why I became interested in self presentation. There are a lot of external determinants of my interest in self presentation. I am perhaps better known for the attribution work, but I think that I keep coming back to self presentation. I feel that there I have a more unique perspective to offer. I feel it is more part of my marrow."

Training Students

Jones remembers being fascinated by the methodology of psychology when he was an undergraduate at Harvard. He said, "Whenever somebody talked about the psychometric method or the method of average error or something like that, I would be fairly intrigued, even though I don't think of myself particularly as a methodologist - but to me that is what distinguishes us from journalism."

> In the old days, I never wrote anything up - or almost never - during the year. I would collect data and put them aside. I would then wallow in them during the summer with my trusty calculator. This was in the days before computers. I am still very nervous about data analysis on a computer. I loved taking those data from an experiment and just analyzing the hell out of them. You really got to know what every number was and where it came from. You can identify subjects on each of the dependent variables - there was a familiarity with the data so that by the time you wrote up the study, you really had a sense of what was there and you had a sense that you were describing something that was like an old friend. And I don't have that feeling any more. I don't think our graduate students do. Now you can go and in a day or two

> do all the major analyses of a complicated study, analyses that would have taken three months in the old days. Naturally you don't have as much time to think about what's going on in the study. Now you look at some end product - you get into statistical packages and get a big printout and I think you really miss something. I don't know how to recapture that. I used to just love that part of the research process.

Jones said he gives his students "a lot of tether and I think they like that, but I also give them a lot of help at crucial times." He said that his own work is in a broad enough framework to allow students a variety of topics.

> If a somebody wants to study self handicapping, great, that's fine. I don't have any ideas right now, but if somebody wants to do it, I would be happy to talk to them about it and maybe together we can get some ideas about it. Or if somebody wants so study self presentation or attribution - any of those things, there are so many thing that fall within the general framework of my interests and my research that there is no problem.
>
> I have supervised twenty-five Ph.D. students who got their degrees. I didn't just come up with that number, I happened to count them last year just out of curiosity. They are scattered around the country and I communicate with them and I read their work and I basically keep in touch. I have lost a few - some of them are working in community health clinics and they don't publish any more but most of them are academic and most of them are doing very well.

He said he is very proud of his students and takes pride in "being able to work with bright students and give them whatever I have because without them it wouldn't have amounted to very much. I really think that my work has largely been a series of collaborations with several generations of graduate students."

PHIL ZIMBARDO

Phil Zimbardo was an undergraduate sociology major at Brooklyn College in New York in the early fifties. As a sociology student he conducted research on racial patterns of seating in the school cafeteria and on the dynamics of Puerto Rican-Black interaction in the South Bronx, where he grew up. "They were survey studies, but to me, the interesting thing in both of them was the dynamics of human interaction," he said. It wasn't until Zimbardo was a senior and took a course in experimental psychology that he overcame the negative effect of a C grade in an introductory psychology course he had taken as a freshman. The research methodology he learned in the experimental course excited him because, he explained, "sociologists seemed to be able to ask good questions but never come up with an answer." So, in his senior year he shifted to social psychology.

Zimbardo took a course in Industrial Psychology with the idea of becoming a personnel manager to satisfy his father's concern that he stop being a student forever and go to work. The instructor of that course encouraged him to go on to graduate school. "I was the only one who ever went to college, let alone graduate school, in a whole generation of Sicilian immigrants. So I talked my father out of having me go to work. I just said, 'Well, I need a Masters degree.' Then after the Masters degree I went on and got a Ph.D. and he gave up on me, saying, 'Well, it's obvious you don't want to work.'"

Once the decision was made to go on to graduate school, he began investigating various programs - looking at catalogues and talking to people about places where he could pursue his interests.

> I was all set to go to Minnesota to work with Stanley Schachter - I had been accepted and had a fellowship or something. I was about to send in my letter of acceptance when I got a call from a professor at Yale saying he wanted to interview me

> at the Eastern Psychological Association which was meeting at the New York Hotel the next day. And I went. He interviewed me and said he would like to offer me a position as a research assistant.
>
> Well, you know to a kid from the Bronx, Yale was *special*. It was Yale and it was close to home. My mother would say it was an "Ivory league" school and that really counted. The research, the social lab at Minnesota would have been exciting to be involved with, but this was *Yale* and all there was, besides Brooklyn College, was Yale and Harvard.
>
> For me Yale turned out to be the ideal place. That kind of hard experimental work was an important lesson in terms of thinking more precisely and more rigorously - going from the broad focus of group dynamics and race relations to precise analysis of a limited environment in a y-maze.
>
> My original focus was sociological, where you ask these molar questions and come up with these molar answers and you haven't said very much. The experimental training at Yale was to ask more limited questions and come up with molecular ways of analyzing and it *did* have an effect on the precise experimental research I learned to do in social psychology.

Zimbardo was an experimental psychologist until well into his third year of graduate study. "I had the biggest rat colony at Yale," he said. About that time, the professor he was working for died. Zimbardo, in what he described as his "first big chutzpah step" wrote to NSF and asked for the grant to be assigned to him to continue the work they had been doing together. "I got the money and now I was totally dedicated. I lived and slept in my white lab coat," he recalled.

During his third year, Zimbardo did research with another graduate student on sexual behavior and drugs. "We got very dramatic results," he said. "Again, the next chutzpah step, what do you do with dramatic results? We sent them to *Science*." At this point, he was a third year experimental psychology graduate student with a grant and a publication in *Science* . And then he met Bob Cohen.

Zimbardo met Cohen in the calculator room while he was re-analyzing data for his *Science* article. He then took a course Cohen was co-teaching with Jack Brehm. As part of the course, they were reading "manuscripts of some new book being written on the west coast on the theory of cognitive dissonance." Brehm had been a Festinger student at Minnesota and Cohen came out of the Group Dynamics tradition at Michigan. Brehm and Cohen "were wonderful together," Zimbardo recalled. "Bob was more the generalist, asking profound questions and Brehm was more the experimentalist, more rigorous, and it was a *wonderful* combination. Bob was open and gregarious and Jack was more introverted and they just worked together well."

This was very exciting to him because he had just finished a course with Carl Hovland on attitude change and here was a whole new approach to that topic.

> Hovland's approach was very behavioral, rational, very categorical, descriptive, nontheoretical and it was really not that different from what we were doing with rats in one sense. You analyze what are the input variables, what are all the output variables, what are the mediating variables and you set up a study where you vary one or two at a time. Now here was this exciting theory which starts with very little - a need for consistency and a few assumptions and some postulates and suddenly you have these nonobvious predictions. And that was very exciting.
>
> Then they invited Festinger to come for a colloquium. He came and here was this charismatic person with all these theoretical ideas with really imaginative ways - dramatic ways of testing them. And I thought, "Now, that really fits into my personal style." My style was not to be running rats in the basement in a lab coat. So there was this immediate affininty to both the *way* of thinking

about behavior as well as the dramatic style of doing experimental, laboratory research.

The force of his presentation, the way he thought, the research, the theory - I was convinced this was the person I wanted to work with and I asked if I could do a post-doctoral fellowship with him and he said, "Sure, if you can get the money." Sad to say, I couldn't get the money.

Zimbardo's dissertation research was an attitude study which compared a dissonance theory prediction with a Sherif and Hovland latitude of acceptance and rejection prediction.

My reading of dissonance theory said that under the right circumstances if you get someone to consider a discrepant position which they had said they would reject, you might create more dissonance and you might get them to change more than if a positive communicator advocated a slightly discrepant a position they said they would accept. The way I saw it, it was pitting the rational approach vs. the irrational approach. And the irrational won.

"Part of this is the *style* of doing research. Part I got from Brehm and Cohen and part of it from reading the Lewin-Festinger Group Dynamics scenario approach - you want the immediacy of the social situation." This style of research included a "quality of the dramatic - of the stage setting," he said. This appealed to him.

What I took away from Yale was the importance of doing rigorous research that would lead you and other people to have confidence in your data. That was the important thing. What is important about the behavioral approach was that the methodology has to be sufficiently rigorous, that the data you generate from any experiment is the kind in which you and other people have confidence. And that means being obsessive about having the right controls, the right measurement procedures and being concerned about all the "minor details" and

> potential artifacts and confounds. There is nothing too insignificant to worry about or figure out.
>
> And then you have what at that point was kind of the "Michigan approach" which was to ask vital questions. Not the cosmic questions of the sociologists scaled down a little bit, but still questions of importance. So this to me has been a wonderful blessing. The research I did had this concern for coming up with the right methodology and putting it in the service of answering what I thought were interesting questions.

The Festinger and Schachter styles:

Zimbardo nearly went to Minnesota to study with Stanley Schachter. Instead he went to Yale and Leon Festinger's style came to him.

> I see Schachter starting out with the dependent variable. Starting out saying, "Isn't it interesting that some people affiliate and others don't. Isn't it interesting that some people are fat and some people are not." And so he starts with an observational difference and then he asks, "I wonder why there is this difference." So he starts with a behavioral difference or a demonstrative difference in the case of obesity and then essentially he ends up constructing a theory which will illuminate the causal processes involved.
>
> Festinger is doing exactly the opposite saying, "I wonder how the human mind works," or "I wonder how human dynamics work in a group setting." He starts out with factors that influence the input to the phenomenon of interest and then ends up with a prediction of some dependent measure. Together they are really a wonderful approach.

> Now I see a third approach as the more dominant one in psychology in which people really start with the intervening variables. You start with a process that you are interested in - attribution for example - neither the output nor the input. So I see Festinger and Schachter as really *very* different in starting with what I think of typically as the end-points in the overall functional analysis.

Zimbardo is not sure he could have worked successfully with Festinger - he said he "didn't have enough self-esteem points in the bank yet." He had occasion, in 1963 when he was at Stanford teaching summer school, to sit in on Festinger's sessions with his graduate students. "It was just absolutely masterful what he could bring out of them," he said. "But he starts with the best students. It's an elitist point of view. He said he was not there to train the average. He was there to take the best and make them better - or take the best and make them realize how good they are. And maybe to some extent Schachter does that too." Zimbardo described Festinger as, "an intellectual game player."

> He will challenge you and if you keep playing the game, will end up extending you. At some point, if your self-confidence or self-esteem begins to be shaky, then you drop out and he lets you go. Schachter's style on the other hand is to simply lay the thing out saying, "Here's what I think ought to be. Here's the way I think the world is arranged." His students are encouraged to think about it, go out and collect data. And if you brought back data that didn't fit, he might say, "You must have done something wrong - try looking elsewhere for the right data." And it is never the kind of direct intellectual confrontation (as with Festinger.) There was the challenge of, "This is the way I think the world ought to function and if you can't find it, then there must be something wrong with your data." The question (for Schachter) becomes, "Why can't you find the difference that I know ought to exist out there."

Zimbardo described his time at Yale as, "four years to exploit the environment." He worked with an array of professors on a variety of the topics they were interested in.

> I was looking at each of them in terms of their research style: how did they ask a question, why did they ask this question this way and then how did they go about trying to get an answer? That was the main thing - what kind of question did they ask and then how did they go from the question they were asking to a way of testing it. What became data for them. I was like a street urchin taking a little bit from here and a little bit from there, saying, "All this can help."
>
> I see all those years as training, knowing that I did not want to get imprinted to one way of working, one way of doing things - in that sense, my training was really as a generalist and it stood me in good stead now writing Introductory Psychology and teaching Introductory Psychology in the broadest sense. It allows you to see issues *across* disciplines - across social into developmental, into cognitive, into psychopathology which is where I am going now.
>
> I think the biggest influences were essentially Neal Miller's approach to the importance of rigorous analysis and setting up of conditions to test an idea and being aware of all the biases. That, plus the Brehm/Cohen "dynamic-duo" influence. I see them as a combination of more imaginative questions, more imaginatively studied.

Although Hovland was Zimbardo's thesis advisor, "until he got cancer," he pointed to Bob Cohen as his mentor. He describes the relationship as, "friendly and close but always respectful." The general environment at Yale at the time had "this incredible resource of people who would be accessible - if you dared approach them. There was just a high level of intellectual stimulation."

> The thing about being at Yale was there was this incredible richness of talent. When I started it was Hovland, Janis and Kelley. And there was Brehm and Cohen and Bob Abelson and Bill McGuire was there along with Irv Sarnoff and Milt Rosenberg. Don Campbell was also there my first year. Hovland had all these grants to bring in staff and visitors. Sherif was always around and so was Herb Kelman - it was incredible.

Zimbardo received his degree from Yale in 1959. He continued collaborating with Cohen until Cohen's death in 1963. He described their work:

> Jack Brehm's classic study was if you get people to commit themselves to food deprivation under high dissonance conditions; high choice and low justification then they ought to reduce their perceived hunger. They ought to say they are less hungry, they ought to eat less and at a physiological level (the measure they took was the amount of free fatty acids in the blood), that should also be reduced.
>
> Bob Cohen and I were interested in how far this kind of dissonance induced motivational control could be extended. We had begun to outline the studies to do that when he died. So I went on solo from 1963 to 1968, for those five years to do a whole set of these studies. We took traditional experimental models of motivation and learning and put the dissonance conditions in and we got very dramatic results with psycho-physiological measures, behavioral measures, cognitive measures. I published The Cognitive Control of Motivation in 1969 and was excited by the anti-behaviorist implications of these powerful demonstrations - but nobody else was. Sadly, at that time dissonance theory had died out. It was no longer mainstream.

He feels the book might have had more impact on the field if it had come out several years earlier. By 1969, the field had shifted away from dissonance.

Training students

Zimbardo tells every first year student, "You are going to need three letters of recommendation - you have to work with at least three people and your training should be as broad as possible: You want to understand *how* people do research." However, students usually find one person to work with and stay with that person. He believes this is a mistake.

> From one person you get a sense of how to ask questions, from somebody else a sense of importance of rigorous dependent measures and from somebody else, a sense of how you reduce data, and typically you can't get all of that from any one person. And you can't get it once you graduate because then you have to be giving it.

Describing his current style of working with graduate students he said, "Since I have been at Stanford, I think I have had seventeen Ph.D. students - only four of whom worked on anything in which I was interested. Many worked on areas in which I had little interest. I am the universal donor in our department and students who are disaffected or non-traditional gravitate to me - I gave them support, feedback, help them shape their experiments, but I haven't benefited personally in any way, I mean it does not help my thinking or my research." This style is a change from when he was at NYU in the late sixties working on the cognitive control of motivation. He described that environment:

> That was very exciting because we were doing a set of studies around a common theme. The studies were working out and there were four or five students doing dissertations. I think it was the ideal system where there was a student working on dissonance theory and thirst, and someone was working on eyelid conditioning and dissonance, and

> I was working with several other students on pain and dissonance. And we would meet and talk about these things, learning from one another - somebody uses a measure that works so we incorporate it, somebody has developed a good choice manipulation so we are all using it, and we were all working on a shared high because all the research was panning out - solid gold. It was an exciting climate. I provided a high level of energy and enthusiasm, a physical presence and the overview that was infectious.
>
> What you get from good graduate students is that they extend your ideas. They take them places you might not have thought of because any one person thinks in a limited way and that is what you don't get from a good undergraduate (even those I worked with, like Ebbe Ebbeson and Barry Schwartz.) A good undergraduate can execute your ideas the way you would like them to be executed and a good graduate student takes them and runs with them in a different direction than you might have thought of and that's what makes you grow.

Zimbardo is also "heavily invested" in teaching. He uses teaching as a way to get ideas. The prison study as well as his work on deindividuation and on shyness all came from issues arising in undergraduate courses he was teaching at NYU and Stanford.

> Every well-informed, knowledgeable person will come up with interesting ideas - will say, "gee that's interesting, I wonder what would happen if..." But they are either not trained or don't have the ability to take the next step which is to say, "How could I answer that question in other than logical terms or purely verbal terms?" And that is the training that we get as psychologists.
>
> But most psychologists don't open themselves to potential sources of ideas that are non-traditional, such as their own lives or novels. So it is always being on the lookout for what might be an

> interesting idea and phrasing it in a testable way. It is taking an idea, whether it is yours or somebody else's, and putting it in an interesting context. And then step two is taking that interestingly stated idea and saying "How can I translate it so it is studyable so we can begin to look at the causes and some consequences and maybe the processes in between."
>
> For me, the kind of research I do is interesting enough and dramatic enough that I can easily put it back into teaching. And when I do research, while it is going on, I always think about how I can present it to my class, to colloquia - how can I teach this to skeptics?

Current work:

Recently, Zimbardo has been working on what he described as a "madness model." It began with an interest in the way people go about explaining discontinuities in their lives. He sees this as a key concept in Lewin's work - the perception of a discontinuity of an individual's standards or attitude and that of the group. He traces this idea through Festinger's work.

> If you look at Festinger's work you see that he begins with this difference - perceived discontinuity between the individual and the group in his informal social communication, which came *directly* from Lewin. Then the next step in social comparison theory is the discontinuity between you and some other person and in dissonance theory it is now discontinuity between two cognitions within a single person.

Zimbardo is working on the way in which people explain perceived discontinuities to themselves. One of the discontinuities he has been exploring is unexplained arousal, another is undetected hearing loss as a source of paranoia. Using as a springboard a study done in England which showed that a large percentage of elderly people hospitalized for paranoia have undetected hearing loss, he thought:

> What would it be like to be an elderly person who is developing hearing loss and was unaware that the reason they couldn't hear was because of an organic problem. And what it would look like is - people are whispering. Then you ask, "Why are you whispering?" and they "lie" and say, "We are not whispering." Then you ask yourself, "*Why* are they lying?" And you begin to fill out the content of the scenario: People lie when they want something from you or they are plotting against you, and so forth.

Following this line of reasoning, he designed experiments in which subjects who are "psychiatrically normal" are introduced to a discontinuity analogous to the undetected hearing loss. He is excited about this work.

> Because it combines lots of different strands of my thinking: the dissonance work, social comparison, attribution and it also has tremendous practical significance. For example, with elderly people the first time you notice paranoid symptoms, have their hearing checked. Maybe the treatment is a hearing aid rather than psychotherapy. Or you might be able to change the initial diagnostic interview to one where you look for time-based discontinuities.

Summing up:

Zimbardo said he believes that often when faculty matures they become theorists, scholars, and critics - and are no longer out on the front lines collecting data or working closely with research assistants. "They don't run subjects any more and they don't even necessarily have students who run subjects. But I enjoy the process and am still 'into it.'"

I don't think you can teach the subtleties of experimental social psychology except in an apprentice relationship because lots of things seem very superficial if you just say them out of the on-line context. The people working with you must begin to see it is important to think about every detail as well as the general theory if an experiment is to "work" as planned - the transitions, the wording, the flow, the timing of each event. And I think if you say it in a class, where it is not connected with the actual practice of doing research, it seems kind of trivial and you get, "Oh yeah, here's somebody who is obsessive." But most important is to convey enthusiasm for the *process* That is what is crucial. There is an endless number of interesting problems to work in, and each of us must select a piece of the pie. The joy of psychology is not only digesting it, but the delicious process of eating it - and serving it to others.

INTERVIEWS

The Schachter Group

The following interviews are with Stanley Schachter and four of his students. The first four interviews are with Schachter's students. Peter Schonbach was Schachter's first Ph.D. at Minnesota. Following the Schonbach interview are interviews with Jerome Singer, Lee Ross and Neil Grunberg. Singer was a Schachter student at Minnesota after Schonbach finished. Ross and Grunberg were students at Columbia a decade apart. Last is the interview with Stanley Schachter.

PETER SCHONBACH

Peter Schonbach began his studies as a student of German philology, literature and history at the University of Frankfurt in 1949. He was also interested in sociology and attended seminars at the Institute of Social Research in Frankfurt. This institute had been re-established by Horkheimer and Adorno, who had just returned to Germany from his wartime stay in the United States. Schonbach's work caught the attention of Dr. Osmer at the Institute who recommended him for a research job there.

At that time the Institute in Frankfurt was the German headquarters of a study being conducted in several European nations by Stanley Schachter. Schonbach worked as a student assistant on the study which was a replication of Schachter's doctoral thesis - the deviation/rejection study (Schachter, 1951).

> At the time nobody knew anything about social psychology in Germany nor anywhere else in Europe. So Stan had to frantically run around and teach us how to do a t-test or a u-test in order to be able to function. And one day he looked at me and said, "Peter, you don't learn a damn thing here, why don't you come to America." And I said yes and he offered a research assistantship at the University of Minnesota. Leon Festinger also came and saw me and supported this proposition and so in 1953, September, I went on an old liberty ship from Rotterdam to New York and then on a Greyhound bus to Minnesota.
>
> They all were very nice to me, supported me, helped me and so I really dipped in it. I never had any psychology in my life before this, some sociology but no psychology. So I went into it and I learned. I did a paper in a seminar with Richard Elliot, one of the senior people at Minnesota and it was a classic comparison of Hull, Skinner and

> Tolman. He liked the paper - he gave me an A and said it was an excellent paper. I was first in the statistics class in my first semester and they thought - "Well, here is a good boy, we'll keep him," and so they asked me if I would stay on and get my Ph.D. and that's what I did.

When Schonbach first arrived in Minnesota, Schachter was still in Europe and so he was assigned to Ben Willerman until Schachter's return. He also worked frequently with Leon Festinger. He said, "I took courses with Leon as I did with Stan and we did this car advertising study, the Ehrlich, Guttman, Schonbach and Mills (1957) study together as an outcome of one of Leon's seminars. That was the seminar where he had the mimeographed version of his dissonance book discussed with us."

Schonbach described the environment at Minnesota:

> There was a group of senior staff members from different departments. The psychologists were Leon Festinger, Stanley Schachter and Ben Willerman. There was the economist Papandreou who is now the prime minister of Greece and Nat Flanders from education. There was also May Brodbeck from philosophy and Herb McClosky. There were about the same number of research assistants coming from these different groups.
>
> The set-up was very loose. The first month they did not give me anything to do and I was angry about this. They wanted to give me time to get into the system and I didn't have any trouble - I got my A's right away. So I was impatient and finally Jack Darley, who was executive secretary saw that and got them to give me work. Then Leon assigned me as an observer to run together with Denuta Ehrlich the gambling study which is mentioned in the dissonance book. That was one of the first experiments on dissonance theory and we did that under Leon's supervision.

Every Wednesday afternoon there was a meeting of the staff. There, somebody would present and Leon would sit there and listen for a while and then would start throwing daggers. He was very very sharp and mercilessly clear in his criticism. I learned lots from him. You could not mistake the informality of the situation for being loose in your thinking. *Then*, Leon certainly would cut in very quickly.

We were housed on the fourth floor of Ford Hall. It was a rectangular building. On the fourth floor was a long hall going down the corridor. On one side were sociologists and then at one end of it was one big room across almost the whole building and that is where the two secretaries and the research assistants were. There was one little room on the side for the departmental secretary, the next room was Stan's, the next room Leon's and on the other side of the elevator there were maybe one or two more rooms and laboratory space. And there was a big observation room. The other people had their rooms at their departments. It was Leon and Stan who I remember having rooms within Ford Hall *besides* having rooms at the psych department.

People would keep the doors of their offices open unless they had work to do. We had coffee hours. Andy Papandreou did not like the coffee they had so he would make Greek drip grind coffee.

In addition to affiliation with the university, the group at Ford Hall also had "independent means." He was not sure exactly the source of these funds.

Schonbach believes that Schachter was "not so much interested in developing a theory and testing it. He was interested always in phenomena and curious about phenomena and he wanted to know why." He said Schachter was "not at all shy about developing different methods and different approaches" to explore what he was interested in.

He would certainly not stand there in reverence for some sheet of data. He would remain a creative, intelligent man and try to put them together. That is what he always used to do. I think this is something I learned from Stan and I operate the same way.

I also have felt encouraged both from Leon and Stan that you are certainly not swamped by the fact that something is barely not significant or significant. You look at significance levels as just some other piece of evidence that you take into account, you present it and you look at the data and you say: "Here I have got this several times, you know it is just barely significant, I am going to keep that bit of data because..." Or else you may say, "This one looks significant but it is so contradictory, I will set it aside, I will not forget it but I will have to do them first - I will follow this line of research, I will take that seriously, I will do that because -." It is this kind of dealing in a certain sovereign manner, you know. Without being irresponsible, you always have to keep your standards - but, to be as honest as you can, to present your data clearly as you can and finally leave it to the judgment of the reader if he is willing to share your conclusions or not. It always comes down to some kind of consensus being established among the people who know. And who is going to say who are the people who know is again something to be established by consensus.

But the best thing you can do and there is nothing else - is you can be sensitive. This is my basic conviction. And that I have learned from Leon and Stan.

At the time Schonbach was at Minnesota, the advanced seminars concentrated on Festinger's social comparison version (1954) of his 1950 theory and Schachter's work on deviation and rejection. He also learned about Lewin's food studies during the war but apart from that, there was very little Lewinian residue in the courses. He said, "Sometimes Stanley would talk about hodology and those kind of things. He was fond of drawing bathtubs - making kind of weird figure and they looked very much like Lewinian figures."

> If I would have to make a guess, I would think Lewin's greatest influence in this group - John Thibaut, Hal Kelley, John French, Leon Festinger, Stan Schachter - was liberating in them and fostering creativity and intelligence that was there already among these guys but just opened it up for them. That is the best thing that you can do as an academic teacher. You can do it a little bit by example, you can listen carefully to some problem somebody has and help unlock the door. Maybe you can do that, but you certainly cannot put it into their head like that.

In addition to these lessons regarding basic research, Schonbach said he always tries to take into account the application of research. Many of the problems he has worked on such as prejudice or account episodes have origins in history. Schonbach's interest in doing research that was useful, "beyond the ivory tower," has resulted in his choosing topics and methods which are quasi-experimental in design. He pointed out that much of the early work in social psychology also had such origins.

> If you look at the work of pressures to uniformity, the first Festinger piece in 1950, what you really have is the first layer of foundation beyond Lewin. You might say that is pure basic research and yet if you look back at it from the distance of over thirty years, you see that this was a part of a concern with conformity, with cooperation that was highly salient in American history and it may have had its origins there. It was only later that so much emphasis on conformity attracted the criticism of European social psychologists - you are always concerned about the majority, you forget about the minority. So I think Festinger, as well as Asch and Sherif and all those people were not clearly independent from their background.

Schonbach received his Ph.D. in 1956 and returned to Germany where he has remained. He believes it was Schachter's intention that Schonbach help build social psychology in Europe when he invited him to Minnesota. He is active in the European Association of Experimental Social Psychology, a group organized with the help of Festinger, Schachter and others during the sixties.

> People like Hal Kelley, John Thibaut and Leon Festinger said to us, you guys know *us*, but you don't know each other. I knew the psychologist in Oslo because he had been on this Schachter replication but there were so many other people and we didn't know each other. There were conferences in the sixties and now we have about 150 members and social psychology has grown partly due to the Association and the journal and the monograph series.
>
> The Associations in Italy, Austria, Spain and the eastern European countries. It works with Poland and it works with Hungary to some extent, it is less influential with the east Germans, the Czechs and the Russians but some... Some are allowed to come to the east/west meetings partly funded. They get permission to come, preferably to the eastern countries. The European scene has one beneficial effect, there is no competition. You will get criticism, but it will be friendly - it will not be tinged with competition.

When Schonbach returned to Europe, he said it took him a while to get established. "With my American Ph.D., I was sort of an odd man. It was highly salient and interesting but people didn't know quite what to do with me." In the German system, in order to become a professor in a university there are requirements beyond the doctorate. He explained, "You have to write a second thesis, even more involved than the first and this establishes you as a professor and you are then allowed to teach in your own right." When he returned to Germany he married and went to work as a market researcher. Then he got a chance to return to the Institute as an assistant.

I was a fringe member at the Institute because they were marxist oriented and so it was very high brow and theoretical and they sort of started to look at the people who were doing the empirical work in the laboratory as being necessary in order to keep going. There was a slightly arrogant, condescending attitude toward the empirical. After a while I began to establish myself as a person to be recognized. I once did a piece of qualitative analysis of right wing newspapers on anti-semitism and communism as part of a bigger project and Adorno liked that. He saw that I was not only a nose counter but that I could do a qualitative analysis and from then on they accepted me as a person and let me do my own thing. I think what I established was sort of extending the boundaries of the niche I was in.

Now, I was an empiricist sitting in a niche doing empirical work that was helpful to them. But the mainstream of the Institute, of course, was political theory, marxist oriented, and that of course had a flavor. And there I was, an American Ph.D. sitting in this marxist oriented institute trying to accomplish this second thesis on language and attitudes for a Faculty of Philosophy. It was a bit difficult, to put it mildly. But eventually, in 1968, I made it.

In 1963 Schonbach spent a year visiting at Duke at the invitation of former colleague, Jack Brehm. Brehm had finished his degree with Leon Festinger the year before Schonbach received his from Schachter.

Training Students

Most of the students Schonbach works with are diploma students who chose to write a thesis with him rather than with the professor of clinical psychology or animal psychology.

When he finally got his chair as a professor in 1969, at the Ruhr-Universitat in Bochum it was the third chair in social psychology in western Germany.

> The Institute of Psychology at Bochum has a core set of eight professors and thirty assistants on various levels. There is also nonscientific staff. I will now describe one of these eight working units which is social psychology, which is me plus two assistants (each holding a doctorate) and a part time secretary. There is another half time secretary who mostly works for the two and I have a technical assistant working full time. There are also four paid student assistants. These students are close to receiving their diploma which is roughly the equivalent of a masters degree - that is our standard finish. We don't have a bachelors degree, the diploma is it.

He said the students he works with are those who come through his seminar and are bright and sufficiently motivated. "I would expect a student to have come into my seminar and show some work before asking to work. I am willing to spend much time with them and expect from them in return a decent thesis - the necessary empirical work connected with my theory or whatever I am working on," he explained. Beyond being smart and motivated, he looks for students who, "would fit congenially in our group. They must have a sense of humor. I like them to be friendly." He considers his former students to be friends. He said, "we are on a first name basis which is not so customary as it would be in the United States." He said he has the reputation of being a nice guy, easy going and relaxed yet tough. "In an examination, I cannot be fooled. It is a good reputation to have."

Recalling his own training:

> I still have a feeling of being in a special group. Even though it is now thirty years later, I still have very vivid memories and would consider myself to be a student of Leon Festinger and Stan Schachter.

JEROME SINGER

Jerome Singer began his undergraduate career studying Naval Architecture at the University of Michigan. This lasted only until his first year drafting teacher, whom Singer described as "a very kindly man," said to him: "Singer, you are not the worst draftsman I have ever had, but easily since the end of the war." So Singer spent the next three years studying materials and chemical engineering. He remembered, "The science part was ok, but I didn't like the engineering aspects at all." After that he dropped out for a year, "to try to figure out what to do." Once Singer returned to college, he eventually finished with a double degree in sociology and anthropology and the knowledge that he wanted to go on to graduate school.

He was attracted to the new Behavioral Sciences Training program at the University of Minnesota run by John G. Darley. Leon Festinger had just left Minnesota for Stanford but Stanley Schachter, Harold Kelley and Henry Reicken were all still there. He said his sociology background made him "putatively a sociologist" and he spent the first two years taking courses and doing research.

> There were three of us who were taking a sociology of conflict course. Instead of doing a term paper, we talked the instructor into letting us do a study on renegades and heretics and some other notions in the sociology of conflict.
>
> Lew Coser, a sociologist, had just published a revision of George Simmel's theory of conflict in which he argued that when groups are in conflict you build up in-group sentiment and out-group dislike. The renegade, somebody who moves from your group and joins the enemy is more disliked than the enemy. And disliked most of all was the heretic - somebody who remains in your group but

> espouses the values of the enemy. We ran a study to try and test that and we found some results that differed from Coser's. We wrote it up separately as term papers and it wasn't until I got my first job a few years later that I wrote it up and got it published in Sociometry. So that was my first year of graduate school - we did things of that sort - we decided we would rather do an experiment than write a term paper.

During his second year Singer helped political scientist Herb McClosky analyze data from a survey which included, "one thousand Republican elite, one thousand Democratic elite, which he had acquired during the 1956 conventions, and a random national sample of two thousand which he had acquired from the Gallop Poll," he said. He also worked with Henry Reicken. "At the end of my second year, Reicken had left I wasn't a political scientist and I wasn't all that thrilled with the sociology department there."

> I wanted to do more experimental work, I found sociologists dreary so I decided to work - Stan Schachter was gone, but I decided to switch into psychology. Hal Kelley was there and I liked the psychology program better, so I applied to the psych department in my third year in graduate school. I had three courses in psychology in my first two years there.
>
> In my third year, Stan came back and I started out as his research assistant and we started working. Stan asked some of his people - he had been gone for a year - who among the new people were any good. Some of my friends said, "take him." Stan picked me and I was assigned to him. Whether Hal was my advisor or Stan was my advisor didn't matter because I was on this crazy program where the courses were all outlined anyhow.
>
> So I started working for Stan - his system for picking people was terror. I don't argue a lot, but I am not easily terrorized and so it worked out. We

> got to be friendly. I started being his research assistant on a number of experiments and after two years when I was in the middle of my thesis, he went off on sabbatical to Stanford. While he was gone, he insisted that my wife and I rent his house and take care of Harold the cat.

The physical arrangements in the Behavioral Sciences program at Minnesota were such that, "Hal's students and Stan's students and Ben Willerman's students all were in the same place and we had an identity as a social unit as well as by advisor - so we were all friendly across advisors as well."

> We learned to do things because we would have group meetings which meant we would go in to discuss a study and plan it as a group and talk with Stanley - mostly late afternoon, playing cribbage - which preceded backgammon.

Schachter ran a tight-knit lab. Singer described a Group Dynamics course Schachter offered, "which consisted of his and Leon's work." Because the course was listed in the course catalog, according to Singer the first order of business was to discourage "all the people from the school of education who wanted all sorts of things." Because he couldn't just tell them to leave, Schachter did this by taking the students he was sure of - his students - and running a "very hostile, insulting session where he yelled at them, humiliated them and treated them in such a way that the others dropped out before their turn came. And then he went on with the seminar because that was all over," Singer laughed.

> We worked as a group. Usually two or three people. In the case of the emotion study it was Stanley, Bibb and I mostly. In the concluding chapter of the affiliation book there is a notion: Would people affiliate in order to evaluate something totally ambiguous like an internal state? And so Stanley thought, "How about you give people adrenalin and find out will they want to wait together or alone." The situation he used was the one Peter Schonbach used for his food and hunger evaluation which was you give them tasks: "visual

diplocity" and "binocular redundency" - which one did they want. The only difference between what you do is, one you wait with other people and one you wait alone. Then there were two auditory tasks, "oral angular displacement" and "auditory peripherality."

> My first task with Stanley was to go over to the psych department's store of old apparatus and get things that could be *called* a visual diplocity and we made up this crazy apparatus. We had a good time. There were also *very* bright people there and it was just fun only - they were people who were interested in more than just psychology. Stanley and Leon selected people who were not only smart but enjoy that kind of schmoozing.

When he finished his degree, Singer took a postdoc in biochemistry. His undergraduate experience in chemistry and engineering furnished him with some of the prerequisites he needed.

> A lot of our work had involved injecting humans or animals with drugs and we decided - or I decided it would be nice to have studies that went the other way. Studies where you did something behaviorally and then extracted and measured the free flowing hormones instead of injecting hormones and seeing what they would do. In the middle of that year, the man with whom I had the postdoc announced he was moving the lab to Stanford and I was welcome to go along. I didn't want to be a psychologist who was a third rate biochemist in somebody else's shop, so I started job hunting late in the year. I had one offer.

Training students:

"I am not a particularly good trainer of students," he said. "It never interested me. I would rather be a student than a teacher." He went on to say that he is "good at training assistant professors." This he does by being a good colleague. "I am interested and listen to what other people are doing and I am curious about their work as well as about my own. I got tenure that way," he laughed. He explained that he had been an assistant professor at Penn State for several years and was in New York giving a colloquium when his wife called to say he had received a letter from the dean. She wanted to know if she should open it. "I said, 'sure' and she opened it and it said I had been promoted. I didn't even know I was up."

Some of Singer's work at Penn state was on Machiavellianism. It was his first work independent from Schachter. He had heard Christie talk about the Machiavellianism scale and said, "I used it and published using the scale before he did. Then he kept referring people to me." Because of this, Singer wound up handling the paper work on the Scale.

Singer said his favorite part of the research process is, "working out the script and the spiel and the debriefing."

> Debriefing is not just cooling the mark, which some people have called it. It is also, in a very real sense - especially in a deception experiment or a complicated experiment - it is educating the subject into what you are doing. I find a lot of people I have run through studies, no matter how outrageous the deception was - liked it.
>
> You take a subject who goes for a straight experimental psych experiment. They are sitting in front of a memory drum in a room by themselves for two hours going over lists. Its over and somebody gives them a routine explanation of what they have done which is totally accurate and they are bored as hell.

> They come into our study, they have been the star in a drama. The answer is not to make them think that you are running a candid camera show but to explain what you have done and why and let them see how their behavior in this situation was constrained by the setting that occurred. And they really *learn* something about what has happened.

Singer enjoys teaching. He said, "I don't resent taking away from research but I resented teaching introductory psychology eight times in a row - I don't like being a patsy." All he requires is to have "a little variety and cycle on and off" with some courses.

He said there are "two different kind of faculty members. A department cannot exist with Stanleys or Leons entirely. And for very good reason." Because of the way they run their labs which are very tightly focused, there have to be other people in a department for students who have their own interests. Singer said he has functioned as one of those people in the various departments he has been associated with. He is currently chairman of the Department of Medical Psychology at Uniformed Services University of the Health Sciences. He teaches statistics and methodology in a program of approximately sixteen graduate students.

He said when he writes something he doesn't care who reads it. "I just want to say it. I know who *should* read it, but they don't often." His major audience are his colleagues and his friends who are the people he went to graduate school with and, "people I am *now* friendly with who were ahead of me, like Stanley and Leon and that group."

He said he has never worried about having ideas. "There are some people who think intellectual life is a zero sum game, who begrudge somebody an idea because it is one less that they can have." He believes if he has anything to contribute, he will have another idea. "If I am not about to go file an NIH grant on it, I don't care who does it. It is just an interesting idea." This attitude is one Singer shares with Schachter. He described a conversation between Schachter and a perceptual psychologist who was going to be coming to Columbia to visit for a year.

> Julie, who worries about these things went to lunch with Stanley and said, "You know I am going to come to the department of social psychology and I am really in perception - social perception but it's perception. I decided I would read what you people wrote so I would know what sort of work was done and whether I would fit in. I am very puzzled. I have read your work. I like it, it's interesting but I am really bothered - in one sense it is not programmatic. You start a field, you run a couple of studies and then you just leave it and go on to something else." And he said, "You never really follow up on things."
>
> He pointed to some of Stanley's work on rumor for instance and Stanley said, "Ok, was that an interesting problem, something that was really fascinating?" And Julie said, "Yeah." Stanley said, "Fine, if it that fascinating, somebody else will do it, I don't want to bother with the details. Give me another one." And Julie gave him another one. Stanley said, "Was *that* interesting?" He said, "Not particularly." Stanley said, "Why should I spend my life doing something not interesting?"

Working with Festinger:

While on leave from Penn State working at the Educational Testing Service and Personality Research Center, Singer was asked to join the Transnational Social Psychology Committee as a temporary staff person. According to Singer the committee was formed, "when Leon and Stanley and a number of others got the notion that all over Europe you found social psychologists all of whom knew what was happening in Ann Arbor but the people in Paris didn't know what was happening in Brussels. So they formed at SSRC a committee called Transnational Social Psychology which was half Western Europe and half United States. They ran conferences and out of that came the European Association for Experimental Social Psychology." The position was open because of the sudden death of Ben Willerman, and

Singer was recommended for the job by Stanley Schachter. Leon Festinger was chairman. Singer recalled, "Even though I knew of Leon, and one time Stanley was trying to get me a postdoc with Leon, that was the first time I met him and became friendly with him."

Schachter and Festinger:

> Much of the difficulty that social psychology had getting accepted in many departments had to do with Leon's explicit and Stanley's implicit disagreement with a lot of what was going on. There were two major centers in social psychology: there was the Group Dynamics bunch, the Lewinians, and there was the learning theory group at Yale. The learning theory group got into the hypothetico-deductive method at the beginning and that soon petered out. There was some crossover, Hal Kelley was at Yale for six years before coming to Minnesota, but by and large you had a foot in two camps.
>
> One of the major contributions of Leon and Stanley was that their kind of theory is not the geometry or topology of Lewin in that way. It was: you take an idea and you say, "If this idea and *only* this idea works, what implications does it have?" And you *very* tightly say, "If *only* this is working, what would you predict?" Then you try and test that out - They were very tightly theoretical in that sense, which is not the common mode.
>
> They were also very much attached to a foot in the real world. I don't mean real world in terms of Lewinian applied work but real world in terms of phenomena. For example, take a look at the introduction to the dissonance book where he talks about how he started. It was when Leon was doing a review for the Social Science Research Council on rumors and he was reviewing a finding in India

> that seemed puzzling. It was a real world phenomena that bothered him. And from that he said, "Maybe people start rumors in order to justify their feeling afraid." From that he got to incongruities and dissonance and pushed that as far as he could. *that* is a real world phenomenon as opposed to the learning theory where you said, "If habit strength goes up and drive goes down, what happens to the product of the two?"
>
> What happened then was that people who hadn't studied with Leon latched onto dissonance theory and ran drudgerous experiments in which they picked one particular word and tested it against another particular word. You will *never* see a Festinger or a Schachter experiment look like that. You will see that all of them are concerned with real world phenomena. It is the way we were all trained - keep an eye on what is interesting and then when you get an idea about what is happening, test your idea and push it as rigorously as possible as if that is the *only* factor at work to see what the implications are and how much it overrides. The argument is that if your idea is powerful, it will override other things. Jack Brehm sometimes says, "I don't believe in individual differences." And what he means by that of course is that if your idea is worth anything it is going to ride over the individual differences. And that is the way we learned to do things.

Singer rejected the idea that Festinger and Schachter were wedded to the laboratory. He pointed to Festinger's field experiments and Schachter's birth order work as examples of nonlaboratory studies. He said, "It is just a canard of people who didn't like the way they worked. They were always for simplification. Take one idea, push it as far as you can. When you change it or make it more complex, it was made only as *least* complex as possible."

According to Singer, another thing that set Schachter and Festinger apart from the rest of the field was their habit of citing only work that was relevant to the study at hand.

> There *is* sort of a trading relationship among people on citations. If two people work in an area, even if you disagree with somebody, you cite "in contradistinction to this view, the reader might see..." and you cite somebody else. Back and forth, people cite each other as a courtesy to acknowledge that somebody else has worked in the field. Leon and Stanley never did that. They cited just their own work. What this means is that if an idea doesn't pertain, you don't cite somebody just because they wrote on that topic if you don't think much of their ideas.

One personal characteristic Schachter and Festinger share is a passion for games - backgammon and chess respectively. According to Singer, "They are both enormously competitive."

Singer believes part of Schachter and Festinger's success in producing good students is in selection. He said, "They don't pick a student out because they have a theory about what is going to make the student... They do it because, 'This is the only kind of person I can be around. I want somebody who is bright, who is willing to learn, who is not a know-it-all but yet I can get some interest and enjoyment out of.' They are looking for students, in a sense, who they can enjoy as friends when the student-ship is over."

He described Schachter's attitude toward his students:

> It's if you are good and have a certain kind of personality that I am going to enjoy being with, that it is fine, then we can be friends. If I call you schmuck and I yell at you and all the rest, it is only because I have granted you a fundamental degree of respect. People I am polite to I have not use for. It's a Jewish family - you yell and scream at each other - but of course you wouldn't do that to a stranger, that would be crude.
>
> The issue is whether you are stamping people who don't belong in that mold or you are selecting people for whom you know that training is

> appropriate. Stanley's success has been only working with people who he feels happy with, which means who *he* thinks are good. He has had some errors, he has had some people who haven't made it, who quit or what have you. His success has been in having a style which he calls selfish, rigid or unwilling to change and imposing it not on everybody who walks through the door but only on those people who he thinks match that style.

Singer said the key to this system is having a large enough talent pool come through the department so even though Schachter may have "a very narrow filter," a few people get through. He pointed out that Schachter and Festinger were both at top universities which attracted the very best students to begin with. He said, "Look at where Leon was. He was at Stanford, getting some of the brightest students in the country with the most rigorous entrance criteria and *still* only picking three or four students coming through." Comparing this process with that found in musical organizations, Singer said that Schachter and Festinger were training soloists, not section players.

LEE ROSS

Lee Ross said he "always had the feeling that psychology wasn't very hard" and that is one reason he thinks he majored in it as an undergraduate. He said, "I always felt this is a great subject that you don't really have to study, all you have to do was write down the way it is." But there were other reasons for his choice. First, he said he found psychology "endlessly fascinating; more important you could actually do psychology as an undergraduate and you couldn't do that in any other field." This was possible because Ross was an undergraduate at the University of Toronto in the middle sixties. He said, "It was truly outstanding - as impressive a group of undergraduate mentors as you could have anywhere. There was a professionally oriented honors program so you were taking a large number of psychology courses in classes where everyone else was taking the same program."

Although he described the department at Toronto as "heavily Hullian," Ross worked with John Arrowood on cognitive dissonance. Arrowood had worked with Harold Kelley and Stanley Schachter at Minnesota.

> I was very interested and very full of Hullian psychology and very aware of the longstanding battle between the cognitivists and the old fashioned learning theorists. And I knew which side I was on - Despite the lessons of my undergraduate teachers, I was on the side of the cognitivists from the beginning. In fact, a lot of the subsequent interests that I developed, I think can be traced to my growing appreciation of the cognitive critique of learning theory.

He went to Columbia for graduate school because Arrowood, who was also his undergraduate advisor, said to him, "If I was going to graduate school, I would want to go to Columbia and work with Stanley Schachter." Ross said, "That just seemed like a very sensible thing to do and so I only applied to one graduate school." With Arrowood's help and the fact that he had won a Woodrow Wilson fellowship, Ross was admitted. He was particularly attracted to Schachter's work on emotion.

> It was the *ultimate* in what seemed to me cognitive social psychology. It was saying that in order to understand the effect of the stimulus of the situation on the actor, you had to understand its meaning to that actor. In other words it was speaking to the main thing that seemed wrong and frustrating about Hullian psychology - even the particular kind of Hullian psychology I had been exposed to.

Once at Columbia, however, Ross spent his first year working with Bibb Latane. He chose Latane because he was impressed with what Latane was doing and wasn't initially very interested in the obesity research that Schachter was working on at the time. He also noted that "Latane had just finished doing work on sociopathy and I though maybe I could get to do with Bibb, who was Stanley's student after all, what I had hoped to do with Stanley." But things didn't work out as he had hoped.

> The work with Latane (on bystander intervention and on rat affiliation) was quite interesting and quite satisfying, but I really was envious of the people who were working with Schachter. There were many reasons. First of all, of course, there was Stan's charisma and his ability to convey the idea that his work really "mattered" - was really at the "cutting edge" of the field. Also, it was Stan's students who became my friends. I found myself talking with them a lot about their work and I felt that I had more interesting ideas about *their* work than I did about my own. In part it was that I envied their style and the esprit de corp of the group - the way they all spent so much time just sitting around thinking about their research problems and talking about possible experiments. I found myself getting interested. I found myself having ideas and reactions, saying things to myself like, "Why would you want to build an animal whose, feeding

behavior was controlled in that way" or, "How can we tease apart situational and cultural factors from physiological and psychological ones?"

There was a sense that it was a cohesive group, and also a bit of elitism - the feeling that the *most* promising students seemed almost all to be working with Stan. I don't really know what all the reasons were, but I do know that it wasn't the research topic itself because I actually wasn't that interested in obesity. I knew that for some reason or other the kinds of studies that Stanley was doing and the way he was conceiving of the problem made us think of exciting possibilties but it wasn't that I had any abiding interest in obesity - I wasn't fat, I didn't know anybody who was fat, I didn't *care* about fat (although I did like eating!)

Ross switched advisors, "with great pain and discomfort, because Stan was reluctant to encourage defection by one of Bibb's students." One of Schachter's advanced graduate students at the time, Richard Nisbett, helped "broker" the switch and they eventually became close friends. According to Ross, "We actually became friends more in the three subsequent years after Dick left. He was at Yale, which is close to New York, and he came back frequently. I think the real secret was I was married, and unlike most Columbia students at the time, had a 'real home.' Anyway, Dick and I were very interested in getting to know each other, and we did eventually become very close friends. But I think we became respectful colleagues long before we became personal friends."

Schachter's Style:

Ross described Schachter as being very single minded and serious about his work but not certain of the answers he was seeking. Ross said, "He was really convinced he had an interesting *puzzle* to unravel, and he was quite excited about finding out what the answer to this puzzle was going to be." He described the way Schachter would follow a problem:

One interesting aspect of the obesity work was that it initially got its impetus from a *failed* hypothesis. Schachter originally got into obesity because he was trying to show that overeating and obesity were the results of a special kind of mislabeling phenomenon - namely that people who were fat mislabeled lots of other emotional things as hunger.

This idea had been around to some extent in the literature. In the psychoanalytic literature for instance, Hilda Bruche had talked this way. I think Stan's initial idea was that if mama gives you a cookie every time you are upset, like when the other kids don't play with you and you feel sad and feel rejected, you will associate almost any aversive internal state with eating and hunger. So you reach the point where sadness, anger, anxiety, loneliness, or the like all lead you to say: "*Aha* , I must be feeling hunger." So you go out and eat. That was a clinical syndrome Schachter was thinking about and he wanted to demonstrate some version of it in the laboratory.

The results that got him off and flying were findings that manipulations of internal states, whether through manipulating how anxious people were, or afraid, or even how food deprived they were - didn't seem to have any effect on obese subjects. However, these manipulations *did* have an effect on normal subjects. How was one going to explain that? The interesting thing is that Stanley at that point *totally* changed gears. Instead of saying, "No, no let's do the study in a different way, lets get the right results," he somehow understood that the results suggested a more interesting idea, and a more profound one, than the one he had been pursuing initially. He said, "Aha, we seem to have people (obese people) who are *insensitive* to their internal states and lets go with that." In some ways reminiscent of his earlier work with Latane on sociopathy, where again the notion was that the thing that might characterize sociopaths was their

> insensitivity to their internal state. So Schachter was somewhat prepared to think along those lines.
>
> People often accuse him at least of having fixed hypotheses and then doing great violence to the data - throwing out subjects or whatever in order to *make* the hypothesis work. But that really does not capture the *essence* of his style *at all.* After the fact - after he has done seven or eight studies and he knows very clearly the story that he wants to tell, he works very hard to make all the data fit with that larger story. But that is *after* the data is in. Schachter is not someone who gets an idea and then runs one study, and simply tries to make the study work out so it's publishable. On every major area he worked at, I think, the idea that Schachter ended up using to give coherence to the work was *not* the idea he started out with.

Ross believes that Schachter and Festinger train their students in a similar fashion.

> There's a real tradition. Partly it is just a love of craftsmanship, in the same way that good artists had a real appreciation for what it was that a good painter was supposed to be able to do -- handle draperies, nude figures, reflections in water, the play of light and shadow and whatever. I think that there is some tradition here too about the display of craftsmanship that should be shown in the measures, cover story, and manipulation of a "good experiment."
>
> The way it worked with Schachter and Festinger was interesting. They actually didn't give a lot of feedback - there usually weren't detailed comments, feedback and criticism. And there were no general discussions of methodology or paradigms. We *never* got that kind of thing. Basically, we learned by apprenticeship - by doing what *they* were doing. If you did something wrong, Stan would look at you kind of incredulously, like he was sort of hurt or

> disappointed slightly - but mainly conveying to you that you weren't supposed to waste his time or yours. You were supposed to be *serious.* It was perfectly permissible to make a mistake, but you weren't expected to waste his time discussing the obstacles to getting your work done. It was acknowledged that it is always hard to do something right; you were supposed to keep working til you get it right, and *then* show you work to the "master."
>
> Stanley never criticized, he would just start looking bored when he thought you were off the track. He would start looking distracted, basically conveying the message that if it wasn't for the fact that you had *enormous* credit built up from all of the hard work you had done in the past, and for his overall relationship with you, he *certainly* wouldn't be suffering through sitting here while you talk drivel. Generally, the way it worked was that you came in to see Stan whenever you had gotten to the next step of whatever you were working on or if you had an idea about a study on phenomena. You rarely sought him out just "to chat." Sometimes he would come by your office and try things out on you: Sometimes you would do the same with him. Also he ate lunch together with one or more of his students probably four days a week. Arrangements were informal and there were few "appointments."

At lunch, the talk was not necessarily about ongoing research. There was "a lot of gossip, some talk about politics, or phenomena in the world. Usually it was very ordinary talk, but it was still talk that was influenced by the fact that it was psychologists doing the talking."

Ross said he thinks Schachter's secret to working with graduate students is that he "always makes students think they are probably a little smarter than he is, or at least that they have more 'pure g' than he does."

> You get the idea that he knows some valuable secrets and has some special skills, but that he can teach them to you, or at least that you can learn by watching. Somewhere along the line you will learn his secrets, and especially his incredible instincts for what's interesting and important. That, coupled with your pure g will make you very good indeed - maybe even better than he is. That, at least, is what we somehow came to believe.

Schachter's students spent a lot of time together both in and out of the lab. Ross believes the senior students played a "very very important role in socializing the junior students." They would help the younger students, "anticipate whether a given idea really was one you wanted to go talk to Stanley about, or not; and that was quite important."

According to Ross, the only real social psychology he did at Columbia was done during one year when Schachter was on leave and Phil Zimbardo replaced him. Zimbardo taught a course on deindividuation which required a research project. Ross was eager to work with Zimbardo, because he was "so creative as a methodologist," but was hoping to work with him on affiliation and emotion, which Zimbardo had done quite a bit on during the previous few years.

> It was a chance to do what I had initially thought I would be doing with Stanley when I came there. In fact I had one particular study at the back of my mind, right from the time I came to Columbia. I had a version of the study in mind, and after some major changes, it produced the basis for an experiment Phil and Judy Rodin and I published in 1969. Phil was eager to teach a research-oriented course on deindividuation, but when I made it clear that I was hot to do an emotional mislabelling study, he was very gracious and very flexible. He said, "All right then, we'll make it a course on deindividuation *and* emotion." Several of us ended up doing studies on emotion rather than on deindividuation, and it was a great opportunity to finally take the lead in designing a study, and to see

> how another fine experimentalist (i.e., Phil Zimbardo) went about the business of doing research.

When Ross finished his degree at Columbia, he took his first job at Stanford. He is still there. The job was offered without his ever interviewing. "I think that wouldn't happen now," he said.

> There was more of a patronage system then, and I had both push and pull. Phil Zimbardo was at Stanford, and he had just finished working with me. Schachter was pushing me a little bit, so between the two of them I was in good shape, even though I had relatively few publications - at least few by today's standards.

Once at Stanford, Ross followed his interest in emotion. In this case it was emotional attribution and emotional misattribution. He believes, however, that it was "a paradigm whose time had passed a little bit." But it kept alive his interest in attribution issues.

The environment at Stanford is very supportive. Ross said the institutional attitude is, "Do significant work and get well known, publish, and exert an impact on the field; we will take care of the rest." He said the environment is enriched by the quality of the faculty - some are important colleagues with whom he works regularly. Others are, "good colleagues who are smart people," interested in ideas and willing to give some feedback even if their work is not similar enough to his own for there to be a "direct impact." He said there is a "strong tradition of civility" in the department and a "very strong ethic against being a prima donna."

Training Students:

When graduate students come to Stanford, according to Ross, "they talk to everyone and some kind of assortative mating goes on where, if they are particularly interested in working with someone, they usually get their way." Students are encouraged to work with more than one person during their stay.

Ross discussed the way the constricted job market has affected the of training graduate students and in turn the field.

> I think a lot of students first of all are disillusioned when they see students who they thought were pretty good, not getting good jobs. That kind of scares them. Or alternatively, they may be scared because the student who got the good job was so *impossibly* good and hard working that they say, "Oh, I see, only people like *that* get good jobs." And I think there is a socialization process that goes on in graduate school, whereby a lot of people came in thinking they were going to get a very good academic job at a splendid place and spend their lives supervising the running of experiments and doing a little teaching. They find out that such privileged status will not be achieved by everyone. That is appropriately scary to some of them.
>
> There is obviously more emphasis on publication than there was when I was coming up. You worry a little with regard to graduate students, a lot with regard to new assistant professors, that young people no longer have the luxury to follow the Festinger-Schachter tradition - i.e., to look around for some big questions and not worry. In that tradition it was ok if it took a year or two years to run a study; in fact, if you are publishing seven papers a year that's probably a sign you are doing too much, none of it really well. I am willing to bet that even Leon Festinger, as a junior faculty member, was not publishing as much as lots and lots of mediocre assistant professors do nowadays. And that is despite the fact that it was a lot easier to get manuscripts accepted for publiction in those days than it is now.
>
> There is an emphasis on quantity now that is hard to escape. It is hard to have an impact on the field if you haven't done a lot of research. But it is impossible to have impact on the field if you haven't done anything creative. The emphasis at

> Stanford is more on quality than on quantity but it is important to understand that the mere absence of quantity isn't necessarily evidence of quality. Some people do only a little bit of work, and all of it is second rate.

He said the way students learn is by being around someone who is a "very serious scientist." These scientists shape behavior by being interested, or not interested in what the student is doing.

> It isn't someone "telling" you how to be a creative scientist, it's seeing someone do it, seeing what a real success looks like, and seeing someone who does it in a series of studies that take on some direction. It is important to see work done with a kind of vaunting ambition that suggests, "What I am doing is *really* going to make a difference."

During at least one quarter every year (sometimes more), Ross meets with his students once a week in a research meeting. This meeting is open-ended. He has a core group of four or five students whom he described as, "clearly *my* students." Also attending are two or three other students who "may or may not do something with me." So the meetings are usually attended by about seven students. He said he sometimes asks a couple of students to report on their planned or completed research in some detail and, "we usually try and save some time to just go around the table and have everyone give us a quick update on what they are planning or running - but most of the collaboration is carried on by my dropping in their office or their dropping in mine."

> I think a lot of advisors believe their role is to be brakes on enthusiasm, that students are disposed to "overclaim," to overestimate the importance and originality of their ideas, not to think of all the alternative explanations. The advisors believe their job is to make their students more modest and sober. And I think one way in which Stanley was a really good advisor was that he did not see his role in such terms at all. He saw his role, I think, to help you get more excited about things and recognize what might be worth doing and teach you to

appreciate good ideas and good solutions to problems.

> The one thing I think is important for advisors to avoid is the constant putting down of students, cutting people down to size - making them realize their ideas aren't as good as they thought, making them realize that they have to be more modest about their claims, and recognize all the alternative possibilities. They encourage students to consider the way in which their ideas may be *less* important than they seem. I think there are a lot of advisors who do that, and a lot of advisors who feel a continuing need to prove they are better than any of their students.
>
> Stanley and some other senior figures in our field who I respect greatly (notably Ned Jones) insist that it's hard to be a successful graduate advisor until you can stop competing with your students.

Ross works on his own program of research and students participate in that. If they have other interests, "there is usually someone else who is more appropriate for them to work with," he said. "I do insist that we work on projects that are coherent with each other." I warn students that there are always a lot of studies that *could* be done, and just because you have a clever idea for a study doesn't mean you get to do it. It has to have something to do with where we are going in research. If a student has a genuinely clever idea that lies outside our current research program I say, '*by all means* go off and do it on your own.' I encourage my students to do studies with other faculty members. I also encourage my students to collaborate with each other and to do things I don't even know about or only know enough about to kibbitz." Ross commented that he doesn't usually become personal friends with his students, "but there have been one or two exceptions."

He conceives of the role of advisor as "making someone better than they were, and making them confident they have what it takes to be an important contributing psychologist." He said he doesn't feel particularly fatherly toward his students. "Quite the contrary, my students probably feel they look after me in a lot of ways," he laughed.

> I always like the fact that my students will educate each other early as to what you have to do to get along with me. It is very useful. I would say my relationship with them is more like an older sibling. Like most relationships with older siblings, they are more dependent on you than vice versa, but there are always some particular ways in which the reverse is true.

Experimentation:

Ross said that he does not restrict his work to experiments, and noted that he has received some recognition for work that "organizes" fields of inquiry. Nevertheless, he insists he is primarily an experimentalist. He described experiments as parables and said, "the point of an experiment isn't to prove that an idea is correct; the point of an experiment is to illustrate and explain an idea. If you are trying to show something, then you have to control it - you have to make the story work right. The next level is to look for parables in the real world and describe what you think is going on there."

> When I show you an experiment, what that should do is make you understand what it was I was telling you about in the introduction. Conversely, a good experiment should have the property that it is interesting even if you never read the introduction and never read the discussion - upon reading method and results one should be able to say, "*Oh*! People *do* that," and then one should be able to make the connections between demonstrations and other phenomena.
>
> If you have to tell what a bunch of other psychologists did in order to make a piece of work interesting, in general - not always but generally - it isn't an interesting piece of work. I don't know

> whether that reflects something about the unique status of psychology or whether it is something about the immaturity of the field, but I think an examination of the "classics" will bear me out.
>
> Most of the important experiments in psychology could be described in such a way that you never refer to any other piece of research. Consider the Asch experiment, I could tell you about it, talk about the real world and the Asch experiment and *not discuss any other psychology.* The same thing is true about the Milgram experiment. The same thing is true about Festinger and Carlsmith - there are lots of studies that have that property of being interesting all by themselves. They can readily be connected to real world phenomena - and it is that connection, and not the connection between them and any other experiment, that accounts for their "classic" status.
>
> Good experiments are plays, they are pieces of drama that convince you that the author is saying something important not just because they strike a resonant chord, but because that author was right about what people were going to do, or at least he showed that they would behave the way he said. The drama shows, "There really are *some* people who really *did this thing*, or some percentage of people *did this thing*." A dramatist who does not do experiments can merely ask you to accept the fact that you can behave in a particular way under at least some circumstances.

Ross said he continues to be influenced by the classic experiments in social psychology. He said he is more influenced by them than by theory. "I still treat the Asch experiment (Asch, 1956), the Milgram experiment (Milgram, 1963), the Festinger and Carlsmith experiment (Festinger & Carlsmith, 1959) and some others as points on a compass when I think of a new idea," he said.

To him, the remarkable thing about the classic experiments is they "stay alive regardless of the context in which you think about them." He believes both the Asch experiment and the Milgram experiment are about people trying to figure out what is going on in a situation. "The Festinger and Carlsmith experiment could be explained as being about subjects who made a wrong correspondent inference - they are not responding in a way controlled by their attitudes, they were attributing an attitude or a belief to themselves that did not correspond to their behavior. It isn't that it is *really* a study about attribution error and not a study about what the guys who did it originally thought it was about, it's about many different things at the same time." "But," he said, "I am interested in attributional errors, and all of a sudden when I look at that study I see it is also a study about attribution error. Truly classic sound psychology experiments just have that property. You can be a role theorist, or a reinforcement theorist, or almost any kind of theorist; and still think that the class experiment is *really about* (or at least *partially* about) the types of processes and mechanisms embraced by your pet theoretical perspective."

Ross feels that experimentation is important.

> I think that is one of the main things I owe to that Lewin-Festinger-Schachter tradition. I think if I had gone to a different kind of place, I might very well have been someone who loved to pontificate and have grand theories and grand schemes that never forced me to actually get in and do anything. I think one of the real strong Lewinian traditions was to make you appreciate the value of a good experiment and to make you appreciate how *hard* it was to do a good experiment - that you *really had to understand something* to do a good experiment. There was a way in which it was almost an engineering trick. An engineer proves that he understood important theoretical information every time he or she actually makes something work. And I think that a good psychology experiment is almost always a similar triumph of engineering.
>
> I think that's what I got from Schachter - being around people who really thought very hard about how do to an experiment and what the right way to do it and what the wrong way to do it was...that

there were aesthetics involved and it wasn't just a matter of making an experiment work in the sense of getting a significant result - it is to tell a story, it is to be a parable that illustrates some larger truth.

So what are all the different components that enter into that? Who should your subjects be? What should they be doing? How much should you control? How much should you not control? Should you use behavioral measures? Should you use self-report measures? Do you want the subjects to tell you why they are doing what they are doing? *All* these kinds of questions, you have to think about *beforehand*. You don't just fluke a good experiment and it's no accident that everyone in that tradition will tell you the same thing. In fact they are kind of annoyed that people think of them as being "mere experimenters," as people who merely do "demonstrations," with an implicit comparison to researchers who painstakingly test alternative explanations or pit different theories against each other. I am willing to bet that Elliot Aronson has never done any study that he didn't think about for four or five *months*. Any experiment. And it usually involves, minimally, having thought of some wrong ways to do it - and having the experimenter try and run you as a subject to see what you were thinking and doing. All those things which people who turn their nose up at mere "demonstrations of phenomena" usually fail to do.

What always shocks me is how much research, to me, looks like people ran the first draft - that they had this idea and then they ran that study because that is what their idea was and they didn't think through what *really* was their idea and, given this idea, was it really the best possible study. Most people just didn't do very much of that. I learned to place a value on it.

I often tell my students when they are playing with an idea, "How does the study read?" In fact, I often tell my students when they are playing with an idea, "How would you write that up?" Or I will say, "Make me the graph or picture in the result section so I can work backwards from there. What could happen that would be interesting here, how would it look?" If you can't imagine how the study will read, and satisfy yourself that it will make an interesting story, you haven't figures out how to do the study.

Much of Ross' current work is in "the judgment tradition" which doesn't require a lot of "heavy staging." He has been working on belief perseverance which he described as, "the fact that the way you expect to see the world, the way you believe the world is, influences the way you see the world." When an experiment is ready to go, he has his students run him as a subject to help work out the bugs. Most of the ideas evolve from what he is thinking about, but he said, "I don't place a lot of emphasis on ideas. Ideas are cheap, and many of the best ones have been around for a long time without being 'used up.' Once you have the paradigm or the approach working well, the ideas will come and it doesn't even matter who they come to."

Collaborations:

Ross's major collaboration has been with Richard Nisbett. He said they make a point of getting together and talking about psychology. They have been friends for so long that when the idea of their book, The Intuitive Psychologist (Nisbett & Ross, 1980), came up, he said "we worried a lot about whether the kind of intellectual play we engaged in, the fun of bouncing wild ideas off of each other and not feeling we had to produce products - would be lost." But he added, "When you know someone very well and you have worked together for a long time, and you have thrashed out ideas, you both know what the other person is going to write." At that point there is little worry about surprising the other or being surprised by material that causes disagreement.

The book was fun to have written. It was enormous fun to talk about writing it. It was enormous fun to

> think it was being written. But *writing* it wasn't fun at all, it was drudgery..

Ross also has a close collaborative relationship with Mark Lepper which began when they co-taught social psychology at Stanford. About collaborations, he said:

> I think the best way to put it - and I think the same points apply equally to my collaboration with Dick and with Mark - is that we always valued some aspects of the graduate student experience. We have always thought it important to to have graduate students who were good and so we thought the best way to solve that problem was to be each other's graduate students. In some ways we take turns. Whenever Dick did something he would send it to me in somewhat the same way he might have sent it to his advisor and vice versa. And Mark and I simiarly take turns using each other as advisors and prize graduate students.

Ross believes what he took from his training with Schachter was a commitment to being interested in big questions.

> We felt we were involved in a serious attempt to carve nature at the joints, to figure out the right way to parse experience, and to capture phenomena. There was very very strong emphasis on mundane realism. That is, you wanted to get effects occurring in a context or situation where the background noise was somehow representative of what you find in the real world. The conviction was that the right way to do a study was to do it in such a way that there were *lots* of things that could make it not work. If the effect you were looking for wasn't strong relative to everything else going on, it wasn't going to work because there was a lot of noise. I came to Stanford wanting to work like that, but I wanted two other things: first I didn't want to work on individual differences variables (such as obesity) any more; I wanted to start with phenomena that lent themselves to manipulation.

Second, I wanted to work on things that were big and real, even if these were not as subtle or non-obvious as those that Schachter excelled at.

What I have difficulty in conveying is the way in which the actual content of the research was not terribly important to what you got from working with Stanley - it was incidental. It is a little bit like if you met someone who was terrific and you would go on a vacation together. Well the particular *texture* of the relationship as it unfolded would owe something to where you went on this vacation together, but in the long run of course, what was much more important was the *person* with whom you went on the vacation. And you wouldn't say, "Oh, that was great, I'm going to go back there;" you would say, "No, no, I want to be with *you*."

NEIL GRUNBERG

Neil Grunberg was an undergraduate premed student at Stanford in the early seventies, pursuing a medical microbiology degree. It was his intention to go into medical research, a field in which his father is well known. Grunberg was also interested in psychology and took a few courses in it, "but my family was clearly down on it," he said. One of those courses was a social psychology course taught from the standpoint of extreme behaviorism and which Grunberg said, "was totally banal, obvious and I swore off psychology forever." He continued in microbiology and worked for Nobel laureate Joshua Lederberg in his genetics lab. But after a time he found he missed psychology.

He spoke to Ernest Hilgard about some research on hypnosis that was going on at the time which interested him. Grunberg took an independent study with Hilgard over the summer. During the next two years Grunberg worked in the hypnosis research lab as well as Lederberg's genetics lab. But he was still avoiding psychology courses.

Then one summer he took a course at UCLA in psychobiology. He said, *I loved* it, it was *great* and the woman teaching it saw my background - I had by that time had all those hard science courses such as advanced calculus and physics and chemistry. She called me in and told me I should go into psychobiology. I had never heard of psychobiology because they didn't call it that at Stanford." He returned to Stanford and took their course in physiological psychology and enjoyed it. When the time came to decide about graduate school, he was faced with a choice between medical school, graduate school in microbiology and, he said, "I was *even* toying with the idea of graduate school in psychology."

> Actually it was my wife and Joshua Lederberg, each of them independently, who strongly encouraged me to go into psychology. My wife basically took the position that those were the courses I really

> enjoyed even though I had extreme reactions to some of them - some positive, some negative.
>
> Lederberg basically said, "Neil, don't go on in microbiology. You like research, don't go to medical school. The place to go is psychology. The future is integrating psychology and biology and medicine. And no one else was saying that at the time. This was now 1974 or 1975.
>
> I bit the bullet and decided to go to graduate school. My wife and I were both going to go on to graduate school, she in history, and the two places we both got in were Harvard and Columbia and we were trying to decide between them. Then I talked to people at Stanford and I was given very strong advice to not go to Harvard but to go to Columbia. I took that advice and went off to Columbia. When I arrived, I was planning to go on in physiological psychology.

When he arrived at Columbia, there was a system set up in which the director of graduate studies, who at that time was Robert Krauss, looked over the transcripts of the incoming graduate students and asked a few questions about their interests and intentions. After that, appointments were made with various faculty whose interests overlap with those of the incoming student. Grunberg had appointments with "all the physiological psychologists and even the mathematical psychologists," he said. There were four or five in all. While Grunberg was sitting in Krauss' office he said, "We were almost done and then a man walked into the office, I remember it well, it was very hot and it was the end of the summer and this guy had a tie on and a white shirt and he was incredibly tan. He breezed in, mumbled something to Krauss and then breezed out." And Krauss said, "We should put Stan Schachter on your list."

> Like any timid graduate student, I went to my meetings - four or five of them - I just went down the list. Typically I would arrive at the meeting, "Hello," and I would give my name and the professor would be very polite and would know

who I was and to different extents had looked over my transcript. Then they would sit there and give me a ten minute recitation on what they did. But they were clearly scientists and I started to realized, that this is what graduate school is about, you really do study small things.

I got through my list and I was trying to decide - this all took a couple of days. Finally, I saw at the bottom of my list the name Stanley Schachter. When I found out Schachter's office was in the social psychology area, I thought, after my experience at Stanford, "Oh no, not social psychology, *no way*!" But I didn't want to get in trouble so I went.

I got to that big corner office and I knocked on the door and he said, "Yes?" I walked in and said, "Dr. Schachter, my name is Neil Grunberg and I am supposed to talk with you." "Come on in, son." I came in. I walked in this office in which I am sure to this day the rug is crumpled up and the desk is piled high, two or three feet high with paper. There is no way you can imagine he could find anything in there. The man sitting there was in a suit and a tie that I bet he still wears, that he wore every day. So I sat down and he began the standard spiel. The he started telling me what he did. I listened some but I was so nervous I barely processed. To my surprise instead of talking just about a small point in social psychology, he was talking about cigarette smoking and stress. And then I understood why I had been sent there - because of my background in physiology and biology.

He went on for about ten minutes and then he stopped and he looked at me and he said, "I told you about my work. So what did I find?" I said, "Pardon me?" He repeated, "What did I find? I told you about the work, what are my results? I told you the theory..." I didn't know what to say. I will never forget, he then took a manila envelope, a number two pencil and a manila envelope and drew two perpendicular axes and thrust the pencil in my hand. "What did I find, I will even label the axes for you." He wrote "urinary ph" and "cigarette smoking." Well I drew something, I don't even remember what it was, I was totally blitzed. So I drew some line. He looked at me, paused and said - apparently I got it right - and then he said, "So what did I do next?" I spent 45 minutes in there with him just grilling me, posing questions, asking what the result is, based on that proposing what should be the next experiment.

I came out of there and I went home to my wife. We went jogging and I said, "I can't believe it. I have interviewed with all these people. With each person I spent 10 minutes. It was all right. And with this guy Schachter, I spent 45 minutes and I learned a lot. And I said I can't believe that is social psychology - the one area of psychology I had found trivial. And I said to my wife, "If I can learn that much in 45 minutes, there is just no question which way I have to decide." I was upset because this was the absolutely polar opposite from what I was planning to do.

The physiology professors were calling me and asking when I could start and this guy didn't seem to care. Columbia had a matching program so the professor had to agree to have you. I found from talking to other students that, at least in those years, there usually would be five or six people starting in social - who came in social and *all* would interview with Schachter. I came and they had me pegged as physiological and so they didn't even think I would be in the running. Schachter would interview the five or six and take one or two of them. So I realized I had to tell him, or ask his permission. So I went in to see him the next day. I went in and knocked on the door and he said, "Come on in." And I said, "Dr. Schachter, I have met all the people and I decided I would like very much to work with

> you." He had been really gruff up until then and he jumped up from his desk and he shook my hand and he said, "I would be delighted to have you." I was very excited, but I didn't know what I had done.
>
> Then we sat down and I said, "Well, there is one thing. I said that if I worked for him, besides being trained by him I wanted to get full training in physiological psychology as well. And he just said, "Fine with me." That type of approach repeated over the years because he was always open. He would say, "Fine, you can do whatever, as long as it doesn't interfere with my work."

This last request reflects Grunberg's strong belief in multi-disciplinary research in psychology. During his years in Schachter's lab, he did animal research, human research, and psychophysiology, "all under Stan's umbrella," he said.

According to Grunberg, Schachter works with his students as a group. Each student would have a separate assignment which would be related to the overall work being done in the lab. "From my perception, I felt responsible for the other fellow's assignments too," he said. This was because the assignment would generally overlap in that they related to the same question. "Everything with Schachter is a problem or question orientation, which is the key. That is, he is following a question rather than being methodologically parametric," Grunberg said.

When Grunberg arrived at Columbia, Schachter was winding down his work on smoking. By that time he was concerning himself with what was happening to nicotine in the body. So the first assignment Grunberg was given was to teach Schachter everything there is to know about the liver.

> I didn't know *anything* about the liver - but he didn't either and that was my assignment. I raced to the medical library and got out every book I could find and started a series of tutorials - even to the point that I developed my own biochemical model of the process and how it relates to psychological events.

> We would have meetings roughly once a week. Every one of Stan's students would be there. He would call on you to present what you had learned from library and laboratory research. When I was at Stanford, before I went to grad school, before I worked for Stan I thought I was obsessive. When I got there, I found out I was just right.

Grunberg said that for Schachter, "the main emphasis of the work was for it to be meaningful." In the research meetings Schachter would question students about everything without using many words. "He was very quiet and he would sit there and a student would say something. He would say, 'Go over that again, now how are you going to...' The student would respond and he would simply say, 'Why?' With Stan there were always certain questions that you would get knocked into your head. One of the questions was, '*so*?' So what? is the big question...so what does this mean?" And to Grunberg, this was fascinating because he was able to see the scientific similarities between Schachter and Joshua Lederberg. Both of these men were similar in approach to his father, also a scientist. Grunberg said, "For years in my home I listened to 'science has to be thoughtful.'" So even without an extensive background in psychology, Grunberg could value the kind of science Schachter was doing.

Besides the library assignment, within the first month of Grunberg's arrival Schachter assigned him an experiment that hadn't worked. Grunberg said in addition to the way in which Schachter selects his students, getting them to work doing research *right away* was another characteristic which stood out.

Grunberg was given the failed study and told to redesign and run it. Everything had to be checked with Schachter. Grunberg would take the study home, rethink, rewrite and redesign. The next day he would give it to Schachter. "He would say, ok leave it with me. Then he would call me in maybe an hour or two later and he would have written on it and he would throw it at me and say, 'Well, this is what is wrong with it.' Then I would go back to my desk and start working on it and give him a new version the next day." By early November of his first year in graduate school, Grunberg was running an experiment.

The coursework consisted of statistics and a proseminar series, "which they called A and B but the students called hard and soft psychology. There were three in each category during the first year," he recalled. One of the seminars was in social psychology. This course was very different from the one Grunberg had been exposed to at Stanford.

> Bob Krauss gave the first lecture. It was on social facilitation and it was just excellent. It was a different social psychology - I was astonished. We read a dozen original pieces from Triplett's 1897 piece on. It was one of the best seminars.
>
> Then in that seminar series Stan taught only two or three sessions. He came in and the seminar started with Group Dynamics. It was some work of Lewin and his students. Basically Stan would come in and run the seminar in his distinctive style. He knows the work thoroughly but he doesn't simply explain it to you. He asks you direct questions on what it means. You also get a very detailed handout in advance, hypothetically so you can have some questions prepared. The way he started is, he passed a piece of paper around and you signed your name. After that he would call on you by your last name and say, "First question, do it." In that first session, I remember, he called on someone else to answer a question having to do with Lewinian derivation and he wanted us to be able to do it formally. The student did it - really did an excellent job. He said, "Do you others think that's ok?" I remember barely nodding my head and he looked at me and said, "Grunberg, you are nodding" and I was getting ready for the next question and I said, "Yes." He said, "Do it again." It was a very difficult question and he wanted it explained again and that's the way it was - always understanding. If something was right, he would have me do it again, if something was wrong, he would have me do it again. Just zap - make sure you are there, thinking about it.

It was Schachter's practice to pack up and leave the city each summer. He would take with him all the work that had been done in the lab over the year and spend the summer writing. It was the student's job to put together all the material he would need.

At the end of Grunberg's first summer, Schachter camc back with a surprise.

> Now I had a co-enzyme theory of how the liver metabolized the nicotine and how it relates to smoking. He had asked me to learn all about free fatty acids, so I studied up on esterified and nonesterified fat and how it might relate to smoking. I showed up and was ready to make a presentation.
>
> I will never forget his entrance that summer, because he came back incredibly tan and back in the white shirt and tie and now I had all this stuff for him. He walked into my office and said, "Why are some people misers? My kid is a miser, why?" And then he left. I said, "What?" I looked at the other student who was there and said, "What is going on here?" The next day, he came back and asked, "Well, did you figure it out?" And I said, "Figure what out?" "My son the miser." And I said, "I really don't know." And he said, "That's what we are going to study." I couldn't believe it. I couldn't *believe* it. And then I found out he was serious. At the next meeting he decided we were going to study the psychology of money.

Schachter had been about ready to give up the smoking research - he had taken it as far as he could - down to the ph level of the urine. Then Grunberg showed up with his physiology expertise and he believes that kept it going for a little bit longer. The extension of this work is what Grunberg has been doing since leaving graduate school. He said, "My dream is to do everything Schachter could do and more, or at least make my attempt. I don't have his particular creativity but I will use my own in whatever way I can. I have an animal behavior lab, a human social psych Schachterian lab and I have a biochemistry lab. I do them all, I pull them all together. They are all here. I learned it all from him but he wouldn't go that other step into biology and the chemistry."

Grunberg felt responsible for what what was getting done in the lab. In addition to his own work, he helped another student finish his masters paper on blood pressure and heart rate responsivity to smoking in smokers and nonsmokers. "He would yell at both of us even if it wasn't my study," Grunberg explained. His own masters paper was the study he was asked to redesign and run early in his first year. It was designed to try to use physical exercise to manipulate urinary ph which, according to Schachter's theory, would make it more acidic and more acidic urine should increase smoking. "It was a nice counter-intuitive experiment because who would expect people to smoke right after they exercised," he said. "Unfortunately it was confounded by the fact that people were absolutely exhausted and therefore did not feel like puffing on a cigarette.

> There are a number of things that were critical in the makeup of the lab. First off all the original cohort selected by the school was always excellent. Second was Schachter's own interviewing style. For example some students would interview with him and say, "I just don't want to deal with this guy." The 45 minutes I *loved*, others hated and didn't want any part of it. Finally, students would drop out or transfer so over the years there was a self-selection - or imposed selection. We used to figure that for every four who were assigned to Schachter, one would finish with him.
>
> As far as his selection is concerned, you have to be above a certain threshold of intellect and that's it. And then it is how you approach things.
>
> He conducted one graduate seminar every couple of years on appetitive behaviors. He basically followed his work from emotions through obesity and to smoking. Students would have to see him to get his permission just to be in the course. He asked me to find and encourage good students. I knew all the students in the experimental program

> and had some of my best friends - who I thought were the best in the program at Columbia working for other professors - come and take the course. At the end of that course, he selected from that group and invited them to stay on in another graduate seminar.

It was in preparation for the second in this two seminar series that the lab started their work on money. They began by focusing on misers because that is what had triggered Schachter's interest. Grunberg said, "He had us read books ranging from *Theory of the Leisure Class* to *Escape from Evil.* We would read the books and discuss them - we always did that." Then the seminar started.

> We sat down as a group and he said, "I am interested in studying the psychology of money. Neil and John and I have looked into this a little bit and we are just starting to formulate some ideas. Over the first few weeks of the course we would meet weekly and basically brainstorm: What are all the issues? What are all the questions? - Just the questions - always the questions first. What are all the questions one might address in psychology of money? Why do people like money? What do people get out of money? Why do people hoard money? Why do people spend money - developmentally, anthropologically, sociologically? And this went on for weeks.
>
> Finally, when we had this whole list, then we went to the next step and this is the way I do all my research now. The next thing after drawing from reading, from experience, from discussions and getting all the questions up - then we organize those questions. What are the topic areas? That took a couple of weeks. We ended up with specific topic areas such as the development of the psychology of money. Then Schachter asked for volunteers to work in each area. Each of these people worked in their own area and I volunteered for everything.

One of the projects Grunberg worked on extensively was to try to develop an animal miser. A student in the course, Rick Straub, was an operant psychologist. The two of them trained rats to press bars to get tokens and used various pay off schedules in try to create the animal analog of a miser. He said, "Rats hoard food, which would be a primary reinforcer. Money is a secondary reinforcer. What makes that transition is that the secondary reinforcer becomes a primary reinforcer - in operant terms." Schachter only saw the rats once but he was very interested in the data they yielded.

Another project they worked on had to do with mood and money. One of the students had some clinical background and had pointed out that one characteristic of mania is to throw or give away money. "We spent a lot of time trying to figure out how to measure the mood of the general population and how to measure spending." This led to research correlating Macy's receipts with the number of news stories on the front page of the New York Times. During Grunberg's third year in the lab, a student, Paul Andreassen, came in who had a strong background in economics and the research focus expanded to include the stock market. By this time, Grunberg was planning his dissertation, which was going to return him to work on smoking. The money project was passed on to this new student.

> The emphasis for us and for me was learning how to do research - how to ask questions. He (Schachter) always taught didactically - read, ask questions - why did we do the experiment this way? The best example is his Affiliation book (Schachter, 1959). It is a beautiful road map for how to do research. Even now, I do not do animal research the way most people do it. We let the question guide us, not the technique. So we use all different techniques in my lab.

His dissertation combined two of Schachter's former research interests as well as a personal one. Grunberg said, "By that time Schachter had quit smoking and was gaining a lot of weight. So one of the questions I wanted to ask was 'why do people who quit smoking get fat?'" Grungerg decided he wanted to be able to do

"Schachter style social psychology on humans and parallel animal work," he said. So he did studies on both animals and humans.

He approached his dissertation the same way Schachter approached his money interest. Grunberg read everything in the literature, organized the questions and found what answers had been suggested. He found three possibilities. People gain weight when they quit smoking because, "they eat a lot. It's a banal, obvious kind of explanation, if true. Second, because their metabolism changes, and the third suggestion is that they change their consumption of certain foods - pastries and so forth," he explained. "So I designed animal and human studies that complemented, to address all these facets." Since then he has been following up on these studies in the way he was trained to do.

After receiving his degree, Grunberg took a job at Uniformed Services University of Health Sciences. Jerome Singer is head of the department.

> By the time I left graduate school, I had zero publications. I had learned a tremendous amount and Jerry Singer was willing to take a chance on me based on what Schachter said and what I seemed to know. The fact that I was well trained, not number of publications, was Jerry's criterion for selection of a new faculty member.

He has continued his interest in appetitive and addictive behaviors and has collaborated on a study on bulimia with former Schachter student Judy Rodin. He has also collaborated with Lynn Kozlowski a Schachter student who finished six years before Grunberg. He said they made a connection because, "all of the people who were involved in the smoking period would come back to Columbia because they were working on the manuscript at the time. We would have meetings with them and present what we were doing." He believes that collaborations among Schachter students work particularly well because they have the same approach to research. He said, "these collaborations create lots of pressure, there is a lot of quickness to it - It is like working with a sibling which is a rivalry but a very happy rivalry."

Training Students

The training of graduate students is very important to Grunberg and he has given the topic a great deal of thought. His ambition is to influence the field through his students. He said, "I think it would be presumptuous to assume that my individual contributions will even come close to the potential contribution of a whole line of students. I hope to train students in my approach." Grunberg has consciously adopted Schachter's style of training, adding components from his own experience to create a rigorous program for his students.

> If I am only going to do one thing successfully as a professor, it would be to train students. If I train ten good students and they could each train ten good students - that is how it is going to proliferate. It worked for Schachter.

What gets handed down is the approach - philosophical and methodological.

> It is extremely purposeful for me with my students. I don't know how purposeful Stan was. I *think* it was, but I don't know. In my first year, I worked on projects he assigned. Second year, I started contributing to the research ideas - on money. Third year, I was running many studies in the lab. Also, I was expected to train students junior to me.
>
> I remember battling over one point continuously. He would say that the reason some of his students left in my years was me. And I would say that the reason some of his students left in my years was him. I think people left because of his demands but he thinks, and it may be true, that what I *thought* he wanted was so high - such high goals that that is what I lived by and that is what I would tell other students were the standards of the lab. I would bum people out, I am sure. I thought I was being brutally honest, he thought I was being overly competitive.

During Grunberg's fourth year, Schachter called him in and made him promise to be supportive of the new students - only supportive. Grunberg said he replied, "'I just tell them when they are screwing up.' And he said, 'Leave that to me, you just be supportive.' So I did. I didn't agree with it, I thought it was wrong, but I did."

Now he has his own lab and can do it the way he feels is most effective. To begin with he takes great interest in the applicants to the program. They generally select four people from an applicant pool of about seventy. He looks for students with psychology majors and who have strong biology background, "because I believe that is the way to work in anything," he said. They have a strong applicant pool because health psychology is on the upswing and they are a center for health psychology. He said, "I think we have the best graduate program in it by far and that's to Jerry's and Andy Baum's credit." Students are assigned to faculty according to interests - "the same kind of matching program as at Columbia," he said.

Grunberg's teaching responsibilities include participating in a course taught by the entire department - he gives four lectures. Beyond that he said, "you teach whatever you want." He runs a seminar in social psychology of which he teaches half and the rest are guest lectures. He also teaches a graduate seminar every other year in appetitive behaviors and psychopharmacology. He said it is exactly the same load that Schachter taught at Columbia. "Jerry treats you as though you were a full professor anywhere else. Now it is up to you - with all that rope, to build a bridge or hang yourself." Grunberg has been in the department since 1979 and has produced two Ph.D.'s so far and is bringing along two others. He likes to have one student every other year. He has what he describes as a "very purposeful system - within the flexiblity of the individual."

> The department has certain requirements and I have additional requirements. The department requires certain graduate seminars: statistics, methods, social, learning and developmental - all the standard psych courses. In addition they require physiology and pharmacology. The department requires a year of physiology and half a year of pharmacology. So

> I require for my students a year of each. And those are the minimal requirements.
>
> I also encourage - they may say insist - that they take other advanced seminars. Also they are immediately in the lab. The first month, without any question.

His students work as teams on every project, animal or human. The students have different amounts of responsibility according to their level but all students work in all of his labs. He said, "I don't want them to be narrowly trained. I went them to know that they can do Schachterian social psychology, they can do animal studies and they can do biochemistry and psychophysiology."

He sees research as a process that includes seven steps: coming up with the original concept, formulating the question, designing the study, designing the nuts and bolts of the study (after the overall design), performing the study, analyzing the data, interpreting the data and writing it up. The way he begins training his students is to have the first year student learn how to do the middle four steps. By the time a student is ready for the dissertation, he said, "I set them up so their dissertation - they have learned all the pieces of the puzzle and the dissertation can then be their own interest."

> Typically in the first year, the student is assigned to whatever experiment is on line. This is a study which has been planned the summer or spring before. Say it is an animal experiment - they learn how to handle the animals, how to perform all the methods appropriate to that study plus the keeping of the data.
>
> The data book style I use is not Schachterian. This is all Lederberg, I copied that from Lederberg. Stan had no prescribed system. He had just envelopes with data. If you didn't give him what he needed when he was ready, he would yell at you. But he didn't teach you how to keep a notebook so I teach my students what Lederberg taught me. For every experiment we do there are two books. One of the books is always with me and in this office and then

there is a rotating one. There is a methods section, a timeline of the experiment, all the raw data broken down into subsections, literature and the summary data. Then we have different analyses. I have this on every one of our experiments. So when an experiment doesn't turn out or we are not going to write it up, we will have the study. I have a whole cabinet here full of studies. The first thing a student learns is how to do the measurements and the first year student learns how to make a lab notebook.

We use old Minnesota tablets for summary sheets - Schachter used them, Jerry used them in the sixties. My students fill them out and give me xerox copies of them. This is the way Stan always had us do it on these kind of sheets. And then this was something that was always with Stan. All the original data is in black ink, all the stats we do in pencil. There is one person responsible for every study. Everybody knows that doesn't mean the others can close their eyes to it but that is the pivot person.

All of the things that I did that worked for me, I have now made part of my program. So the first year student works on a couple of experiments, learns a tremendous amount and then becomes responsible for a notebook. Then gradually, by the beginning of the second year the student is put in charge of a study - at least logistically in charge.

We have weekly meetings and we always go through what I am thinking. I do the theory, the research and then the really "how to." Stan would go over with us, with me, how to do a study one on one but he would never explain how to keep the data or this or that. I brought that from Stanford. Now, I tell my students "you figure out how to keep the data and propose it to me." I don't say, "I want this sheet this way." I pose it as a question. I ask questions so the student figures everything out and

> if they don't get it, I tell them because obviously I don't want the research to suffer.

Another thing Grunberg learned from Schachter was his way of working with statistics. He said one of the criticisms of Schachter has been the way he used statistics.

> I spent years at Columbia arguing with fellow students the relative merits of punching numbers into a computer and using SPSS packages. I had to do everything by hand, on my hand calculator. Well, I understand what I was doing and I used statistical tests as they were appropriate. I didn't use any canned program in any of my work, including my dissertation. Everything was done with hand calculators. It wasn't that Schachter was purposely ignoring other methodology, he just knows that forms and methods serve the question, where most of the people - and you particularly see it in the biomedical sciences, they are even worse than psychology - serve their paradigm, they serve their approach. Sophistication in statistics should be used thoughtfully where appropriate.
>
> If an electron microscopist spends years learning electron microscopy techniques, they tend to take that very sophisticated machine and point it at different things. If they use electron microscopy to study (by analogy) pencils, lamps or telephones, they are using the method or paradigm to drive the research instead of the question driving it.

At one time Grunberg was a "fairly serious" musician and was trained as a jazz drummer as well as a tympanist. He said, "I studied with a number of drummers and the most famous drummer who I was studying with , Joe Morello, used a similar approach." He compared his training as a musician with the way he trains his students. Technique comes first and it has to be learned to the extent that it becomes automatic before the student can participate with other artists.

There is plenty of room for creativity - improvising jazz music, you *have to have* all the basics down *cold.* And that is what I try to teach my students. They have to learn how to do research and any first or second year student should not waste their time doing their own projects. The students who have been allowed to have, in my judgment, been failures. It never works. They *never learn* how to play their scales. And if you can't play your scales and you don't understand everything about them and all the rudiments, you can't do it - you can't be great. You can be very good, but you can't be great.

You have to learn the self-discipline and the control and all the rudimentary scales to such an extent that they become part of you - they become non-conscious. Only when they are non-conscious can you play with them. Can you turn a phrase? Can you stick them together in other ways? Can you approach new questions? And you have to have a certain command over your instrument which is seemingly non-conscious so that you can hear in your head what you want to play and it just comes out. It just comes. But that takes an enormous amount of practice. *then* you can go and sit in with other people - that's like research collaboration. If I sit in with other investigators, I am not sitting there trying to understand. If I am trying to think, "Gee, how could I do this in my stuff," it would never come. I have to know *my* approach, *my* technique but I have to address their question. I have to play their *theme*, but I always play their theme in my style and that style has to be *so well* learned, so automatic that you can just address anything.

Current Work:

Grunberg is very dedicated to his work on smoking. He began his undergraduate career with an interest in doing medical research and he is doing that - broadly defined. He believes that health issues such as cancer and drugs of addiction other than cigarettes are the "questions of our time." He said, "The questions I grew up with in the late sixties and the seventies were all non-medical answers addressing a number of questions which are a cross between biology, behavioral medicine and psychology. For example, why did I have so many friends who got so heavily into drugs of addiction? Why did some friends freak out? Why were they interested in it?" He believes that all addictions have some commonalities. He said, "We are studying smoking as a way of cutting into the question of addiction in general."

He pointed out that the important medical questions being addressed earlier in the century were the ones that had to do with infectious diseases - "the single most preventable cause of death during the twenties and thirties. The problems of the forties were clearly the horrors of the Holocaust, the Nuremberg Trials and when we learned what was going on - the questions of those times were questions addressed by social psychology," he said. "Today, thirty percent of cancer deaths in the country are caused by cigarette smoking. The leading killers, the leading issues in medicine and of preventable death, are behavioral. We find that sixty percent of cancer is attributable to specific diet. Smoking and diet, if we changed those two behaviors, we could prevent between fifty and seventy percent of cancer." Grunberg said he wishes social psychologists would spend less time in cognitive psychology and work more on compliance issues with regard to health practices. He said, "Even if we know what people should eat, we don't know how to influence them to change."

Grunberg believes he has been fairly successful at achieving his goal of maintaining the Schachter approach while adding to it animal and biochemical research. But nobody believed he could do it. He said when he was first hired he wrote a grant proposal and was encouraged to send it to NIH. He didn't have any publications at the time and the grant was turned down with the comment that said basically, "This is all very interesting but it is not possible. One person cannot do animal and human research, behavioral and biochemical all at once. Particularly somebody with no track record."

Well, they didn't give me a dime of support and by disapproving me they really slowed me down and I had to go these other routes and now, not only am I doing it, have done it successfully, I have trained, I have graduated Ph.D.'s who can do it. I have proved it. And I guess that is the main thing because the approach is more of our own lasting contribution to science through our students - it has to be through our students. You can't count on being that one great scientist and even if you are, it is only one set of contributions. Through your dynasty of students, you can have dozens and dozens of contributions.

Schachter and Festinger:

For a course in statistics taken when he was a graduate student at Columbia, Grunberg wrote a critique of Lewin's Topological Psychology (Lewin, 1936). He said, "Then I read Field Theory (Lewin, 1951) and after that Stan used to tease me that I had been the only person in the last twenty years to have read both books." Grunberg said he had considered himself as part of a "Schachterian" line of students rather than part of a Lewinian line because he "didn't see that the students of most of the others have followed a given style."

> You can clearly see Lewin's approach in Festinger's work. Particularly when you go back to the theory of social communication - it's so formal. Also, the theory of social comparison when Leon first wrote it - hypothesis I, Ia, Ib, II and so forth. You can see that training in Mort Deutsch. And for me, the "so what?" is missing. In *my* view, when I compare Festinger and Schachter, is that Leon's great theoretical contributions weren't implemented, he didn't follow the lines as thoroughly as Schachter did.

According to Grunberg, this difference can be seen in the work of students trained by the two men. What he misses in the work of Festinger's students is the added step of, "so what does this mean, where do we go from here. The spark is, 'so what?'"

You have to be very careful, meticulous, in the laboratory doing your work but you have to keep the big questions in mind. You have to be driven by the questions. "What does it mean?" "Where does it go?"

For example, during my research meetings a student will present and we will have a discussion critiquing the study. And then we will say - I always ask the next question, which I learned from Schachter - and that is, Ok, lets say the study works the way you say and we get the following findings. What else - what *next* would we want to know, what would be the next question." And every time we keep pushing and if we can figure what the next question is, then we incorporate it into the experiment. If we can't figure out the next question and it going to be the end, I don't know if the study is worth doing, it is too boring. To me, everything has to lead to more information and that more information could be basic, could be applied, and we will go macro or micro - whatever is called for.

Grunberg said he thought Schachter's greatest talent is the ability to "both use a theory and to operationalize. He is just a genius at addressing interesting questions and then designing studies to answer those questions."

I have a version of Schachter in my head. He is my Yoda, colloquially. I know the question and I say, "So what?" I am constantly asking those question. I can see him sitting there, I can hear him asking questions. It is always, "So what? Why are we doing it, What is the question?" It has got to be the question, and then comes, "So what?" - whatever result - or "Why?", in any reality. So the question, "Why is my kid a miser? is followed by, "Why do some people become misers and others don't" and then, "Does it matter?" And if the answer to the "So what?" question is that it doesn't matter, it doesn't mean anything, then you don't bother with the question and you study something else.

It really goes back to an old story. The passover seder. One of the stories told in the seder has to do with different kinds of sons. The question is finally posed by the rabbi, "Who is the worst son?" The way my father always told the story was, "Who is the most *evil*?" Who is the worst son? Is it the smart alec, is it the stupid son with a very low IQ, what is it? And the answer finally comes, "The worst son is the son who doesn't even know how to ask a question." If you can't ask a question - you know, it is over before you begin.

STANLEY SCHACHTER

Stanley Schachter said, "Immediately before I went to MIT, I was at war with the Germans." He was stationed in the Aero-Medical Laboratory at Wright Field during the war where he worked on problems in vision. "I was busy designing airplanes for the *next* war," he explained.

Before being drafted Schachter had spent a year in graduate school at Yale - running rats with Clark Hull. He had been an undergraduate art history major at Yale and stayed on, "with Donald Marquis' encouragement," because he was too young to go into the army. "Being young and ideological," he said, "you sort of feel like you ought to do something. I had been an art history major before and decided I would go into psychology." He worked as a research assistant to Walter Miles, "who was in vision," he explained. "He had invented red goggles for helping the flyers at night adapt to night vision quickly and it just seemed to me I ought to be doing something useful, so when Lewin started this whole thing I was attracted to that and instead of going back to Yale, I joined this group at MIT."

Of Lewin he said:

> I really had no first hand contact with his work, God knows we were never required to read him when I was at Yale - but he was kind of inspirational. He was ideological and very smart and wanted to apply his things to real social problems. It just sounded a lot more my sort of thing at that time than going back to Yale was.

At MIT:

Schachter arrived at MIT in the fall of 1946 - the second year of the Research Center for Group Dynamics' tenure there. The students each worked with one senior faculty. "I think there was a sort of mutual feeling out process," he recalled. "I kind of liked and respected Festinger and some of the people who worked with him and so I went to work with them."

> Leon had a grant to study this housing community called Westgate and we simply got these interviews and combined sociometry with a set of questionnaires. It was presumably to be a study of housing satisfaction which couldn't have interested any of us less, but it was the basis on which I think the grant was given to him.
>
> We did a complete survey of the community and a complete sociometric and we started finding all these nice relationships and took off. That particular study led to Leon's whole theory of pressures to conformity and social influence, which in turn led to dissonance.
>
> This group, which was in essence "Leon's boys," simply worked out the whole theory of pressures to uniformity. We each did - starting from the Westgate book and later theorizing about it - we each did a thesis related to part of it, which Leon then integrated and had this rather nice theoretical scheme which, I think, led him into all his other work.

Kurt Lewin died just five months after the arrival of Schachter's class at MIT and Schachter recalls little contact with him. "I took a course from him and there was a tight geographical unit so you inevitably saw him and schmoozed with him. He was always there as a presence in general seminars, but we barely knew him."

During those years, Schachter was primarily influenced by Leon Festinger. He believes Festinger to be "literally the father of experimental social psychology."

> Social psychology experiments before he came along were essentially morasses. In the democracy-autocracy study for example, they were attempting to create the experimental parallel to what is democracy and compare it with the autocratic. They were manipulating a million things.
>
> Leon, I think for the first time, introduced really strong manipulations of the independent variables, tight controls, good measures of the dependent variables and a great deal of precision in what you are looking for.

The working relationship with Festinger was collegial. Schachter said, "He ain't a status type, never was." Schachter thinks once it became clear to Festinger that he could "do things on my own, we worked in a very collaborative fashion."

> We worked on his program. He was very clever about it and I think I modeled myself as a teacher on him. He involved you totally. He expected an immense amount out of you but it never was explicit. You got totally immersed in this and it was yours as much as his.

Schachter believes the group at MIT was not particularly unique at the time - that the hiatus created by the war resulted in a highly motivated and talented cohort of graduate students everywhere.

> Everybody was being swept out of college to go kill Germans and Japs. There was no one in graduate school Now all at once the war is over and there is four years worth of applicants to graduate school which allowed *fantastic* selection. I mean, you didn't have to scrape the bottom of the barrel to make sure that you were filling your department with the right number of research assistants or teaching assistants as one has to sort of do these days. I mean, you were really able to get the cream of the crop.

> Secondly, they were all considerably older, more mature and with their own ideas than the typical graduate student. They were by then, far better educated having spent four years of hideous boredom, interrupted occasionally by some outrage, but mostly boredom. So you had a group, and this isn't true only of the MIT group - I mean the people who were at Harvard at the same time were a *marvelous* group.
>
> Lewin may have attracted people who were certainly different simply because it was a brand new enterprise with a strong ideological bent at the same time insisting on the scientific part of it. He may have attracted different *sorts* of people but I don't think as far as talent goes, were they any better or worse than the people who were coming back to any of the other graduate schools in the country.

Schachter pointed out that at that time, immediately after the war, the universities were expanding and the government was pouring money into the sciences. This meant there were jobs available and research money to support assistants. It was an expanding system and that added to the excitement.

Beyond MIT: Schachter's Style

After Lewin's death, Schachter moved with the group to Michigan. There he completed his thesis and received his degree from Michigan in 1950.

In 1949 he took his first job at the University of Minnesota. Leon Festinger followed in 1951 and they were "true colleagues," until Festinger's departure for Stanford. Schachter remained at Minnesota until 1961 when he moved to Columbia where he has remained.

> My first job I really couldn't believe, given conditions now. I taught one graduate course and

> that was it. I had all the money I wanted provided by the university for research and it was also a cinch to get grants in those days because there was simply more money than people available to spend it. All of that really kept up for ten or fifteen years after I got my degree and Leon and I never had any problem placing our students.

Training Students:

"Maybe they learned from me what I learned from Leon," Schachter offered as a possible explanation for the well known productivity of his students. "I work with my kids the way Leon worked with me."

> I am convinced, and I think Leon is too, - and this is something I feel very strongly about - that is there is no point in doing research if I really know the answer - I rarely do - or have my kids do a project that will essentially prove that I was right or where it is a test of banality. I don't see the point of the entire scientific research enterprise except to learn something that nobody knew before.

"The kids who work with me tend to work as a group - almost always," he said. He pointed to the friendships and collaborations which still exist between people who worked together in his lab ten or fifteen years ago. He said, "They continue working for a while in these problems (Schachter's problems) and then the usual sequence is about five years. After about five years they start getting off on their own and then they are their own man. If they didn't, I would be ashamed."

He continued to describe his style of working and teaching:

> The main thing I think that kids get out of me which is possibly slightly different from Leon is that when we get our hands on a phenomenon, we really follow it down to where the hell it leads - what follows from what. If there is any Lewinian touch

to it, I suppose it is: What are the implications in real life, which is kind of fun. That's something that Leon and I got working with Lewin.

My style of working has always been to sink my teeth into a problem and then follow it wherever it leads me. All of my work really has gone the line. I expect it may not seem that way but everything is connected to everything else, including the Wall Street work. I think if the kids get anything out of this, it is that particular style of working.

I teach through terror. I have a device for teaching which I believe is extrordinarily effective. I swiped it from Clark Hull who used this as a means to teach.

You give students homework as if you were Miss Goldberg in the second grade. And that homework isn't excessive, it is two or three pages, perhaps. You give them a two page handout in which you discuss the homework and you ask questions about it. These homework sheets all start off in essence with, "Ok, here is what you know now from these readings, what happens next? Where does it lead, what are necessary next steps, what should follow in particular experiments, how would you go about testing it." They are all designed that way.

Then you ask them questions designed first to make *sure* they have read it. These questions are designed to see how well they have understood the material by seeing how well can they *predict* what would follow in either real or fake experiments. Usually they are real experiments and so there is a real answer as to what should follow next and so on.

I then teach the class as if indeed, I were Miss Goldberg in the second grade. Nobody volunteers and it doesn't much matter if they do. I call on people. They know this and they know they have to read the material and they know they have got to think about it and they know the entire discussion will be based on these two or three pages of notes, comments, jokes and questions. And one does not suffer fools gladly - or people who haven't done this.

Nobody ever misses a class. Nobody ever works less than a day preparing for it and usually the kids get together before-hand, and I encourage this. There are no exams, but there are take home exams which usually say, "Take it home and spend a week or so and tell me what should follow given everything you now know." The amount of involvement in this technique is just staggering. Every kid has to know everything, to have thought about every issue that I consider important and so on. Practically every student I have had swiped that technique from me just as I swiped it from Hull.

Schachter is careful in his selection of students and looks for those who have talent as well as this ability he requires - thinking a problem through and understanding what should come next. His students must to be able to catch on to the research process quickly and also have "some vague imagination." But there is another condition. "First, I have got to like them - if I don't like them, then the whole thing isn't going to work," he said. Obviously they need a *minimum* of ability in this domain, but my first requirement, I think, is I have got to like them."

His style of teaching is to structure the research process, "as a matter of, 'look, here are the facts so far, what has to follow next, what will illuminate this, how do we understand it.'" He said that once they, as a team, get to this point, "then you are pretty much in virgin territory and I am no better than they are at getting good ideas as to how we might want to test this or what could be the variable. It is then the idea comes through that the research process is really to discover something and that discovery means it is something *new.*"

Collaborations:

Schachter pointed to his students as his "major intellectual community." He said , "Even if it is not a brand new problem or anything of that sort, their slant is usually different." Also, he is still in close contact with Leon Festinger.

> I use Leon constantly to talk things over with, even if we are not working in the same area. We have influenced each other a lot. He and I have worked together a little on the stock market research I am doing and I have worked a little bit with him on his passion which is at the moment canon law in the eleventh century church. I have taken a wonderful seminar which he and a professor of religion here at Columbia gave on the schisms in the Catholic church in the eleventh and twelfth century and it is kind of fun.

The work he is currently involved with has brought him back to social psychology, "for the first time in probably twenty years." He became interested in "aggregate variables" as a result of his work on smoking. "I got very interested in whether a single number that summarizes the behavior of an entire population can be meaningfully related to the kind of psychology that I have embraced." He and his students have for a two year period correlated the number of articles about violent crime on the front page of the New York Times with sales figures from Macy's. "There is nothing surprising about it except the fact that it worked," he said. He then began searching for other aggregate variables and settled on Wall Street - exploring the relationship between the Dow Jones or some other index of stock prices and the volume of stock transactions.

> This is purely correlational and we find lots of wonderful things, but I haven't the faintest idea why they really occur because they *are* correlational. It has been great fun comparing economist's views of stock market activity to what a psychologist might say. Most of what I have been doing is examining what happens when you take what the economists say dead seriously and what happens when you take

> what psychologists say dead seriously and under what conditions which approach to take in the marketplace.

His favorite part of the research process is "writing it up." He said it is only when he begins to write, "that I really begin to understand what it was all about."

> In writing, you must simply be so precise about what this is about that I think you are forced to think in a way you have not been forced to think before. I mean in setting up an experiment there is always a lot of room for wobbling around, getting lots more things than you really need, and in analyzing the data, you can always fool around with the data and analyze endlessly this and that and so on. In writing it up, if it is to make any sense at all, you have got to know what it is about.
>
> I think when you start writing it up, you still have all of the presumed standards and pomposities and pretensions as to what science is supposed to be about so you tend to write up things as if they sprang intact from the godhead and as if what you found is really what you were predicting and the experiment was designed to precisely test this. Which, I think most anyone will tell you, is pure nonsense. I mean it is really a guided hit and miss kind of process. There is an awful lot of stumbling around and a lot of errors. After a long time you really find out what it was about. For me, that tends to be the stage when I am forced to write it up.
>
> I also greatly enjoy the data analysis - if it is coming out. If we are working on an experiment I almost invariably keep track of the data. The kids who are doing it will have the data and I will sort of have a running knowledge of what's happening. They do the hard work of course, if it is anything that is very complicated. Some of the stuff I have been working on recently requires *major* computer - use

> of the computer, then I am totally helpless. I am in their power.

"I am a lousy theoretician," Schachter laughed. "I really need a phenomenon before I worry how would I bother explaining it." He contrasted this style of working with Festinger's, which is more theory-driven. He said, "Leon was an *excellent* theoretician but that wasn't his main schtick - you needed data first and phenomena before you did anything theoretical."

> With Festinger's kind of theory, he starts with a phenomenon and then he asks himself what is behind this - what's it all about. He then comes through with, usually one grand insight and goes to work from there and says, "Ok, if this insight is true, what follows, what relates to it, what variables are affected."

In contrast, Schachter's way of working is to stay in close relationship to the data. "I am willing to let a piece of data change any theory I have," he laughed.

Of his students he concludes:

> I must concede I have great pride in my students. I think they have great pride, I don't know about affection but... First, I make awfully sure that they get very good - the *best* job that's available and that is a hell of a start for any of us. And I hound them to publish their thesis.
>
> They almost invariably will come back the first year or two to just tell me what they are doing. The second year they start telling me where I was wrong and by the fifth year, they are on their own.
>
> I watch them very closely, I am very fond of them - I pay very close attention. So does Leon.

INTERVIEWS

The Festinger Group

The first two interviews are with two students trained by Elliot Aronson: John Darley and Harold Sigall. Darley was an Aronson student at Harvard and followed him to Minnesota. Sigall worked with Aronson at Texas. Following these is an interview with Elliot Aronson.

After the Aronson group, there is an interview with Judson Mills who, along with Aronson was trained by Leon Festinger. Mills began working with Festinger at Minnesota and followed when Festinger moved to Stanford. Aronson and Festinger came to Stanford the same year. Aronson and Mills were contemporaries in Festinger's lab at Stanford. Following these two is an interview with Leon Festinger.

JOHN DARLEY

When John Darley was a boy, his father ran the program at the University of Minnesota in which Leon Festinger and Stanley Schachter worked.

> They were frequently in and out of my house when I was eight, nine, ten, eleven and so forth. And clearly, without being able to understand completely what they were doing, they were up to something that fascinated me. Here were these men who were engaged with their problem, enjoying themselves, intellectually committed and all of these things I found very attractive.

When Darley set out to choose a graduate school, he knew he wanted to do "social psychology, broadly defined." He had been an undergraduate psychology major at Swarthmore, where he pursued briefly an interest in "the reigning discipline of learning theory" and explored the gestalt tradition, which existed there. He said, "The questions that seemed to interest me were the ones on the human side of psychology and somebody told me that was called social psychology." So that is what he decided to pursue.

His sister was a student at Radcliffe when Darley went to investigate Harvard as a place to continue his education. During his visit, she introduced him to Elliot Aronson, who had recently completed his degree with Leon Festinger and was then in his first year teaching at Harvard. "Knowing both that Harvard was a place of some considerable prestige in general and that there was somebody as exciting as Elliot to work with, I decided that I would go there and I never regretted it," he recalled. "I went there to be at Harvard and Elliot was the the thing that made Harvard human and possible."

> Elliot had more or less inherited one of those small houses into which psychology was satellited out and were really very important. So there was a sort of

> Elliot building - 9 Bow Street. There were some older graduate students working with him and I was challenged to think about what made a sensible next study in a series of studies they were working on. I managed to do that, happily. I ran that study and off we went, talking about all sorts of possible studies.

In the beginning, Darley relied heavily on Aronson to sort out suggestions and help him decide which made sense and which didn't "in how this whole business should be encapsulated to present to the subject," he said. The senior graduate students, Merrill Carlsmith and Tony Greenwald, were also helpful to him in that respect.

> I think Elliot's skills were clearly so vast in that particular dimension that we were all a bit in awe of him and simply modeled on him, but we also used him as a kind of consultant. So it wasn't, I think, until I got *out* of graduate school and had to stand on my own legs that I had to think those things through finally in my own way and find my own particular patterns within it.

He described Aronson as "an overwhelmingly impressive model" when it came to the "creative processes of the experiment." These he listed as being: The importance of the problem addressed, the tight theoretical derivations which result in interesting answers to that problem and finally, the creation of an experiment which is compelling for the subject.

Darley worked with Aronson for several years and followed along when Aronson moved from Harvard to Minnesota. There, he said, "the legends of Schachter, Latane, Wheeler, and Singer were still alive," although they had moved on.

He described Aronson as an "excellent graduate trainer and always has been."

> There was a very tightly knit gang. We were quite isolated both in this house at Harvard and in other ways. They did not press you to take thousands of

> courses and there wasn't a lot of formal training in craft. Aronson was giving that so we felt like - perhaps a deviant subgroup of some sort but we really valued that. Merrill Carlsmith and Tony Greenwald are both effective individuals but reasonably competitive ones so there was a certain amount of sibling rivalry but there was training too. I learned a good many things from Tony *and* from Merrill but there was a certain amount of rivalry and productive tension there also.

Carlsmith was in his third year at Harvard when Darley arrived. Greenwald had been there a year. Darley said he had "no idea" how Aronson chose his students. "One simply gravitated to him and if you were interested, you started." If things didn't work out, then "there were other models at Harvard and people would gravitate toward them."

Darley believes, "The handing down of the method was absolutely critical." He said that if he "had not felt comfortable with a reasonable spectrum of experimental techniques and the craft associated with those I don't think I could have been able to realize any of my ideas."

He has worked in areas such as Oxford linguistic analysis which requires different methods, but he sees a problem with being able "to make the results of that method convincing to one's colleagues." Among those he wants to convince are "the gatekeepers who run journals." He said, "You need to do things in ways that make a difference to them. Since experimental methodology is the "lead method in the particular kind of psychology we do - it's not irrelevant."

He defines his intellectual community as being "the people who I regard as being sophisticated and creative experimental social psychologists themselves, first." These people don't necessarily have to work in the same area, and include both older and younger scientists. In addition to the people in this group, there are some he would like to reach "for policy reasons."

> I see the importance and the force of doing policy research so I am often drawn to it. But, I also find

> my own satisfactions in the sense of wonder and curiosity being rather more engaged with the sudden insight that is demonstrable and then the creation of some kind of experimental demonstration of it. Then, I guess I don't particularly worry about the policy implications. It seems to me that something that is interesting about human functioning is what I care about.

Training Students:

The graduate program at Princeton, where Darley is currently teaching, is "specifically an apprentice system," and not heavily dependent on courses. The formal requirements are one course in statistics and a one year seminar in which "faculty members in the department teach various areas. There is very little emphasis on course work and much more on 'hands on' or 'hands over' training."

> What we tend to do, and what every place that uses sort of an apprenticeship system does, is to hand problems to graduate students in the beginning year or so of their career and then try to give them more and more freedom with the larger and larger aspects of the study including its conceptualization and what topics it should be about as they move up. So towards thesis time, they should be moving toward that. But it is usually the case that the thesis has something to do with the advisor's interest defined in some very general sense.
>
> I continue to find graduate training the most mysterious thing that we all do and my rules for it might simply be statements of what worked well with the individual with who I am currently working and won't work well with the next one. So I *really* have no idea of the process or how that process can be made to go well. I think daily of Elliot and various things he did. How one gives them sufficient independence and sufficient

training, weaning, flying from the nest - all those metaphors - is terribly difficult.

One of the problems with graduate students is to avoid creating somebody exactly in your own image, and Elliot at certain points would forcefully say, "Ok, that's what I have got to give you, now you have got to get on with it," and would in some way sort of wean you - push you out of the nest by telling you it was time for you to go try something.

The qualities that indicate a student will be successful once they finish their degrees are those traditionally characterized as motivational. These Darley defined as, "intellect, excitement, some willingness to stick to it in a situation where more sensible people would go away." He said, "Basically, those for whom it works best are those who can get tremendously excited about the whole process."

His relationship with his graduate students is "a very close, collegial one," he said. "But there is almost going to be some components of hierarchy. Although there will be younger faculty, older faculty, senior graduate students, junior graduate students but once it is all sorted out as siblings somewhat, there needn't be hierarchical relationships that create barriers between levels."

The quality of interaction with graduate students, "is different at different times in your life," Darley believes. "When the faculty have kids and all those other agendas, I think the back and forth of the relationship is a little less but I think it is still a close relationship and there the parental one describes it. You don't necessarily want to go and and have a beer with daddy. Nonetheless, the model is there."

Subsequent Work and Current Environment:

Darley said the thread that links his body of work could be described as "the individual in the process of constructing his or her own world. Constructing those things using the cues available which are often social cues and then in some ways internalizing some of those constructions and taking the chances that implies - sometimes having them go awry but living as we have to do, as individuals have to, in groups."

He is currently working on "whether interaction goals affect self-fulfilling prophecies." That is, when a person interacts with other people there are different purposes involved, "and those turn out to affect the course of the interaction in ways that modern social psychology seems to be forgetting," he explained.

Darley points to three aspects of his working environment at Princeton which facilitate his work. First, many of the graduate students are supported by National Science Foundation training grants which relieves him of some of the pressure to keep grants coming in. Second, all of his colleagues in the department are themselves experimental psychologists "of one sort or another and there is a shared orientation there that is very valuable." And third, he said, "Princeton is a university that lets you get about your research, indeed expects it." He said there are some "deep splits about how to teach - the value of certain things, but we do share these working traditions and that is terribly valuable."

Another enriching aspect of the environment is that at Princeton, undergraduate teaching is considered to be very important.

> A good many of our ideas initially come up within teaching contexts. You have to lecture about something that you haven't been thinking about and in thinking about it, we think about it in some new way and that convinces, at least us. And so you go out and do an experiment about it.
>
> At Princeton, every undergraduate does a thesis. Some of those end up being published and we *do* involve them in research quite heavily. One needs to be careful because there is no point in trying to give them a Ph.D. training or all the craft training one does to a graduate student. Nevertheless, there are things they could do that are valuable.

Darley described three ways of going about doing research: Starting with an observation or some phenomenon, starting with a theoretical formulation, or, finally, starting by questioning some piece of conventional wisdom or rule of thumb.

> Bibb Latane and I one evening in New York, after a woman had been stabbed, were sitting around and talking and we came to realize that a good deal of what we mean by group processes really applied to the inhibition of bystanders in a case like that. So in that case, you start with something that happens and you realize that you have some principles that will make a difference in the process in question.
>
> The dissonance studies were a little bit different - they were saying that in a good many real world processes there is an underlying dissonance process. That too seems to me to be very creative. And I suppose I would like to think some of the deviance studies that I worked on were more like that.
>
> A third way of doing things, of course, is to take what the real world conventional wisdom is saying about something and discover that it causes a person difficulty - so you have objections to that.

Discussing "The Family:"

Darley describes himself as feeling fatherly toward his students. He said. "You see each other at various meetings, you follow their achievements with very considerable pride and you perform various mentoring activities - references and so on."

> That task is to give your intellectual offspring positions so that they can have an exciting time. If they are excited about what you are excited about, you want them to be in some kind of setting in which they can do what they are excited about. That translates into a "good job." The job doesn't have to be one at a high prestige university, there are some very good smaller universities of kind of modest rank that are excellent places for

> psychology to get done and those would be just fine.

Darley believes the "Lewin family" metaphor is a "*very* active conceptualization. For me, it has always been a very positive one. I have always felt very lucky in the people with whom I trained - in their continuing contact and support of me." It is especially active for those in his age group, he believes. He continued, "I think it is for our students as well. But, like all families, when the property gets divided and you get second, third and fourth cousins, the relationship get a bit attenuated."

He suggested another way of conceptualizing the origins of the group:

> If you want to look at this whole business as a social movement, Lewin is something of a Christ figure but certainly Festinger played the role of St. Paul who made the thing happen. Festinger, who was a very competitive fellow, demonstrated that we in social psychology could do as good, well reasoned, methodologically sophisticated experiments as people working with infrahuman subjects. And by God, all of us still feel that tradition. One of the very important claims we would make is exactly that claim. And that was Festinger's role, to show that we could be as rigorous as the others and I think he did that very successfully.

HAROLD SIGALL

Harold Sigall was an undergraduate psychology major at City College of New York. The course he took in social psychology was taught by a graduate student who was just finishing up at Columbia. "He was a clinician by training but he had to have some courses from Stanley Schachter," Sigall recalled. What was significant about this course was that, unlike most introductory courses, the students were assigned primary research material in the form of a reader by Maccoby, Newcomb and Hartley (1958) - there was no textbook. Each of the students were assigned to present an article to the class and to analyze it critically.

> That was my first crack at that kind of thing. Because I *had* an experimental course, I can't remember now if it was before or after, but there was nothing original about it. It might have been a whole year doing experiments but you were told exactly what to do. It was really sort of Chem I lab - how to mix this chemical and that and reaction time and that kind of thing.

He described City College: "In many ways it was just like a high school for 18 to 22 year olds, unless you were terribly motivated as a student and really got involved. And I wasn't and didn't. You really had very little contact with faculty." Sigall became attached to the teacher of the social course. In addition to having taught a good course, this instructor had been at one time a jazz musician and a friend of Lenny Bruce's - all of which Sigall found fascinating. "He was just fun. Even after that course I never thought of myself as being a university teacher. I think he must have planted the seeds of possibility for it."

By the time Sigall was finishing college, the Vietnam war was heating up. Interested in staying out of the draft, he considered graduate school. With the goal of getting a job, he thought he might go into industrial psychology. His advisor suggested he apply to Purdue, but a friend was applying to Texas and suggested that as a place to go.

> I thought, Texas, that's ridiculous. At that time I probably hadn't been more than a hundred miles from New York - except for a trip to Washington, D.C. once. So I went to this guy who had taught that good course a couple of years earlier and I chatted with him and I said I heard this thing about Texas. And he said, "Yeah Gardner Lindzey is going to be going there" and he named some other names. I didn't even know who Gardner Lindzey was - his name was on a personality textbook and that was it. But it sounded good to this teacher and that sounded good. In any event I went off to Texas. And I went there and I remember getting there thinking I was going to be in industrial psychology and they didn't have industrial psychology.

Once he arrived at Texas he was given a choice between experimental psychology and clinical. He chose experimental. He said, "I ended up taking a social course which I liked. But I wasn't wedded to social, I think I was more interested in designing research." He also found out that there really wasn't a masters degree program.

> It was a very brutal system actually. You didn't have to take any course, you didn't have to do anything. You just had to pass these qualifying exams. And lots of people had failed them. The previous semester only four people out of 24 had passed. Others had passed some of them. So there was just this terrible morale among the students in this place when our class got there. What I was presented with was the notion that there was no sense in deciding you were going to go for a masters degree. You entered a graduate program, take the qualifying exams and it is not distinct but I have a vague recollection of making this conscious decision - I am going to redefine myself as getting a Ph.D. Now that again had *no* connection for me

> with ever teaching in a university. I didn't know what it meant. I was very immature and unknowing - not thoughtful.

In the fall of Sigall's first year at Texas, Elliot Aronson visited and gave a talk. Immediately Sigall asked Aronson if he was coming to Texas and assumed they would work together. He recalled, "I just assumed it would be. It was another part of that naivete and it happened to be true and it worked out and was nice but I realized at some point, probably long after I left Texas, that it was an assumption on my part and it wasn't necessarily something I could control."

> I think that when he got there, I followed up. I probably made a big pest of myself. I came around and I said "I want to do research." And he gave me things to read and I read it and came back with ideas for research. And he said, "no, they were dumb," and I came back with more and finally there was something worth shaping and we shaped it and did the study and kept at it. Then I got a research assistantship and I worked on his grant. I think that was my third year, maybe the second half of my second year. Then he helped me get a fellowship my last year. But essentially, I worked with him for two years very closely and was really mentored and I learned a lot from him.

Sigall describes the other graduate students as "terrific." He said the students who worked with Aronson felt "special. We were all together in one little room. We got what we wanted, we never had any problem getting resources - maybe we didn't want anything outlandish..." Sigall said Aronson had research grants during that time and was able to hire graduate students as assistants. Students came to work with Aronson who were recommended by friends and former colleagues at other universities.

During Sigall's last year at Texas, Aronson's interests shifted and he began to work on t-groups with a colleague of his, Michael Kahn. During that year, Ned Jones was visiting Texas and Sigall collaborated with him.

Sigall was nearly finished with his dissertation by Christmas of that year, which allowed him time to work with Jones and get to know him.

> I had pretty much planned it (his dissertation research) during the summer before. And I went to one of those Tuesday night meetings and presented it. It got criticized and kind of recast very early - it was probably one of the first two or three meetings of the year. So it was probably recast by September. I was ready to go. I had the background under control and it was just a question of the details of the design. There were radical changes made in it as a result of these meetings but I was really able to function independently. I really needed very little help from Elliot on it at that point. I had gotten all the help on it I needed from Elliot by the time of that meeting and shortly thereafter. So the fact that he went off in the other direction didn't really have an impact on my dissertation. I collected all the data and analyzed it over Christmas vacation and leisurely wrote it up over the spring.

He described Jones as being, "very different in style" from what he was used to. He said, "Elliot was a terrific role model in a lot of ways and Ned complemented that nicely - He had different sorts of strengths." Out of this collaboration came the "bogus pipeline" (Jones & Sigall, 1971). The idea was born at Texas and they began to collect some data but there were problems. When they each went their separate ways, they continued to work on it and published it several years later.

Sigall said, "My first student at Rochester, where I went when I left Texas, was a guy who was very good mechanically and a good experimenter. We did some of the first studies on stereotyping." What made this student a good experimenter in Sigall's view was that "he was able to convince the subject. I think when I say that I am a good experimenter I might use the term a little bit differently. What I mean is that I can design an experiment and come up with the scenario and write the script and do all that kind of direction that I think will involve the subject. This student was good at the other part of the process. He was good at enacting the role and being able to convince the subject what he needs to be convinced of and so on."

> The Tuesday night meetings were an important part of the research process at Texas. They were attended by all people who identified with the social program. Sigall said, "A lot of the meetings were held at Elliot's house but they were also often at other people's homes." Anyone who had a big enough place would host a meeting from time to time.
>
> They were terrific. What happened at them is somebody would present a research idea and in general - at least what I remember and it might not be accurate, but what I remember about it is that there was kind of an unwritten rule that you didn't present stuff that was cast in stone. You always presented stuff that was early in its development - an idea - which I think is a great idea. I think the tremendous advantage of that was that you reduce defensiveness on the part of the presenter and you increase involvement on the part of the non-presenters because there was really room for a contribution. If somebody tells you they have done something and you criticize it, all you are doing in a sense is showing you are smart and that they made a mistake. And the only positive thing that can come out of it is you might persuade them, if they were particularly open, to not publish it. That is about as much as you could do. The other way, you can really make a contribution, you could help the other person, you feel like you are collaborating. Sometimes studies would come out of these meetings - you know, new studies. It was really very very fertile. It was great. You have to be able to take a little heat, I think. You have to stand a little criticism because although nothing is cast in concrete, certainly your ideas were out there and they were vulnerable. And I think there was probably a mixed reaction to those meetings. In the same way I think I was able to handle Elliot's style,

I was able to handle these meetings. For some reason, I didn't feel vulnerable to Elliot's judgment or other people's judgment about my intelligence. I think my ego and my ideas were separated and I didn't have them all wrapped up together.

I think the critical thing for me was that I recognized that I really didn't know anything when I came in. It wasn't that I had had this experience doing research as an undergraduate and when I started working with Elliot, I really felt ok about putting myself in his hands that way. So if he said something wasn't interesting - and interesting was very important - if he thought it wasn't interesting, then I was persuaded. I really respected his ability and judgment as a social psychologist and I didn't get caught up...That is what I mean about keeping it separate. I don't feel like I have any magic, I mean it *was* magic in a way, but I didn't have any formula.

I would just say, "I am going to work on this," and I didn't get the two things confused. There were painful things, though. I really learned a lot. I learned a lot about writing from Elliot. Now that is not to say that it wasn't painful to go in there and give him a draft of something and it came back in shreds - all marked up. But I never - I don't remember thinking that he was being capricious or a bastard. I am sure I might have thought that there was a nicer way to communicate this to me, but somehow I responded to the criticism and not to the form of it because I respected where it was coming from. I think there were other people who were crushed by this - they didn't want to deal with it.

The relationship with Aronson was partly collegial and partly subordinate, with the level of collegiality "increasing over time." Sigall said overall he was very happy as a graduate student - once qualifying exams were over. He laughed, "It was a great time in my life and I have never been able to quite recapture it. I was much more idealistic - I was going to solve the world's problems through social psychology. But there were also some practical things. When I was a graduate student, more or less I didn't do anything I didn't want to do. Once I got past the exam business, all I did was research and I chose what I wanted to do. We were even able to get undergraduates to be the experimenters."

His favorite part of the research process is having the insight - "although I haven't had that many of them," he smiled. "To see some relationship that isn't that obvious and then being able to demonstrate it in a persuasive way by creating the conditions is fun. The rest of it is no fun."

Training Students:

Currently Sigall is at the University of Maryland where he teaches an undergraduate lab course in methods. The course is primarily "the rudiments of research, not just experimental research but research with the emphasis on experimental," he explained. He also teaches a graduate core course in social psychology. Occasionally, he teaches a graduate methods course similar to the one he had as a graduate student.

There is a seminar that is part of the graduate program. But it is closer to a colloquium series than the old Tuesday night meetings. "We talk about the program, people present research and we have a lot of outside speakers. The work we hear about from inside is rarely in the beginning stages. It is almost always completed."

> I have never worked in a way that I did social psychology by myself. I was never locked up in a room working independently, not talking to anyone, just producing social psychology. And what I think I have discovered is that probably if those were the circumstances under which I had to do it, I wouldn't have done it because it wouldn't have been fun. I think that the fun for me has always been...it was *captured*...created? I don't know, but certainly it was there in those Tuesday night meeting settings...or in the back room. It was having an idea, talking to people, speculating about things,

developing the story, creating the story together with someone else and having fun doing it. And *that's* where the fun was. That was not the only motivation I had, but that was a big part of it. I think as I have gotten older it has been harder and harder for me to do that. To get that kind of enthusiasm going.

Designing experiments is just not as rewarding intrinsically as they once were. I think that is partly because I know I can do it, that I am a good experimenter and that I can set the thing up in a way that demonstrates the effect. I am not interested enough to do just "another study" in a sequence of studies - as I might have been.

Currently he is ambivalent about the the prospect of training graduate students. There are some things about the field in general which have contributed to his feeling. First is the job market. He said he had a very good student who wasn't able to get a job and that was "very discouraging" to him. He said, "I *love* training graduate students. I wish the times were fatter so that they could do what they want to do and are capable of doing."

Not only was it demoralizing but it had other consequences: Why spend all this time teaching people how to do research if they are going to end up working for a market research company or doing surveys for the government and never advancing the field at all. So that took a lot of the fun out of it. I had a couple of *very* good students, particularly one guy who got these visiting jobs for a year and he probably could have done a little better if he had stayed with it a little longer, but he didn't and I can't really blame him. Ten years earlier he would have gotten a great job - he was really very good.

Related to that is that I don't feel comfortable recruiting people into the field without making it clear that there is no pot of gold at the end of the rainbow. I can't say, "This is a great, growing, exciting discipline where you are going to be able to

> save the world and make a living while you do." That is just one big set of things that has had a negative effect on my enthusiasm.

Another thing that affected Sigall's attitude was his experience of editing a journal for four years. He said that for the first year or two it was "even fun in some ways. But on the whole it was a terribly depressing experience." What affected him was the atmosphere of publishing in order to be promoted. Too frequently people want to publish work they knew wasn't first rate simply because they believed they needed a certain number of publications in order to get tenure or raises. He said it wasn't that he "was bringing any special standards to it but there was this clawing for tenure." He said the kind of research being done has changed over the years. One small part of that change is due to this situation.

> Most people can't take the time. They can't do work in a way that it takes them an hour to run a subject, or a scenario has to be created - it is just not common. It is not that it isn't done, it is just not common. So much of the research is by and large uninventive, uncreative and non-risktaking. Although, who knows, maybe I would have felt the same way if I had edited a journal twenty years ago. It was such a joyless enterprise, reading that stuff.

Even with the situation in social psychology, Sigall said they have a lot of good students at Maryland. Many of them are women who are "trapped in the area," and are returning to school, he said. He said the kind of hope for the future he had during his training at Texas is available today in only a few elite places.

Looking back, Sigall doesn't feel he made an informed choice back in 1964 when he began in social psychology. He thinks he might as easily have chosen cognitive psychology if it had existed at the time. He saw experimentation in social psychology as the only alternative to traditional experimental psychology. He said, "The human experimentalists were studying verbal learning." It was the chance to do experimentation with people in addition to the possibility of doing some good that attracted him to social psychology in the first place. He said, "I certainly could imagine again falling under the spell of someone like Elliot - I think maybe I would - it's hard to say."

ELLIOT ARONSON

Elliot Aronson went to graduate school at Stanford because two of his friends had gone to Stanford, been successful there and had liked it. Besides, he had never been more than 300 miles from Boston so living on the West Coast was an attraction for him. He had grown up in Revere, Massachussetts and was an undergraduate at Brandeis, studying with Abraham Maslow. He then completed a masters degree at Wesleyan, where he worked with David McClelland on achievement motivation. McClelland was moving to Harvard and invited him to come along as his research assistant but Aronson decided instead to go west. He said, "I didn't even know who was at Stanford. Robert Sears was the only name both of my friends mentioned and he was interested in motivation like I was then. I thought I could go there and he would be interested in what I was interested in. And he was."

During the spring of his first year at Stanford, Aronson was challenged by a friend, Dick Alpert, an acting instructor, to take a seminar with Leon Festinger. Although this was only Festinger's first year at Stanford, he had already acquired a reputation for being "devastating." Aronson said, "Dick implied that the reason I had not signed up for Festinger's seminar was fear. This goaded me into enrolling.

> In retrospect, I think Dick was right. Festinger and I came to Stanford the same year. I didn't know he was coming, I sort of knew who e was because I had read Swanson, Newcomb & Hartley's (1948) *Readings in Social Psychology* when I was at Wesleyan. There were two or three articles by Festinger in it - and he was still in his thirties. I thought, "Wow he must be good if he has stuff reprinted in there." And then after only one or two quarters reports began to circulate among the graduate student grapevine that he was a *killer*.

Aronson said, "I was lucky. I think if it hadn't been for Dick Alpert, I probably would have kept away from Festinger and I wouldn't have known what I had missed. That was a very lucky happenstance for me; once I took that seminar, Festinger's toughness was no problem - I could see the riches."

What Festinger taught was Festinger. "He only taught what he was excited about at the moment so the best of him came out in everything he taught," said Aronson. His attitude was: 'This is what I happen to be thinking about now, you want to take it or not?' This attitude put a lot of people off - I loved it!"

During that first seminar, Festinger was developing dissonance theory and the work focused on broadening the sphere in which dissonance theory was applied. "It was like a fertilization seminar," Aronson said. The students were reading widely - "all kinds of fascinating things like about the Salem witch trials. Festinger had the notion that if we read the transcripts of those trials we would find something relevant," he recalled. They were looking specifically for evidence that witches who confessed without coercion came to believe their own confession while witches who confessed through coercion didn't. The seeds of the Festinger-Carlsmith experiment (1959) were in those three-hundred year old transcripts.

> The project I took on was an anthropological one. John Whiting had done something on initiation - a cross-cultural study that didn't have anything to do with dissonance theory but in reading that, I realized that some cultures require severe initiations - I'll bet those cultures are more cohesive, more patriotic. I thought about that for a while and we discussed it in the seminar and then I thought about how would you test that? I couldn't find the answer in the ethnography literature. So I thought, "Well why don't I do it here?" When you're around Leon, you think in terms of laboratory experiments; that seemed much more exciting than doing a content analysis of ethnographic reports. So Jud Mills and I got together and designed a rather simple experiment.

This led to his first experiment - the Aronson-Mills (1959), severity of initiation experiment - which he said was "one of the most exciting things I have done."

> It made me a believer in social psychology. I believed that social psychology had the methodology to test interesting hypotheses in a way you could be confident about after you did it. And it came so easily to me that I dared to think that I could conceivably be one of those special people who can do research.
>
> The process of building the initiation experiment was exciting as hell - the designing of it and seeing it begin to come out was terrific. It wasn't the data analysis and it wasn't the impact that the results would have on anybody, it wasn't even necessarily the idea - it was the translation of the idea into a researchable problem. For me the artistry is in the that translation.

Aronson was tapped to work as a research assistant in Festinger's lab as a result of his work in the seminar - especially because of the initiation experiment which came out of it. He said, "Once you started working for him he began to take some responsibility for your development."

Aronson said Festinger "had confidence in my abilities as an experimenter long before I did, and once he believed that I was good, we became a junior and senior colleague on an exciting enterprise. He had a great deal of charismatic power and he could be very tough on me but he was also warm and loving. We used to go out drinking occasionally - discussing our ideas and our feelings about each other.

> But I don't want to underplay his toughness. It was important. Initially, I learned to avoid sloppiness because of Leon's sharpness and toughness. If I made a sloppy error in design or procedure, Leon would look at me as if I was a simpleton. It was even worse those few occasions when he made a conscious effort to be kind - a look of pity crept into

> his eyes and I would say to myself "Oh, oh, here it comes!" In order to avoid receiving that look, I'd go the extra mile in designing the experiment. After a while, it became second nature to design it right the first time - on my own.

Festinger worked very closely with his students. He had an office in the basement - which according to Aronson was "sort of a grungy place with yellow walls and the ceiling used to leak a lot because his office was directly under the ladies' room and the toilets would occasionally overflow. But that didn't seem to interfere with Leon's work. There was a secretary across the hall and a cluster of offices for research assistants. In the same corridor was the research space - rooms with one-way mirrors and so forth. All of this took up half the basement of the old psychology building."

> Festinger tended to come in very early in the morning and stay until very late in the day almost every day. He was always behind his desk because he almost never taught and so he was there and he would either put us to work on a problem or wait for us to get an idea. There was always a free feeling - he could bounce in and out of our offices and we could bounce in and out of his. He would encourage us to talk to each other. Whenever we were designing an experiment we would always try out the design on each other. We would run either dummy subjects or each other through the procedure, while he and a couple of other graduate students watched through the one-way mirror, to iron out bugs and to see that we were doing our roles right. And even while we were running subjects, Leon was often in the one-way mirror room eavesdropping and looking in to see if we were getting it right and being convincing. He was interested in the dramaturgical aspects of it - were we really playing our roles well? There were lots of rehearsals. The details were important.

Aronson recalled an incident that happened his first quarter at Stanford before he knew Festinger. He and another teaching assistant were in the "TA room, down at the *other* end of the corridor," when Festinger and one of his students (Judson Mills) walked by. The two of them stopped and Festinger said, "Well, let's see what these guys think." Mills then described the procedure for an experiment he was working on. Aronson said, "I remember saying, 'well, that's not very convincing; perhaps if you say it this way...or that way...' and I remember Festinger saying to Mills, 'Are you writing this down, are you getting this?' It was like that. We didn't have anything to do with those guys or their research project, but they were using us as sort of sophisticated subjects. That was their modus operandi - you try out procedures on people - you find out how people are affected by a procedure before you see your first subject." In this type of research, the procedure has to be involving for the subject.

> Festinger was always concerned about having a scenario that would make sense for the subject and engage his interest while it was testing your hypothesis. You had to keep the subject from falling asleep. It was very clear that Festinger was attending to methodological details that were *absolutely* essential but that most researchers never wrote about. There were things that we never saw written down anyplace in any journal article or methods book.
>
> Most of the ideas that led to experiments simply emerged in the day to day interactions and encounters down in the basement. Leon was always challenging - if one of us got a good idea and thought of doing an experiment, he would turn to the others and say, "Now why can't you come up with a good idea like that." It was somewhat in jest, but also there was the notion among the students that you had better come up with something *soon*. There was a fair amount of external pressure but the pressure was mostly self-generated and there was a lot of enthusiasm around there for getting ideas and turning those ideas into good experiments.
>
> We also had Tuesday night research meetings. We would sit around and drink beer. There was a lot of

> exchange of ideas - it was mostly people batting around ideas, trying out a design for an experiment, trying out a procedure and Festinger was very much *the* person there. Meetings were always at his house; Festinger was very gracious, he was always alive and always on target.
>
> It was my impression that having the meetings at night was our idea. I think if we saw it as just another assignment we might have viewed it as burdensome. But we mostly felt grateful that Leon was giving us his free evening - and we resolved to use it well.
>
> It was a nice atmosphere and I think as I look back on it, the only thing that was really lacking was that there weren't other faculty members in social psychology.

"He was a *wonderful* editor of ideas. He would either shoot it down or build it up - but he would do *something* with it when you brought it up at Tuesday night meetings or in his office. What you never got was a tepid response," said Aronson. Festinger demonstrated his enthusiasm for an idea or a procedure by becoming interested in it. Style was important. What was valued particularly was not just a clever idea - but a clever idea "that was *important* and important not for the world (application) but because it taught us something we didn't know about human nature," he said. But ultimately ideas are easier to come by than a good way of testing them.

> Festinger used to say, "Good ideas are a dime a dozen." While ideas are important and the design was important, what was equally important was how convincing the actual words you used on the subject were and how much they represented and captured the flavor of your hypothesis. *anybody* could come up with designs. Design simply means that if you need a specific control group, you create a control group that fits the requirement. But it's controlling the experience of the subject - having the subject experience the thing you intend for the

subject to experience - *that's* playwrighting. I think if I had to name one thing - *that's* the important thing. Nobody had ever written that down as essential methodology.

That's what Merrill Carlsmith and I tried to capture in our chapter on experimentation in the *Handbook of Social Psychology* (1968). When Carlsmith and I wrote the chapter, we were criticized for having a very cavalier attitude about ideas. Not so. We *assumed* the idea is going to be interesting or else why bother? We weren't going to tell people where to get ideas or how to get ideas - how can you do that? But we assumed the idea was interesting and then we wrote about how to continue. If you read that chapter, you'll see that that's where we spend all our time - how do you write a really good scenario. The details are vitally important.

Festinger also would spend a lot of time engrossed in data.

I remember once a bright sunny California day - when it was a pleasure to be out of doors, I brought an old friend by - somebody who wasn't at Stanford. And we walked by Leon's office and he said, "Who was that grind?" Festinger was sitting there, his nose really close to some pages on his desk, trying to make sense out of some data. And he could *do* that. He could spend three or four hours at a crack immersed in data sheets to see if he could find a distinguishing thread. He *loved* doing things like that. It was sort of like crossword puzzle solving. That is one of the things that I first really liked about him - he sure wasn't afraid to get his hands dirty. He didn't take any executive position in research. He was deeply into it. It was seeing Leon through my friend's eyes that I began to fully appreciate his dedication - which was always far greater than mine.

I once worked for a professor who was an executive. The only one he saw was the head

> research assistant who saw the other research assistants who saw me and we would all feed stuff up the line. And the professor would be sitting there in a suit listening to what all of the subjects were doing second hand but he never went to the lab. And Festinger was always in it, in it, in it.

Festinger didn't normally run subjects in the experiment itself, although Aronson thinks he may have run some of the pilot subject in a few experiments - like the Festinger-Carlsmith experiment, "to get the feel for it" he said. "He was very much looking over your shoulder as you were doing it. Every once in a while he would be in the one-way room watching me run, although I wasn't sure exactly when, and this is something I learned from him. Experimenters are fallible human beings and if we're not careful one might not perform the same way in week six of an experiment as in week one. It is quality control."

> When I began to have students of my own I began to realize how many hundreds of things a novice, a first year graduate student will not take into consideration. And you can't explain them all. And even if you could - even if you wrote them down - all of them, for each experiment, they would miss it because they wouldn't realize how important some things were compared to others. The only way to do it is to know there is something askew and call it to their attention. And that is what I learned from Festinger. It is a special kind of learning. It isn't a casual, "Oh, that's how you are supposed to do it," it's an insightful "*oh yeah*, it would be *terrible* if you *hadn't* done that."

In addition to working with Festinger, Aronson put time and energy into teaching while he was a graduate student - "Something" he said, "which always puzzled Leon." Aronson had a special TA assignment which he allowed him to pull talented undergraduates from the introductory psychology course into a special seminar. In this seminar, instead of reading an introductory text, they read Freud, Skinner, Lewin and others in the original. He said, "I loved teaching that seminar. Leon felt it was taking up too much time. If he had had his way he would have made research my exclusive professional activity. Leon's notion was that there were so few people who really knew how to do experiments that if you were one of those people, then nothing should interfere. It was like a calling. I didn't feel that way at the time."

Aronson said that when he began working in Festinger's lab, his self concept wasn't very high and Festinger's faith in him was, "very enabling." Aronson feared that his first experiment might have been a lucky accident and he said, "Leon was convinced it couldn't have been an accident, it was like somebody playing a violin concerto or something and it was good - how can that be an accident? It took me a while to realize he was right. That was the only criterion he used. If you were a good researcher you - you did a good experiment; you couldn't be good if you didn't do one; and if you did one you couldn't be anything *but* good. He was absolutely right; there are no flukes in this business."

Training Students

When Aronson got his degree, he took his first job at Harvard. There he ran his lab and trained his students in a little house on Bow Street which he said, "was kind of nice, we had our own little enclave after a while. But the kind of research I was doing was not part of the zeitgeist at Harvard at the time, and while I enjoyed my students, I missed having like-minded colleagues." After three years at Harvard he moved to the University of Minnesota, taking one of his Harvard graduate students, John Darley, with him. He said he made the move because, "It was very clear to me that Minnesota had a better atmosphere for doing experiments of the kind I wanted to do and it had a tradition in that. At Harvard, I felt under considerable pressure to defend what I was doing."

"It wasn't until I started teaching that I truly began to appreciate Leon's style. I picked up some of the things Leon did," said Aronson, "but filtered them through my own personality.

> One of the first things I did every place that I went was to set up Tuesday night meetings. At Minnesota it was great to have colleagues who

cared about experiments. Elaine Walster (Hatfield), Ben Willerman, Dana Bramel and I were all there at the same time and we had seven or eight students working with one of more of us. Terrific people like John Darley, Ellen Berscheid, Darwyn Linder and others. Those meetings were very exciting.

Another aspect of Festinger's training that Aronson adopted was to insist on high standards and to "not try to be kind," he said. By this he meant he wouldn't tell a student his work was good simply as an act of kindness. "Festinger was tough, demanding and occasionally devastating. I think I'm a bit softer, but the only time I'm *not* demanding is when I'm convinced a student is not very talented."

Aronson's way of working with students was similar to Festinger's in other respects. At Harvard, Minnesota and Texas the physical arrangements were similar. He and his students had offices close together and they encountered each other continually. He said, "We bounced ideas off each other all the time. We arrived early and stayed late because it was fun to come to work - for everybody." Aronson said this was back when there was a lot of research money available.

I didn't like my students taking a lot of courses. Most of what you need to know you can get out of reading books and journals. Research you learn mostly by doing it, with guidance, in an atmosphere where a lot of people are doing it. If somebody wanted to take a course, say, in philosophy of science, my statement was, "Oh, it probably won't do you much harm." But, by and large you learn the important stuff by doing it.

I *like* the idea of being part of a team with other professionals and graduate students who are in the common enterprise of doing social psychology, where we are excited by it and thinking that we are really pushing the barriers of knowledge. It *is* an exciting enterprise.

Aronson described two kinds of students he has worked with some of whom were energy enhancing and others who were draining.

> I have produced about 15 or 20 students that I'm very proud of. It was a joy to work with them and I follow their careers avidly. When one of these students came in my office for a half hour or 45 minutes, we would do three or four different things: We would discuss a bug that had developed in the procedure of a new experiment, discuss the data analysis from an experiment that was just completed, talk about the write-up of an experiment we had done together that had already been analyzed, and then come up with ideas for a new experiment. These are the kinds of students who got me thinking and were an absolute joy to work with - my energy was enhanced.
>
> Then there would be students who would come in and say, "Well, you know, I don't know, I am thinking about this idea and..." And I could feel my energy drain and I would start daydreaming. I would almost always sit through it because I usually didn't have the stomach to tell the second kind of student, "Hey, you know this is a waste of time, why don't you work with somebody else?" I'm not "kind" in the sense that I don't think I ever told a student that a dumb idea is a good one. But I usually find a way to talk to the student on some level. But you know, these students must notice my eyes glaze over or something - because very few hung around me for very long.

Aronson moved from Minnesota to Texas in 1965. At Texas he set up a lab similar to the one at Minnesota, immediately instituted Tuesday night meetings and continued working on the problems he was working on at Minnesota. He said that when working with graduate students the main goal was always to do the best piece of research possible. "The happy by-product is that the student is going to learn how to do it. Doing research is the only way for students to learn how to do research, but training students isn't the main purpose of the research."

> The best piece of advice I can give a first year graduate student is to make a beeline for the smartest, toughest, most demanding person you can find and work with that person. For at least two reasons. One is that you learn the most from these people and if you develop a tough enough skin, you *really* learn a lot. But beyond that, if you work with a kind person, who is nice to everybody, when push comes to shove that person, I think, is likely not to have a lot of confidence in his own ability to make a judgment and then go to the wall for it. It's nice to have a mentor who is sure of himself and sure of you. When I was ready to leave graduate school, I interviewed at three top places and I was offered all three jobs. Why was I offered all three jobs? Partly because Leon Festinger, who was the hottest thing going, was willing to go out on a limb to support his belief that I was talented.

Aronson believes one reason some researchers have reputations for being tough on students is because they have a primary interest in the task at hand - in the research product. He said, "That's why, in the final analysis, you don't sacrifice being a tough taskmaster in favor of being a nice guy. If you can find a way of doing both simultaneously, that's wonderful. But you don't compromise on quality." He said when he was working in the lab with graduate students at Minnesota and later at Texas, the atmosphere was flexible and generally democratic - but "not *totally* democratic."

> We usually interacted democratically - but when the chips were down it was very clear who was in charge. It was very clear who was most experienced and who had the last word. There *are* better ways and worse ways of doing an experiment. I could almost always explain to a student why one way was better than another - but some things we learn from a lot of experience, and it is not always easy to explain. On those occasions when my explanations were inadequate, I would have to say (with a blush) "Run it *my* way; you will understand why later." In research, if there is a difference of opinion, you don't take a *vote*. At the

> same time, I am also a teacher - and nothing pleases me more than to *lose* an argument to a student or when one of my students comes up with a better way of doing it. That's when I know they're ready.

Training Everybody:

While at Minnesota, Aronson began working with Merrill Carlsmith on a chapter on experimentation for the Handbook of Social Psychology. (Aronson & Carlsmith 1968). Aronson and Carlsmith first met at Stanford when Aronson was a graduate student and Carlsmith was an undergraduate working with Festinger. Carlsmith did his graduate work at Harvard, where he became Aronson's research assistant. Aronson and Carlsmith decided to write the chapter in an attempt to describe and explain how laboratory experiments were actually built. He said they wanted to "open up the technique for a lot of people - make it accessible and to demystify the technique of doing experimental research in social psychology." Aronson said it was the kind of chapter he wished had been available when he was starting to do experiments. "There were literally dozens of problems I encountered and solved, and I imagined that a lot of young people out there were in the process of reinventing the wheel - and probably not reinventing it as well as it had been invented earlier."

> The best way to learn to do experiments is to do them. No one learns to do experiments by reading a book - but the right kind of book can be a useful adjunct if, for no other reason, it counteracts the effect of reading methods sections of journal articles. This is terribly misleading. They present an oversimplified, glossy picture which makes the experimental process look both easier and harder than it really is. Easier because they are written in a cut and dried manner and harder because once you start to do an experiment, you realize that it ain't the same as it looked in the journal article and therefore you quickly develop the feeling that those people out there must be super smart because they got it to work so easily and here I am bumbling

around making these errors that *they* never made...But they *did* make them. I wanted to write a chapter to help students become aware of the problems they would encounter and not feel stupid when they ran into difficulty. People who do good experiments are not *super* smart; they *are* smart, *and* well trained, *and* careful, *and* daring *and* insightful. But almost anyone can do it if they apprentice themselves to someone who knows how.

Beyond the Laboratory:

By the late sixties the field of social psychology was shifting and expanding. Aronson also made a shift in his career - at first, an expansion into t-groups. This came as a result of his association with Michael Kahn who was at the time a colleague at Texas.

> I was aware, of course, that Kurt Lewin had invented the t-group as a way to observe group dynamics - and I found the idea exciting. But I was disappointed and very critical of t-groups because the main thing I knew about them in practice was that the research wasn't very scientific; there weren't any good data on it. It was primarily testimonial type data, so I was rather contemptuous of it. I was being very critical of Michael Kahn's involvement when he threw down the gauntlet. He said, "Well, you are the scientist, I'm surprised that you've drawn conclusions without checking it out. I am starting a group now for people at the counseling center. It's a professional group and you would feel at home there. You might want to come for a few weeks as a participant and then tell me what you think."
>
> I couldn't resist that kind of challenge. I went and after the first session, I was very excited. I thought what was happening there was important for social psychology. It struck me as being genuine and very useful. This was social psychology in the raw.

> People were talking about their feelings and issues that were important to them. The method broke down interpersonal barriers. I was very impressed. There were people there who I had known for a few years - seen at parties, chatted with and didn't know anything about. In contrast, the discussions we were having in the t-group were the kinds of discussions I dreamed of having with these people - where you let down all your defenses and you simply talk about what is important to you and what is going on in the interaction at the moment. I liked it so much that the next summer I went to Bethel - and after a few summers in training, I became an active t-group leader.

As Aronson began to put more energy into t-groups, he believes some of his graduate students felt let down. But he feels that pursuing his interest in t-groups gave him a great many insights into human interaction that he otherwise wouldn't have experienced. He is convinced that these insights informed his subsequent research and made him a better social psychologist. Moreover, this gradual move away from strict laboratory experimentation was broadly based and took other forms. He began to do field experiments on important social problems. He wanted to combine his knowledge of experimental skills with his interest in solving social problems. In addition, he wanted to communicate the material to a wider audience. His interest in teaching resulted in his writing The Social Animal during a year's stay at the Behavior Sciences Center at Stanford.

> There we were right in the middle of the Vietnam war, there was a lot of divorce, there were riots in the streets - society was falling apart and social psychologists were writing pedestrian textbooks as if social psychology doesn't have anything to do with all that. I wanted to write a book about how people could apply what we learned from our laboratory experiments to their day to day lives. I have always believed that social psychology was about how we live our lives and I never got any of that out of the textbooks. It always seemed a step removed.

When I first started to teach introductory social psychology at Harvard, my orientation was to teach these hot-shot premeds and physics majors that social psychology was indeed a science no less than biology or chemistry. I spent a lot of my energy in that effort, in a detailed way describing experiments in social psychology. I did this to combat their general attitude that social psychology was more or less interesting bullshit.

When I got to Texas, what I encountered in the students was not contemptuousness of social psychology as a science, but raw racism. I found myself behaving more like a missionary, recasting my lectures to more closely meet the needs of the current students. The scientific details became subservient to an attempt to vitalize the material on racism, sexism, aggression, war and attraction. I wanted to demonstrate it in their lives because I think I really wanted to change the students. I wanted them to be more tolerant, to be more thoughtful, to be more introspective and to get as excited as I was becoming about the notion that our attitudes and behavior are not all locked up by the time we are fifteen years old - that we can change ourselves and (within limits) become whoever we want to be. This is where my interest in teaching merged with my interest in t-groups; t-groups were not only teaching me things about human interaction but they were increasing my hopefulness about the possiblities of human potential, the possibility that adults could change - that we weren't locked into dungeons called personality.

And I wrote *The Social Animal* (1972). That book is my lectures. It is set up like: Here's a problem. There was a guy painting my house. We were arguing about the Vietnam war - he just came back from Vietnam - and I said, "Yeah, it is ok to make the world safe for democracy but a lot of women and children are getting napalmed over there. People are getting killed - innocent people." And he said, "Hell, doc, those aren't people, those are Vietnamese." *Here's* a problem! Here's a perfectly nice guy who had written a whole group of people out of the human race. How did he come to do that? Who taught him to do that? How did he learn that? And can it be unlearned - can you reverse that? Social psychologists must know about that stuff. It's not useful to think of it as a clinical problem. It's not useful to think of him as crazy; it's more useful to think of it as situationally determined.

And so you take the problem and work back to what do we know - from the laboratory, and then you build those bridges and you come out with a set of hypotheses that have internal validity. The next step is: Ok, how do you test the external validity? Well there is a sense in which the jigsaw classroom was an external validity check on a lot of the research I had been doing on social influence, persuasion, interpersonal attraction and things like that. Some of the mechanisms were different but as a general statement, that was my big venture into external validity. That was the first time I ever started with a problem to be solved. But in the book, I *always* start with problems because that is the hook; that is how I arouse the student's interest. They are not interested in Aronson and Mills, they are interested in - "Hey, here you start to help somebody change their flat tire and you end up really liking the person, how come?" From a didactic point of view, you are dealing with interaction, with live people, and the questions are stated in terms that are meaningful to people. The question should always precede the answer. What the hell do we want to sit there just throwing data at people for? Who cares?

When Aronson returned to Texas after his year away, he began his work on the jigsaw classroom (Aronson et al., 1978), which was an experimental procedure that took him out of the laboratory into the field. In this work, Aronson tackled the problem of racial prejudice in the classroom. By creating a learning situation which required interdependence rather than competitiveness, Aronson and his colleagues were successful at reducing prejudice and also showed that black and Mexican-American students increased substantially their classroom performance as well as their self esteem. Aronson said, "This series of field experiments combined my skills as an experimenter with my skills as a t-group leader; I couldn't have done it without both."

> The jigsaw classroom work was one of my favorite projects. But as an experimental procedure, it is the most pedestrian, boring thing I have ever done. It didn't require nearly the ingenuity of my laboratory experiments, but it was an experiment that succeeded in changing people and helping people with their lives directly. It was also true action research, i.e., a scientific discovery we could leave in the schools so it could continue after I left - for *that* the outcome was paramount. Because the results were so important it was the *data* that was the exciting thing, not the procedure. But unlike my laboratory experiments, the process of the jigsaw classroom experiment was an absolute bore. While I continue to do some research on jigsaw because I think it's important, I need to do other things as well, to avoid the boredom of that process.

In 1974, Aronson moved to his current position at UC Santa Cruz. He made the move in part because it is a beautiful place to live and work, in part because he was excited by the fact that the university was experimenting with new forms of undergraduate education, and in part because he wanted to expand his applied work in social psychology. At Texas he felt limited by a label that said, "experimental social psychologist." He said, "Most of the students coming to Texas expected me to be doing laboratory experiments and to train them to do it. But my interests simply weren't there. I still love the elegance of the laboratory experiment - but in the 1970's it wasn't what I felt like doing. The time seemed ripe to move on, to get re-potted."

Since moving to Santa Cruz, he has continued to do field experiments on issues involving the application of social psychological knowledge to social problems like race relations and the conservation of energy. He has spent some of his time working with policy-makers in Washington, trying to communicate the applicability of social psychological research to social problems.

> These guys need to be educated; they're not going to discover us on their own. Right now, policy decision are being made that have social psychological implications yet are based on the kind of bubba social psychology that economists and other policy makers assume they know. I enjoy trying to communicate with these guys. Actually, it's a three-step process. First, there is a finding from a laboratory experiment (either my own or someone else's), say, that commitment produces attitude change; then, I will perform a small field experiment with high external validity (like train an experimental group of energy auditors to exact greater commitment for conservation from homeowners, and show that these home owners conserve more energy than those audited by "control" auditors); then, I try to convince the policy-makers that they ought to pay attention to this stuff because it's not just some esoteric, academic finding, but it says something about how the human mind works and it checks out in the specific area they're making policy about.

In some of this work, he has collaborated with colleagues from other disciplines - such collaboration is made easy by the special structure of Santa Cruz, where the buildings and faculty are not organized along departmental lines.

> But every silver lining has a cloud: This is a small psychology department and there is no critical mass of experimental social psychologists here. There is no common philosophy that I share with *any* of my colleagues about what the research enterprise is all about. Because I am the only bona fide experimental social psychologist around here, I feel a little bit like I'm in a glass case in a natural history museum..."Oh look, Shirley, come see the

experimental social psychologist!" I have come to realize that it would be a great advantage to have at least one like-minded colleague; two people can create an electrical current. To some extent I can do this with my graduate students - but it's not easy.

But, I like the research I'm doing now because it's so varied. I get bored easily. For some of us old lab people, when we get bored we switch to doing lab experiments on a different topic. I think my boredom is more profound; I need to add a whole different activity. One of my best friends once characterized me as someone who doesn't know very much but who makes full use of what he *does* know. I'll cop to that one. I like combining things I know - and forming new entities in ways that surprise me. I always was excited about teaching social psychology - but I never thought I would combine that with my field experiments and become a teacher to policy makers, but there you have it. I love leading t-groups; and if it weren't for that skill, my experiments in desegregated classrooms might have been impossible. Some of my former students have expressed some regret about my having wandered away from the lab. And occasionally I miss the excitement that can only come from creating and conducting a first-rate laboratory experiment - but, what the hell, I need to follow my nose. And, you know, it turns out, that just about everything I've done is very Lewin-like; I sure as hell didn't plan it that way, but that seems to be how it's working out.

JUDSON MILLS

While Judson Mills was an undergraduate psychology major at Wisconsin, he developed a great interest in the work of Kurt Lewin. Mills said he audited a graduate seminar on Lewin's work which was taught by his advisor. In the fall of Mills' senior year, Leon Festinger came to give a talk at Wisconsin and Mills said he remembers being interested in the topic but it also interested him that Festinger had been a student of Lewin's. When it came time to decide on a graduate school, Mills said his advisor suggested he apply to Minnesota, which is where Festinger was at the time. He said, "I didn't go there to study with Festinger particularly, but when I took a course with him I was very impressed with him and also with Schachter who was there at the same time."

Mills said he quickly came to admire Festinger. "He had a penetrating insight into things, particularly in conversations. I admired his ability to think things through and state them clearly and the incisiveness of his thought." It became important to Mills to be recognized by Festinger and he remembers this made him anxious. Interacting with Festinger brought with it criticism.

> He had very few students. And he didn't really try to attract a lot of students, in my opinion. I had taken a seminar with him in the fall that was actually a course on research methods that Schachter normally taught but Schachter wasn't there so Festinger was teaching it. He was scheduled to teach a seminar in the winter quarter and I asked him if I could attend this seminar because I had to get his permission. He wasn't sure he wanted to let me in. I was very worried that he wouldn't let me in and I thought maybe that he didn't think I was doing well in his other seminar. I don't know how he knew that because we didn't have any exams or anything, but I wasn't one of the senior graduate students. Anyway, he *did* let me in the seminar and it turned out to be a very valuable experience. There were only two other people in

> the seminar, one of them was a postdoctoral fellow and the other was Jack Brehm. During this seminar was when Festinger was writing the first version of dissonance theory. I guess it was then when I became so impressed with him.

Mills said the way Festinger liked to work was to discuss ideas with them. "He would give some ideas - like read this paper, what do you think are the implications of it and so forth." The students would then try to come up with interesting material which he would then react to. For example, in that winter seminar with just three students, according to Mills, Festinger said, "Look for the implications of this (dissonance) theory in different areas of social psychology." Mills said he was interested in the topic of prejudice and examined that literature for material. He said, "I found some things which Festinger hadn't found which he then incorporated in the book."

> One of them was a study on the effect of integrated vs. segregated housing projects on interracial attitudes. I remember reporting on this in the seminar and Festinger said, "Well, you are not giving the right data." And I said, "Well, that's the data." He said, "Oh that can't be right." And he grabbed the book out of my hand and he looked through it to find what he thought was the way they should have analyzed their data. It turned out they didn't analyze it that way, I was right. But he thought they must have because that was the way *he* would have analyzed it and so he blamed me for not presenting the data they should have presented. Well then, he finally admitted I was right. He rarely admitted losing an argument.
>
> And he was always, at that time anyway, very very critical. The thing that I remember which was such a powerful educational experience was that if anybody said anything that could be criticized, Festinger would do it. And so one learned to be very careful about thinking before speaking and being able to formulate a plausible argument before trying to make it. People who were not very clear

> thinkers were usually humiliated. He was *so good* and he had such insight about important things, he knew how to do it so well that being faced with his criticism was something you benefited from. If you continued, you learned how to anticipate that kind of criticism...you couldn't anticipate everything he would say. I learned a lot about how to think clearly from trying to anticipate what he might say.
>
> He had a technique of arguing by ridiculous example. He would say, "Well you are saying so and so - right?" And you would say, "Yeah." And he would say, "Well, if what you are saying is true wouldn't you agree with this?" And then he would construct a situation which would seem to represent the principle which you just espoused but which was obviously absurd. No one could really agree with it but it would seem like what you had just said would lead you to predict that. That was a very common way of arguing in these seminars as I remember.
>
> Also, when people wanted to have him approve their research, the student would get an idea and go talk to him about it. Usually they would be very careful to think it through but he could still find something wrong with it. So a lot of the training came in conversations in his office about research projects. That was a seminar-like experience but it was not a formal class. He had a typical kind of reaction of arguing by example and usually to demolish your position and he wasn't very nice about it. But that was the value of it. If he told us it was good, we knew it was good because he wouldn't do it unless he meant it. He didn't praise us without reason.

Even though Festinger's reaction to a student idea would most often be very critical, Mills said, "He listened and was very attentive to people who were interested in things he was interested in and whom he had some interest in having do research. So he paid very close attention and gave very careful criticism. He was trying to get the ideas clear." This was important because the students were a part of Festinger's own research effort, which was integral to the development of his theory. Festinger set very high standards for his own work and when he reacted to the work of others, he didn't compromise those standards. Mills said he thought this style was very effective in "stimulating whatever abilities people had."

During his second year, Mills had an assistantship and worked on a project with Festinger. He said, "I was always very interested in how he was evaluating my work." He remembers it as "an intense intellectual experience." Mills also remembers being disappointed that Festinger didn't talk about Lewin.

> I expected that he would share some experiences he had had as a student and that there would be sort of a feeling of being part of a tradition that was associated with Lewin. But I don't remember anything like that. Festinger was very interested in what *he* was doing.

When Festinger left Minnesota for Stanford, Mills followed. He said, "I was lucky to be a student of his. I just happened to go to Minnesota and just happened to be around at the time when he went to Stanford. I was there at the right time." Once at Stanford, Mills was Festinger's only student at first.

> It wasn't a sense of thinking, "Well this is going to be good for my career to be a student of Festinger's." I don't think people who thought that way would have lasted because the degree to which it would seem like it would benefit you wasn't that clear and the difficulties were immediately obvious. He was very good at sensing motivation. A student who went there not because they were interested in the ideas but just wanted to be a student of his, I think he would not have been interested in teaching them. You had to be really bound up with the topic.

During the academic year 1955-56 Festinger was at the Behavioral Sciences Center at Stanford. where he wrote his book on cognitive dissonance (Festinger, 1957). He joined the faculty in the

Stanford psychology department the following year. Mills said, "It was a very small faculty, but a very distinguished faculty. They had very few people but they were almost all well known. They had many people who were past presidents of the APA so they had a very distinguished group. Festinger wasn't the *star* of the faculty at that time."

Festinger continued his seminar at Stanford. Mills remembers it being like a course except they met at Festinger's house in the evening. He said, "I remember going to his house and Newcomb was there once and Kelley and various visiting social psychologists would show up."

Mills said overall Festinger didn't have a lot of students. The students he did train all knew each other fairly well. He said, "An analogy that I later remember thinking was very appropriate was that it is like the training of artists. If you want to do something like what someone who is very good is doing, you find the best person and you go there and apprentice - you work with them and learn from them." Mills went on, "As with the training of artists, hopefully people who are successfully trained will go beyond what they did in school."

He remembered the students complaining about Festinger's expectations of how much work they should do. He said, "The expectations were not just to be in the lab, the expectations were - the study was to be done by a certain time, why isn't it done?"

Mills said for about ten years after leaving graduate school he did more field studies than laboratory experiments but since then he has concentrated on laboratory work. He said he believes that the laboratory is "where the best test of a theoretical idea is, and that is something that follows from my training logically but was not in a sense taught me directly." He pointed out that while he was at Minnesota, Festinger, Schachter and Riecken were doing the participant observation study which resulted in the book *When Prophecy Fails* (Festinger, Riecken & Schachter, 1956).

Training students

Mills said he is greatly influenced by the interests of his students. He has done experimental work on reactions to people with a physical disability which was an interest he shared with a student. "I have worked on a distinction between communal and exchange relationships, which was something that evolved gradually, but it really only took off when I had a student (Peggy Clark) who was interested," he said. He contrasted this style with that of fellow graduate student Jack Brehm who has a particular theoretical interest and whose students work on it with him.

At Maryland, where he has been teaching since 1971, Mills said that first year students coming in are all advised about courses by one faculty member. Later they chose the person they want to work on research with. When a student comes to him with an interest in doing research, he said, "I usually try to find something we have in common. Usually they would know that they wanted me to be their advisor because they had been my assistant or had been associated with me on some set project." He discourages students from coming to him with a project because he believes they should develop a project together.

> My idea is that it is a collaboration and that they learn from working with me on it. That is how I learned as a graduate student. In a sense I try to repeat that aspect of my experience but I am not quite so directive about it. I don't have *one* theory that I am working on that every study is about.
>
> To the extent that I have been good at training graduate students it is because I give them a tremendous amount of personal attention - in different ways maybe than Festinger did. Festinger gave a lot of attention to planning and development of the procedure and also the details. If it wasn't working quite right, we would sit down and look at the data and think about how to change things. But I give students much more help in the writing.

Mills teaches an undergraduate class on experimental method in social psychology and has given the process a great deal of thought. One of the examples he used to explain how he believes it should be taught is to compare doing research with learning a card game. "It is better to have them play a few hands and then explain the rules." He believes it is better to have students do some experiments and then start talking about the rules - the concrete experience helps them grasp the rules. Also, he believes it is impossible to explain *all* the rules before the game starts.

> You play a few hands and then you explain the rules. And then something happens and we say, "Oh, that's a new thing we didn't tell you about before." And so gradually you introduce the rules in the context.
>
> The basic philosophy I use in my course is the philosophy I talked about before in terms of apprenticeship. I have a son who goes to a Montessori school - it's learning by doing. You go from the concrete to the abstract. Well, that's the principle I use in my class and that sort of fits in with the idea: you play a few hands and then we will talk about the rules. So we don't give them a whole set of rules about how to do it at the beginning. We start doing it and then we talk about how to do it.

Mills also teaches his students that designing experiments is like solving a chinese puzzle box - each stage leads to a new puzzle. Beginning with the choice of dependent variable, he leads his students through the procedure of designing an experiment that fits together. He likened it to a woman dressing for a party. He said, "She might start with a particular dress and then she might look to see what shoes she should wear with that or what gloves, jewelry, handbag and so on. And she might wind up wearing a different dress because she keeps trying things on - they all have to fit together. So one of the challenges of designing this kind of experiment is that we have to keep a number of things about the procedure in mind at once." These elements include good manipulations, good dependent measures and a good cover story if it is a deception experiment. He said, "There is a lot of originality or puzzle solving to every stage, so that when we go from the conceptualization stage to the design of the procedure there is still a great opportunity for originality and creativity." He doesn't believe everything about an experiment has to be original. "One can learn a lot from solving the puzzles which come from puzzles others have solved."

> I tell students that it is not unusual for people to work on their advisor's hypotheses. It may be a good idea. Like Jack Brehm did his dissertation on a hypothesis Festinger suggested to him. I don't think of it as an indication of Brehm's inability to be creative that he got his idea for his dissertation from Festinger. He learned a lot doing that, he learned how to implement the idea. Then he became a theorist in his own right. Not everybody is as good as Brehm, but the idea is that one would get this training and it wouldn't somehow be stultifying that one wouldn't just keep doing the same thing over and over again. It's important that one would want to go beyond and be original. I think people sometimes feel - students feel like they have got to do it all on their own to demonstrate that they are creative, and they don't get this learning experience which is really, in my opinion, the foundation. It is necessary for their creativity to flourish.

He described the process of designing the Aronson-Mills (1959) experiment while he was at Stanford as an example of the kind of creativity he means. He said, "That experiment is probably better known than it should be for a couple of reasons. One, it does have this *cute* feature. The other is that it is easy for introductory students to latch onto and understand. It is a nice study for teaching purposes because it was one of those studies where the procedure was cleverly designed. Not just that the manipulation was cute but that everything kind of worked in the sense of fitting together - like the woman dressing. It provides a nice example of how to do that kind of thing." He said the "cute" manipulation - reading a list of dirty words as an analog of an initiation rite - wasn't chosen because it was "cute" but because it was the only thing they could think of that seemed to work.

I remember very well sitting down in a room in the basement of the psychology department. We knew we wanted to test this hypothesis and we wanted to get something which was analogous to a severe initiation. I remember that we divided up the roles very explicitly - maybe it just happened. In teaching people I say there are two roles, one is the production of ideas and the other is the criticizing, the evaluation stage and sometimes you have to divide them up because if you start criticizing too soon, you stop the flow of ideas. So I remember in that case, I was playing the role of the critic and Aronson was playing the role of the idea spouter, which he is better at and I am better at being a critic. Anyway, it was a natural division of labor. I remember he said, "Well, lets do this..." and I said, "No, that's no good" and I remember he must have said twenty different things and I didn't like any of them. Then he said "Well, let's have them read a list of dirty words." And I said, "That's it! Good." There is another rule which I have - that the first idea is usually not the best idea. We went through many ideas.

We picked reading a list of dirty words not because we had a whole lot of ideas and it was the "cutest" one. It was the *only* one that seemed like it would do a good job in the context that we were working in. There was a playfulness at the time. I can't remember what Elliot said - at least twenty or thirty different things that I said were no good, but they were, some of them were, humorous. We were having fun while we were talking about it. We enjoyed the process and I think that *is* important - that one feel comfortable about doing it but that's different from when I was a student. I didn't enjoy talking to Festinger about my ideas, but sitting around with Aronson thinking about an experiment - I enjoyed that. That is the most enjoyable part of research.

Mills believes the current emphasis on course work in graduate education detracts somewhat from the kind of informal interaction he was describing. There was very little emphasis placed on coursework when he was a graduate student. In fact when he began to teach, he realized he had never had a course in social psychology from Festinger.

> I didn't know what he thought social psychology was, so I had to use textbooks by people who I thought were intellectually inferior to Festinger because they had written them where Festinger never gave us an overview of the field. He never lectured on social psychology - he would just tell us what he was thinking. We never missed that. I don't think we lost anything - that would have been taking time away from the really important learning. I have no regrets about the way I was taught. It was a difficult period but I can't think of a better way to have someone do it.

He said, "We are dealing with a whole different situation now in social psychology than existed thirty years ago. We have so many more social psychologists, so many more graduate training programs. Thirty years ago there weren't that many places to study social psychology and it was a highly selected group of people in terms of motivation of students and so on. We have just as many good people nowadays but they are spread out in a hundred locations. It has become more bureaucratized and there is more of a set definition of what students should know."

> I don't think Festinger set out to train students. He set out to do good work and if a student came along and wanted to do it with him, because they wanted to do good work too and have his approval, they got training as a result. When we were in graduate school, I don't remember saying, "I better sign up for research credits with Festinger because I will get some training out of it." Most of the time we didn't get research credit. Festinger was not very concerned about grades. I remember the first course I ever took with him, he said - and I was amazed because I was a beginning graduate student

> - he said, "well, I am not going to worry about grades in this course, I will give everybody an A." But we worked very hard anyway because we wanted his approval. It wasn't that we had to do it for credit. Maybe it was because we wanted to show Festinger that we could do it. And then that was a kind of credit.

Mills said he thought this kind of system could only work with someone like Leon Festinger who was someone whose respect was clearly worth having.

Looking back, Mills said his current interests in values and attitudes are the same ones that attracted him to social psychology originally. He thinks the field has shifted, "and some of those things that I think are central to the enterprise are not as important in what people seem to be considering the most exciting work, as they were when I first entered the field."

> I think part of what made me able to be a Festinger student was a combination of objective open mindedness - I had to listen - but also I had a stubborn kind of ability to be independent. It is hard to describe how those things fit together but you have to be able to listen and learn and at the same time not be swayed so easily by what happens to be popular.

LEON FESTINGER

Leon Festinger became a psychologist, in part, because he had run out of sciences. As an undergraduate at City College of New York, he knew he wanted to be a scientist and it was only a question of which kind.

> When I went to college, I was pretty sure I wanted to major in some science. I took a couple of physics courses and they were absolutely dreadful. They bored me. I took some chemistry courses and that was even worse - it was just cookbook. So, by the time I got to my junior year I was becoming concerned about what I was going to do. You have to understand the mentality of people who grew up in the depression.
>
> For a month or so I scoured around in the library, reading books about this science or that science. There was one book in particular, by Clark Hull, which made psychology seem interesting, fascinating, and amenable to experimentation. So I decided to try psychology.
>
> I took an introductory course in psychology, which of course was as bad as the introductory physics courses I had taken and as bad as chemistry, but by that time it was too late. And so I majored in psychology.

While attending CCNY, he encountered Max Hertzman, who introduced Festinger to the work of Kurt Lewin. His first publication was an experiment with Hertzman on Lewin's concept of level of aspiration (Hertzman & Festinger, 1940). After finishing his degree, Festinger "went to Iowa because Kurt Lewin was there." Lewin was not in the psychology department at Iowa but in the Child Welfare Research Station there. Festinger said,

"Because I wanted to work with Kurt Lewin, I registered at the Child Welfare Research Station. So technically my Ph.D. is in child psychology - although I never saw a child," he smiled.

When Festinger arrived at Iowa, he again worked on level of aspiration. "Every student and even every new Ph.D. just wants to do the last study he did, better. And my masters thesis was again on level of aspiration," he explained. According to Festinger, he and Lewin "argued a lot. We didn't agree on a lot of things." This was partly because Lewin was no longer engrossed in the kind of work that had attracted Festinger to Iowa. Festinger was interested in Lewin's earlier work - on "level of aspiration, the Ziegarnik effect, resumption of interrupted tasks and all that kind of theoretical thinking he had done about it." By the time Festinger arrived at Iowa, "there had been a big shift of interest and his *major* interest was centered on social psychology and on practical problems," he recalled. "That wasn't my interest, practical problems have never interested me. And that remained a division at MIT."

While he was at Iowa, Festinger also took a course from Spence who was in the psychology department. "It was essentially an individual study and I did a rat experiment. But I enjoyed doing that rat experiment." He smiled, "It is a lot easier than working with humans."

Festinger said Lewin didn't spend much time in the laboratory. "He was involved," he said, "he would sometimes observe what was going on and we had continual discussions with him about it, but he was not, himself, spending much time in the lab." He contrasted this with the way he and Stanley Schachter later worked with their own students. "We are in the lab with the student and the project is as much theirs as ours." But he said he isn't sure this is the important issue.

> I think the important thing for the student is the atmosphere of research and ideas. What Kurt Lewin understood *very* well, and what he communicated to people who worked with him, was the relationship between theory and the empirical world - which *lot's* of people who do research don't understand and don't ever grasp. There's a sense of

> what is an important problem as compared to what is a trivial problem which is something you can't teach - you can show by example. And the sense of excitement gets communicated. I got a great deal from him.

Festinger earned his Ph.D. in three years. "I rushed it primarily because of the war," he said.

He claimed to be "one of the original draft dodgers. I can't imagine myself in a uniform - with a gun." Festinger received a series of deferrals because of his academic work. After completing his degree, he was again deferred in order to teach in the Army Specialized Training Program. "It might have been 'war relevant' but in my opinion, the best thing I could have done to help the United States to win the war was to stay out of the army."

> The army was drafting people with masters degrees, even people with graduate work beyond their masters degrees and, not very surprisingly, they didn't know what to do with them. So they established the program called the Army Specialized Training Program (ASTP) and they sent groups of these people to various universities to take courses.

One such group came to Iowa and Festinger taught them statistics. When the ASTP ended, he moved to the University of Rochester and worked as a statistician for the Committee on Selection and Training of Aircraft Pilots and was again deferred from the draft.

As the war wound down, Kurt Lewin was organizing the Research Center for Group Dynamics at MIT and he invited Festinger, along with Ronald Lippitt, Dorwin Cartwright and Marian Radke to come as faculty. Festinger also received an offer to return to Iowa as an assistant professor, but he chose to go to MIT. As soon as the war was over, the group assembled in Cambridge.

At MIT:

"I became a social psychologist by fiat, when I went to MIT," Festinger said. "Before, I had done work on level of aspiration and my Ph.D. thesis was really a mathematical theory of decision processes and some psychophysical experiments testing it. Then for quite a while I worked on mathematical statistics and when I came to MIT, by fiat, I was made a social psychologist."

As a faculty member, Festinger was involved in student selection for the Group Dynamics program. He believes the students who came were attracted not only to Kurt Lewin but also to "what the Research Center was about."

> There weren't a huge number of applicants. It was brand new and about the only people who applied to come were the people who had somehow heard about it and it suited them. We didn't take "just anybody" but my memory is that we took a high proportion of those who applied. But it was a very specialized, highly self-selected group. And it was a collection of *very* very able, talented people we had there. It was largely self selection - I don't think anybody *knows* how to do selection that is that good.

Except for Lewin himself, the students and faculty were very close in age. "The only reason I was an assistant professor and they were graduate students was because they didn't have the courage to stay out of the army," he smiled.

From the time of their arrival, students were immersed in research projects. "The training environment was very simple. From the very beginning, students started doing research - working with faculty members on research projects. Teaching went on, of course, but teaching was virtually a secondary activity," Festinger recalled.

During this time, Kurt Lewin was engrossed in Action Research. There was research on training groups, and studies on prejudice for the Commission for Community Interrelations (CCI) which was based in New York. While Lewin was engaged in these activities, Festinger and several of the graduate students were working on the Westgate housing studies which led to a series of laboratory and field studies on informal social communication (Festinger et al., 1950). Festinger said he was "much more interested in, developing theory and opening up new areas."

> I think if you just stay in the laboratory all the time, there is no way you are not going to get barren. Because the only thing you are going to learn out of a laboratory experiment is what you put into it. You are not going to see the effect of any variables that you didn't insert. You are not going to find out about any interactions that might be interesting because you have purified the thing so that you can see whether or not what you are looking for is there. I have *always* wanted to go back and forth between laboratory studies and studies in the real world. Field studies, if you will. The field studies were not being done for a practical purpose. They were being done to clarify theory and get hunches and that kind of thing. The Westgate studies have no practical purpose. We did later studies, like *When Prophecy Fails* (Festinger et al, 1956) for the same kind of reason. But again, there is no practical orientation, that isn't what fascinates me.

Beyond MIT: Festinger's Style

One of Festinger's students called him the father of experimental social psychology. While at MIT, Festinger began to refine his style of laboratory experimentation. One of the hallmarks of this style is a concentration on the experience of the subject - to take exquisite care that the subject is experiencing what the experimenters are interested in investigating, in order that the data be meaningful. This requires the talents of a playwright. "Even though you may have to contrive an artificial or semi-barren situation, you want that situation to be real and important to the subject," he said.

He said one could argue that experimental social psychology started at Iowa with Lewin and the notion of taking, "*very complicated* social processes into the laboratory. While the autocratic/democratic atmosphere studies (Lewin, Lippitt & White, 1939) weren't highly controlled, at least they attempted to deal with complex problems and issues like that. But you want control over the situation, which means you have to do a lot of work."

> The process of creating science - creating new knowledge, is no different than the process of creating any art. I think it is the same thing. The process of creating science is not what makes something scientific. What makes something scientific is the product that you have created and its replicability. Having and idea and executing the idea - that's an art.

Training Students:

Festinger claims he doesn't think anybody really knows how to select students - on paper. Only by working with someone that can there be some basis for selection. He believes, "Every student I never had was self selected." He said, "I suspect that because of the way I behaved and because I maintained a rather closely knit group, that I was somewhat difficult to approach." He thinks a lot of students were frightened of him, and "those who got past all that were self-selected." Occasionally, he said, a student would be "encouraged to work with someone else." He thinks he was probably a "little too dictatorial," for his lab to be characterized as a "family business." But he said it wasn't a platoon either.

> It always amazed me when later on, many years later - I discovered from talking with them that they didn't all love each other, that they weren't all close friends. To me they looked like they were all close friends.

Beyond this, he said, "in what I consider the proper atmosphere for research and for training people to do research, you have no alternative but to be task oriented. It is like you have no alternative but to wake up in the morning." But the content of the training process itself is elusive.

> There are some people who never seem to grasp the idea of what is a theory that is empirically relevant - or never seem to grasp the fact that when they get down to trying to do an experiment they have reduced the thing to trivia. I guess the reason they are unteachable is because they don't learn from what is going on and because nobody is trying to teach them. I think you would have the same difficulty understanding or asking questions about anything where you can't teach it in words, the only way you can learn it is by an apprenticeship and that is what was carried on.

In addition to the apprentice role, Festinger believes it is important for students to have "good people at their own level," - that all the other students be as talented and involved as possible. "It helps create a culture," he said.

Weekly research meetings, usually in the evenings, have always been a key part of the research process for Festinger. The style of meeting was adopted from Lewin's Quasselstrippe and are, he said, "the major way everyone knew what everyone else was doing. Everybody got their say about everything and sometimes the arguments were very illuminating." These meetings were known by his students, and *their* students as "The Tuesday Night Meeting" -although no one can remember whether they were ever on Tuesday night or not. "That's not what was precious," he smiled.

"All the work I ever did with my students was really collaboration. In a very real sense, these were really collaborations," he said. While the thesis was the student's responsibility primarily, it was often carried out in the context of Festinger's research program. "Everybody in the lab was working together - collaborating."

> I don't think I pulled status on people, although there obviously was a status differential and it must have had an impact. I was always in the lab and always looking down everybody's throat because if

> I am vitally concerned with an experiment, I am not going to turn that experiment over to a first or second year student who is still relatively inexperienced without looking over his back all the time. Because if I turn it over to him, what comes out is going to be the product of his talent and his talent may not be fully realized yet, or may be limited and so, of course, I was always around.

In 1968 Festinger left Stanford and social psychology for The New School for Social Research and work in perception, later in archeology, and now in history. Commenting on the current situation in social psychology he smiled and said, "I have left the field and now I am looking back and being objective."

> It seems to me that today it is highly diverted. The reasons are probably many and varied, but I don't think countless studies based on paper and pencil answers to questions upon which to infer information processes will be of great import. In a sense I am talking about a lot of things. I don't think real problems are being addressed. I think attribution theory was one terrible mistake and a snare and a delusion. I mean, for one thing it wasn't a theory and why it dragged the field with it, I don't know. And to what extent people want to do paper and pencil studies because they are easier and quicker and you can get more publications - the assistant professor needs a lot of publications to get tenure - I don't know but it is unfortunate.
>
> Every time I pick up a social psychology journal it seems to me ninety percent of it is cognitive information processing - as if the main thing a human does is process information. And every time somebody can discover a way in which the results of this information processing do not correspond to a rational model, there is big joy at this great discovery.

Current Work and Collaborations:

He said that apart from students, he hasn't collaborated much. However, he still collaborates informally with Stanley Schachter. He believes, "The major thing that permits collaboration are the similarities involved. For a real collaboration that is a real working together, I think you have to have people who really bring the same things to the task but from slightly different viewpoints and with slightly different talents."

Recently Festinger has been "learning medieval history." He believes that the events of medieval period had a profound impact in shaping our present culture. "There are," he said, "many kinds of historians. There are some who are content to simply recount facts from the past as accurately and as exactly as they can. There are others who really think the task of an historian is to understand and explain what happened. There are still others who think the task of an historian is to shed light from history onto contemporary work." It is this last way of being a historian which interests him.

He currently doesn't work with graduate students, but would "if there were any good ones who were interested in what I am interested in." The way he works now, however, would make it difficult for collaboration with a student. "I spend a huge part of my time now reading, talking to specialists and there is no way I can have somebody else help me with it.

> I have now run a number of four or five day meetings of small groups of historians which is a wonderful technique for getting a personal tutorial out of them. The people I brought together do *very* different kinds of history but they know things I want to learn.

Before he became interested in history, he spent about four and a half years writing a book on archeology. He said, "I think it is a book on social psychology, but I don't think there are any psychologists who would agree. What I have been doing the past six years is really trying to look at very large questions - to try to get some new ideas about the nature of man and how our societies and behavior patterns have evolved."

"Pursuing these things is very enjoyable for me because I love learning new things. I do have ideas about them." He expects to spend about another three years learning about the medieval world and will then move on. "Just so long as I am enjoying the process, I am quite happy," he said.

Festinger claims to be driven by "pleasure and excitement." "I have a very low tolerance for boredom," he explained. He continued, "I don't think there is any greater excitement than from internal generation of ideas. It is a very exciting thing to have an idea that seems to be panning out."

Having Ideas:

Festinger said he doesn't think there is a "single good research person in the world, in any field, who isn't periodically *totally* depressed and sure he will never have another idea." Gradually, he said, the researcher learns to respect the fact that ideas can't be forced and it may take several months but an idea *will* come. He continued. "I think one can also develop a sense of 'Well, I will have other ideas but not about *this* topic.'" This gentle respect for ideas includes how they are treated once they happen.

> I have known many people who are so talented analytically and bright enough so that they immediately kill any idea they have. You know, if an idea starts it is going to be a very fragile thing. And it is probably going to remain fragile for a long time. If I have an idea, it is only at some later time that I turn self-critical, but I don't turn self-critical very early. People who *do* turn self-critical early, who are *always* critical - as critical of themselves as of other people - nothing emerges.
>
> I don't think the process by which ideas occur to the scientist and the process by which ideas occur to a poet, an artist or a novelist are different. I don't think the process of inventing or visualizing a way of expressing the idea is any different. In the case

> of a scientist, he has to devise some way in which he can get that idea to be related to the empirical world, and where the empirical world can be induced to show evidence of whether the idea is right or wrong. A painter has to do the same kind of thing. A painter may have an idea and can't find a way to express it on canvas. It is in those processes that I think there is very little distinction between what a scientist does and what an artist does. The techniques are very very different, of course. But I suspect that the applying of that technique is the reason that ninety five percent of the time of some scientists and artists and poets is spent in chore-like activity - it's just a lot of hard work.

Summing up, he said:

> If you want my opinion about why so many people at MIT and so many of my students and so many of Stan's students have turned out to continue doing research - even the one's who aren't terribly talented at it - it is because they entered and remained in a psychotic environment. They are afflicted with a psychosis - doing research is what you *do*. You become involved in it, addicted to it, and it just becomes a way of life. In places where that doesn't happen, students don't emerge dedicated to doing research.
>
> The leadership has to create it. It helps a lot if you have a number of good, talented students but the person who is running the lab and running the training has to provide the excitement and the ideas and guide it and encourage the students to interact.

CONCLUSION

The twenty years after Lewin's death provided a cultural environment that included a great expansion of the universities. Social psychology was a developing enterprise fueled by grant money. Departments of psychology added social psychologists to their staffs - many of them trained by Lewinians.

Today, the Research Center for Group Dynamics remains in a research institute (The Institute for Social Research) and functions as one. These researchers, supported by grants, are only peripherally associated with the academic department at the University of Michigan. Dorwin Cartwright and Alvin Zander spent the balance of their careers in that challenging environment.

Leon Festinger, and later some of his students, worked by defining themselves as scientists within the larger framework of traditional academic departments. They established their tight-knit labs, selected their students carefully, and continued their research. To this traditional scientific form they added such Lewinian touches as task-centered collegiality and the Quasselstrippe. They also contributed their own sensitivity to the aesthetics of the scientific enterprise. This last was a critical contribution to social psychology as it developed over the twenty years after Lewin's death.

Scientists and Professors:

Leon Festinger and his students, taking seriously the "scientist" in social scientist, conducted research in the way of all scientists. They would create a micro-environment within the larger academic department. What was unusual about this was that, rather than simply running rats, they were conducting research on complex social phenomena in the laboratory. Work was carried out by the small, tightly-knit research teams within the traditional academic structure - much the way Lewin operated at MIT. In fact, this pattern began even within the group at MIT - with the Westgate studies conducted by Leon Festinger (Festinger et al., 1950). By the time the Research Center for Group Dynamics moved to Michigan, "Leon's boys" were a self-acknowledged group within the Center.

One of Leon's boys was Stanley Schachter, who took this structure and added to it some of Clark Hull's teaching techniques. Elliot Aronson operated in a similar manner. At Harvard, he had the "little house on Bow Street" and so was even physically separate from the Department.

This "research center mini-culture" style contrasts with another, more common, way of training graduate students in social psychology described by some of the men interviewed. In the research center mini-culture, training of students never interfered with the product. Leon Festinger said "of course" he was always looking over the shoulders of the students. It was to make sure the research wasn't compromised by someone whose "talent might not yet be fully realized." Research is labor intensive and any student who was talented enough and tough enough would get the best training possible. But the product was always scientific understanding, not Ph.D.'s.

In contrast, there is the perspective (often expressed at a departmental level) that the education of the student is to be taken seriously. John Thibaut said the departmental attitude at North Carolina was one of "abjuring ownership" of students. Judson Mills said that he is influenced by the interests of students and tries to collaborate with them on a mutually arrived at topic. Ned Jones said he works within a broad enough framework to offer students a variety of topics they might be interested in. Others have theoretical interests that make it difficult for ambitious students to gain the necessary publications and so work with few graduate students. The perspective expressed by these men is that of educating the graduate student - These men are being professors. It is not that they have not produced excellent students - They produce them in a different way.

Being an Apprentice:

To begin with, all of these operations were made possible by research grants which allowed students to be hired as assistants. As with Lewin, in each of the labs - those established by Festinger and some of his students - graduate students were engaged immediately in research. They were allowed to stay or encouraged to move on based on their performance - the analog of Lewin's relating to people according to how the person related to the task at hand.

Selecting Students: The Audition

The criterion for selecting students was always the student's ability to facilitate work in the lab. Students who wanted to do their own research or weren't blessed with some of the special abilities needed for the research, were encouraged to work with other people in the department. This is why Jerome Singer said "a department can't exist with Stanleys or Leons entirely." Leon Festinger said he doesn't think anyone knows how to select students on paper - only by working with someone can there be some basis for selection. Students were, in a sense, auditioned for the part.

Festinger said of Lewin's MIT group, "It was largely self selection - I don't think anyone *knows* how to do selection that is that good." Perhaps not, but Stanley Schachter comes close. Neil Grunberg described in detail his 45 minute interview with Schachter which motivated him to override his negative experience with social psychology at Stanford and opt to join Schachter's lab.

When Schachter interviews incoming students, he describes his research and asks, "And what did I find." In this way, he is able to probe a student's ability to think problems through, to address questions, and to think about research. This gives him some intuition about whether the student would fit - cognitively - into his style of working. Schachter's seminars are run in a similar way. He formulates the research process as a matter of, "Look, here are the facts so far, what has to follow next, what will illuminate this, how do we understand it." He said that once they get to this point, they are "*all* in virgin territory, and I am no better than they are at getting good ideas as to how we might want to test this or what could be the variable." The other criterion Schachter has, he said, is: "First, I have got to like them - if I don't like them, then the whole thing isn't going to work. Obviously they need a *minimum* of ability in this domain, but my first requirement, I think, is I have got to like them"

Not surprisingly, there is a strong family feeling within the groups - within the individual groups as well as the larger network of Lewinian students. Part of this is explained by Jerome Singer's comment about Festinger and Schachter that "they don't pick a student out because they have a theory about what is going to make the student good. They do it because, 'This is the only kind of person I can be around...'" He concluded, "They are looking for students, in a sense, who they can enjoy as friends when the studentship is over." Other Schachter students spoke of "intellectual offspring" and "the padrone system." This attitude was confirmed by Stanley Schachter when he said, "I must concede I have great pride in my students. I think they have great pride, I don't know about affection..." He continued by explaining that he did everything he could to see that each of his students got the best job available at the time. And then he "hounds" them to publish their thesis. Finally, "They almost invariable will come back the first year or two to just tell me what they are doing. The second year they start telling me where I was wrong and by the fifth year, they are on their own. I watch them very closely, I am very fond of them - I pay close attention. So does Leon."

Schachter's lab was described by a colleague as a "family business." Leon Festinger said he thought he was "probably a little bit too dictatorial" for his lab to be characterized as a family business. But he described it as close-knit and told of his surprise when he later learned that his students hadn't all been fast friends.

Choosing Experience over Topic:

The students selected for these labs were chosen on the basis of talents they had to offer the research task. But why did the student select the training environment? Aronson was tapped by Leon

Festinger after completing a seminar. He said that even though Festinger had a reputation as a "killer," he could "see the riches." Judson Mills was mildly interested in Festinger's connection with Lewin, but after working with him, wanted to stay because he came to admire him. Jerome Singer was recommended to Schachter by his friends. Lee Ross went to Columbia to work with Schachter, chose another advisor and came to regret it. He moved to Schachter "with much pain and discomfort." Neil Grunberg enjoyed Schachter's interview. In none of these cases was the choice on the part of the student based on the topic being studied in the lab. In fact Lee Ross's first adviser had been chosen because of common interest in a topic. He came to feel that he had made a mistake.

This attitude of valuing style over subject was best expressed by Lee Ross when he discussed his wanting to move into Schachter's lab. He said the members of Schachter's lab were the people who became his friends. Ross found he was having ideas about their work and not his own. He said, "I felt that for some reason or other the kinds of studies that Stanley was doing and the way he was conceiving of the problem made us think of exciting possibilities but it wasn't that I had any abiding interest in obesity - I wasn't fat, I didn't know anybody who was fat, I didn't *care* about fat..." This flies in the face of current wisdom about interest matching when it comes to student selection into graduate programs.

The Tuesday Night Meeting:

There was one important aspect of the Festinger training environment that evolved from Kurt Lewin. It was the Quasselstrippe. In Leon Festinger's hands it became known as the Tuesday Night Meeting. Festinger met regularly with his lab and discussed research. By some accounts, these meetings would be at Festinger's home where they would meet, drink beer and discuss the research. Kurt Back described such meetings of "Leon's boys" as early as Michigan.

As far back as the Quasselstrippe in Lewin's time, these meetings were designed to solve problems encountered on the various projects, to generate ideas, and to interpret data. Although they later became became known as the Tuesday Night Meeting, even Leon Festinger can't remember whether they were ever held on Tuesday night or not. "That's not what was precious," he said.

Other Lewin students established such meetings. John Thibaut instituted the Organizational Research Group at North Carolina which he said was consciously modeled on the Quasselstrippe. Ned Jones told of Jack Brehm, a Festinger Ph.D., coming to him at Duke and saying, "You know, our students don't know how to do research, there is something wrong." He told Jones about the Tuesday Night Meetings and they decided to try them. Jones reported that it was "just amazing...it just took off. It was the smartest thing we ever did." Kurt Back told the same story. Elliot Aronson held Tuesday Night Meetings everywhere he worked before moving to Santa Cruz.

The key was that the meetings were always for idea generation and problem solving. Several people noted that among other things this served to undercut the defensiveness of those presenting. Many of Lewin's students started such meetings but in many places they evolved into colloquia with the presentation of finished research as the focus. This happened at Michigan as the Research Center grew.

Festinger and Schachter:

Many of the men interviewed mentioned the importance of the apprenticeship system. For Festinger students it was aided by the heuristic value of Festinger's theories. For Schachter students, the apprenticeship arrangement is supplemented by Schachter's tenacious question-following style. In both cases the highest possible standards were set. Stanley Schachter has managed nearly to institutionalize the best aspects of the master-apprentice relationship with his style of leading students through to the edge of his thinking and then soliciting their ideas. He said that he felt there was no point in doing research if he already knows the answer. In an act of intellectual generosity, Schachter's students are invited into his thought processes. Later, this allows them to build on and adapt the imprinted patterns to whatever problems interest them. He involves them in all phases of the process - including the all important question forming stage.

Neil Grunberg emphasized the importance of the question asked. Often that question was "*So*?" This is similar to Robert Krauss's lesson from Murray Horwitz. Horwitz introduced Krauss to Kurt Lewin's approach to translating a variable such as age or status into a psychological variable: The important questions were always about how something like age or status was represented in the person, what these things meant psychologically. It was this talent of Lewin's, the ability to link theory with data, that Leon Festinger (1980) has pointed to as Lewin's greatest ability. Judson Mills described the fun of sitting with Elliot Aronson and tossing around ideas for possible analogs of initiation for a cognitive dissonance study. They were trying to come up with a psychologically meaningful initiation which could then be tested. The instructions for how to create this kind of experimental fun are to be found in Aronson and Carlsmith's (1968) chapter on Experimentation in Social Psychology. The theoretical base for this kind of fun is found in Lewin's (1935) paper on Aristotelian and Galilean modes of thought.

There were, however, some differences between the way Leon Festinger and Stanley Schachter trained their students once the lab was organized. The differences were in their characteristic approaches to asking questions - Festinger from a theoretical position (although he usually had some phenomenon that led to that position) while Schachter begins with data. Schachter commented that one difference between the way he works and the way Leon Festinger works is "that when we get our hands on a phenomenon, we really follow it down to where the hell it leads - what follows from what. If there is any Lewinian touch to it, I suppose it is: What are the implications in real life." In fact, Schachter described himself as a "lousy theoretician" and said he was willing to let a piece of data change any theory he had. He contrasted his style with that of Festinger. He said, "Leon was an *excellent* theoretician but that wasn't his main schtick - you needed data first and phenomena before you did anything theoretical."

Both Schachter and Festinger had their students read widely outside of psychology to trigger ideas for their work. Aronson described Festinger's seminar as a "fertilization seminar" with the students reading "all kinds of fascinating things." Neil Grunberg described the same process in Schachter's lab. John Thibaut remembered Kurt Lewin advising, "Don't read psychology, read philosophy or history of science, poetry, novels, biographies - those were the places where you will get ideas. Psychology at this point - it will stifle your imagination."

Leon Festinger said he also used field studies to trigger ideas. He described having ideas as "an art" and said he doesn't think there is a "single good research person in the world in any field who isn't periodically *totally* depressed and sure he will never have another idea." Gradually, he said, the researcher learns to respect the fact that ideas can't be forced and it may take several months but an idea *will* come. He continued, "I think one can also develop a sense of 'well, I will have other ideas but not about *this* topic.'" He explained that this was why he left social psychology.

This gentle repsect for ideas includes how they are treated once they happen. Festinger said, "I have known many people who are so talented analytically and bright enough so that they immediately kill any idea they have. If an idea starts, it is going to be a very fragile thing. And is it probably going to remain fragile for a long time. If I have an idea, it is only at some later time that I turn self-critical, but I don't turn self-critical very early. People who *do* turn self-critical early, who are *always* critical - as critical of themselves as of other people - nothing emerges."

The Aesthetics of Social Psychology:

The recognition and valuing of form, the way a question is asked, and the careful construction of an experimental procedure, requires aesthetic taste. It is something that Leon Festinger and Stanley Schachter built on what they got from Kurt Lewin. Festinger understands the important similarites between art and science. He chose science. He contributed to both theory and method - both content and form - while at the same time respecting the artistic (non-verbaliziable he calls it) qualities inherent in having ideas and finding out what he wanted to know. This kind of sensitivity was required because of the nature of the variables these researchers worked with. Much care was given to retaining the link between theory and data - the genotypic and phenotypic in Lewin's terms. Thus, variable construction became an act of metaphor-making requiring the talent of a poet. Added to that was the style of experimentation in which the experience of the subject was carefully considered - which required the abilities of a playwright and a stage director. Robert Krauss said that Stanley Schachter would have made an "incredible" theatre director. Elliot Aronson described the design of a good "impact experiment" as playwrighting.

Being a good experimenter also requried special talent. Several of the men interviewed spoke of Lewin's student Alex Bavelas' amazing ability to involve subjects in an experimental situation. Conversely, there were people who became known as "a dead hand" because they lacked this gift. Leon Festinger took what Lewin had begun - the exploration of complex social situations in the laboratory - and refined it into an art form in the interest of science. The talents required for this task went far beyond those normally associated with being a scientist because of the complexity of the object under study. Kurt Lewin had also tapped abilities useful for his enterprise - illustrated by the heterogeneity of the students selected for the program at MIT. Once the talent is recruited, then the rest is hard work, a fact that Ross, Aronson and Festinger all emphasized.

In the late sixties, Elliot Aronson along with Merrill Carlsmith, an undergraduate student of Leon Festinger's who went to Harvard and worked with Aronson in the little house on Bow Street, wrote a chapter for the Handbook of Social Psychology (1968). In this chapter they explained what they had learned from their experience about doing laboratory experiments in social psychology and set out to demystify the process for others. The hallmark of this kind of experimentation is what Aronson and Carlsmith called "experimental realism." This comes from the care given to the situation a subject confronts in an experiment. This focus is descended from Lewin's concern about the entire life space. Aronson described the help Festinger would solicit from his students at the procedures stage of designing an experiment and how he would try out procedures on anyone who happened to be around. The procedures became little dramas with the subject as both star and audience. These dramas were constructed to insure that the subject was experiencing psychologically what the experimenters were interested in investigating. Giving form to emotional experience is one central function of art. These men were creating art and then testing it. Seen in this light, it is possible to understand some of the frustration expressed by experimental social psychologists when the ethics of their enterprise came into question. They reacted as painters would if deprived of the nude for study, simply on the grounds of moral outrage.

All of these accounts, taken together, give a picture of how a variety of very creative men go about intellectual work. Some of the components of environments that nurture such work have been pointed out. These environments inlclude the simultaneous existence of freedom and formality, whether it was a small group of men inventing methods to investigate complex social phenomena while protected by a permissive institutional environment; or creative minds working within the structure of a flexible theory; or a new idea emerging unjudged in a mind reportedly capable of devastating criticism. In each of these cases there is a formal structure but not a repressive one, allowing the coexistence of flexibility and rigor. There is a sense of when to remain loose (trying out ideas in the Quasselstrippe or the Tuesday Night meetings) and when to become tight (designing the experiment so that the link between theory and data was precise). The tolerance for ambiguity is a quality that is consistently found to characterize creative people. But it would seem that there need also be a simultaneous talent for precision - the coexistence of the artist and the scientist - and a sense of when to be which. The elaboration of such a system begs for a Lewinian analysis. Perhaps it is time to break out the chalkboard and start drawing bathtubs.

REFERENCES

Adorno, T.W., Frenkel-Brunswik, E., Levinson, D.J., & Sanford, R.N. (1950). *The authoritarian personality.* New York: Harper and Row.

Aronson, E. (1972). *The social animal.* San Francisco: W.H. Freeman Co.

Aronson, E., Blaney, N., Stephan, C., Sikes, J. & M. Snapp. (1978). *The jigsaw classroom.* Beverly Hills, CA: Sage.

Aronson, E. & Carlsmith, J.M. (1968). Experimentation in social psychology. In. G. Lindzey & E. Aronson (Eds.), *The handbook of social psychology.* (Vol. II). Reading Mass: Addison Wesley.

Aronson, E. & Mills, J. (1959). The effects of severity of initiation on liking for a group. *Journal of Abnormal and Social Psychology, 59*, 177-181.

Asch, S.E. (1946). Forming impressions of personality. *Journal of Abnormal Psychology, 41*, 258-290.

Asch, S.E. (1956). Studies of independence and conformity: I. A minority of one against a unanimous majority. *Psychological Monographs, 70*, No. 9(Whole No. 416).

Back, K.W. (1951). Influence through social communication. *Journal of Abnormal and Social Psychology, 46*, 9-23.

Barker, R., Dembo, T., & Lewin, K. (1941). Frustration and regression: An experiment with young children. *University of Iowa Studies in Child Welfare, 18*, No. 1.

Brown, J.F. (1936). *Psychology and the social order.* New York: McGraw Hill.

Campbell, D.T. (1979). A tribal model of the social system vehicle carrying scientific knowledge. *Knowledge: Creation, Diffusion, Utilization*, *1*, 181-201.

Cartwright, D. (1959). Lewinian theory as a contemporary systematic framework. In S. Koch (Ed.), *Psychology: A Study of Science*, Vol. II, New York: McGraw-Hill.

Cartwright, D. (1978). Theory and practice. *Journal of Social Issues*, *34*, 168-180

Cartwright, D. (1979). Contemporary social psychology in historical perspective. *Social Psychology Quarterly*, *42*, 82-93.

Cook, S. (1984). *Action research: Its origins and early application.* Paper presented at the American Psychological Association, Toronto, Canada.

Crutchfield, R.S. (1961). The creative process. In *Conference on the creative person.* Berkeley: University of California, Institute of Personality Assessment and Research.

Dembo, T. (1931). Der Aerger als dynamicsches Problem. *Psychologische Forschung*, *15*, 1-44.

DeRivera, J. (1976). *Field theroy as human-science: Contributions of Lewin's Berlin group.* New York: Gardner Press, Inc.

Deutsch, M. (1949). An experimental study of the effects of cooperation and competition upon group process. *Human Relations*, *2*, 199-232.

Ehrlich, D., Guttman, I., Schonback, P., & Mills, J. (1957). Post-decision exposure to relevant information. *Journal of Abnormal and Social Psychology*, *54*, 98-102.

Festinger, L. (1950). Informal social communication. *Psychological Review*, *57*, 271-282.

Festinger, L. (1954). A theory of social comparison processes. *Human Relations*, *7*, 117-140.

Festinger, L. (1957). *A theory of cognitive dissonance*. Evanston, Ill.: Row, Peterson.

Festinger, L. (Ed.) (1980). *Retrospections in social psychology*. New York: Oxford University Press.

Festinger, L. & Carlsmith, J.M. (1959). Cognitive consequences of forced compliance. *Journal of Abnormal and Social Psychology*, *58*, 203-210.

Festinger, L., Riecken, H., & Schachter, S. (1956). *When prophecy fails*. Minneapolis: University of Minnesota Press.

Festinger, L., Schachter, S., & Back, K. (1950). *Social pressure in informal groups: A study of human factors in housing*. New York: Harper & Row.

Festinger, K., & Thibaut, J. (1951). Interpersonal communication in small groups. *Journal of Abnormal and Social Psychology*, 46, 92-99.

French, J.R.P. (1950). Field experiments: Changing group productivity. In. *Experiments in social process*. New York: McGraw-Hill.

Gough, H.G. (1961). Techniques for identifying the creative research scientist. In *Conference on the creative person*. Berkeley: University of California, Institute of Personality Assessment and Research.

Heider, F. (1946). Social perception and phenomenal causality. *Psychological Review*, *51*, 358-374.

Heider, F. (1958). *The psychology of interpersonal relations*. New York: Wiley.

Hertzman, M. & Festinger, L. (1940). Shifts in explicit goals in a level of aspiration experiment. *Journal of Experimental Psychology*, *27*, 439-452.

Helson, R. (1961). Creativity, sex, and mathematics. *Conference on the creative person.* Berkeley: University of California, Institute of Personality Assessment and Research.

Hoppe, F. (1930). Erfolg und Misserfolg. *Psychologische Forschung*, *14*, 1-62.

Jones, E.E. (1978). Biography. *American Psychologist*, 58-62.

Jones, E.E. (1985). Major developments in social psychology during the past five decades. In G. Lindzey & E. Aronson (Eds.), *The handbook of social psychology.* (Vol. I). New York: Random House.

Jones, E.E. & Sigall, H. (1971). The bogus pipeline: A new paradigm for measuring affect and attitude. *Psychology Bulletin*, *76*, 349-364.

Karsten, A. (1928). Psychische Sattigung. *Psychologische Forschung*, *10*, 142-154.

Kelley, H.H. (1950). The warm-cold variable in first impressions of persons. *Journal of Personality*, *18*, 431-439.

Kelley, H.H. & Thibaut, J. (1954). Experimental studies of group problem solving and process. In G. Lindzey (Ed.), *Handbook of social psychology*, Vol 2. (pp. 735-785) Cambridge, Mass.: Addison Wesley.

Kelley, H.H. & Thibaut, J. (1978). *Interpersonal relations: A theory of interdependence.* New York: Wiley.

Lewin, K. (1935). *Dynamic theory of personality.* New York: McGraw-Hill.

Lewin, K. (1936). *Principles of topological psychology.* New York: McGraw Hill.

Lewin, K. (1938). *The conceptual representation and measurement of psychological forces.* Durham, N.C.: Duke University Press.

Lewin, K. (1943). Forces behind food habits and methods of change. *National Research Council Bulletin, 108*, 35-65.

Lewin, K. (1945). The Research Center for Group Dynamics. *Sociometry, 8*, 126-136.

Lewin, K. (1947a). Frontiers in group dynamics: I. Concept, method and reality in social science: Social equilibria and social change. *Human Relations, 1*, 5-41.

Lewin, K. (1947b). Frontiers in group dynamics: II. Challenge of group life: Social planning and action research. *Human Relations, 1*, 143-153.

Lewin, K. (1947c). Group decision and social change. In T.M. Newcomb and E.L. Hartley (Eds.), *Readings in social psychology*. New York: Henry Holt.

Lewin, K. (1948). *Resolving social conflicts*. New York: Harper and Row.

Lewin, K. (1951). *Field theory in social science.* New York: Harper & Brothers.

Lewin, K. (1986). "Everything within me rebels": A letter from Kurt Lewin to Wolfgang Koehler, 1933. *Journal of Social Issues, 4*, 37-57.

Lewin, K., Dembo, T., Festinger, L., & Sears, R. (1944). Level of aspiration. In J.M.V. Hunt (Ed.), *Personality and the Behavior Disorders.* (pp. 333-378) New York: Ronald Press.

Lewin, K., Lippitt, R., & White, R. (1939). Patterns of aggressive behavior in experimentally created "social climates." *Journal of Social Psychology, 10*, 271-299.

Lippitt, R. (1945). Kurt Lewin 1890-1947. Adventures in the exploration of interdependence. *Sociometry*, 87-97.

Lippitt, R. & French, J.R.P. (1948). Research and training: The research program on training and group life at Bethel. *The Group*. 2, 11-15.

Lippitt, R. & Radke, M. (1946). New trends in the investigation of prejudice. *The Annals of the American Academy of Political and Social Science*, *244*, 167-176.

Lippitt, R., & White, R.K. (1947). An experimental study of leadership and group life. In: Newcomb T. & Hartley (Eds.) *Readings in social psychology*. New York: Henry Holt and Co.

Lissner, K. (1935) Die Entspannung von Beduerfnissen durch Ersatzhandlungen. *Psychologische Forschung*, *18*, 218-150.

Luce, D. & Raiffa, H. (1957). *Games and decisions*. New York: Wiley.

Maccoby, N.E., Newcomb, T.M., & Hartley, E.L. (Eds.) (1958). *Readings in Social Psychology*. New York: Henry Holt & Co.

MacKinnon, D.W. (1962). The nature and nurture of creative talent. *American Psychologist*, *17*, 484-495.

Mahler, V. (1933). Ersatzhandlungen verschiedenen Realitatsgardes. *Psychologische Forschung*, *18*, 26-89.

Mandler, J.M. & Mandler, G. (1969). The diaspora of experimental psychology: The gestaltists and others. In: (D.H. Fleming, Ed.) *The intellectual migration*. Cambridge, Mass: Belknap Press. 371-419.

Marrow, A. (1969). *The practical theorist*. New York: Basic Books.

Milgram, S. (1963). Behavioral studies of obedience. *Journal of Abnormal and Social Psychology*, *67*, 371-378.

Nisbett, R.E., & Ross, L. (1980). *Human inference: Strategies and shortcomings of social judgment.* Englewood Cliffs, New Jersey: Prentice Hall.

Ovsiankina, M. (1928). Die Wiederaufnahme unterbrochenen Handlunger. *Psychologische Forschung*, *1,* 302-389.

Pepitone, A. (1950). Motivational effects in social perception. *Human Relations*, 3, 319-348.

Perlman, D. (1984). Recent developments in personality and social psychology: A citation analysis. *Personality and Social Psychology Bulletin*, *10*, 493-501.

Ross, L., J. Rodin, & P. Zimbardo. (1969) Toward an attribution therapy: The reduction of fear through induced cognitive-emotional misattribution. *Journal of Personality and Social Psychology*, *12*, 279-288.

Schachter, S. (1951). Deviation, rejection, and communication. *Journal of Abnormal and Social Psychology*, *46*, 190-208.

Schachter, S. (1959). *The psychology of affiliation.* Stanford, Calif: Stanford University Press.

Swanson, G.E., Newcomb, T.M., & Hartley, E.L. (Eds.) (1952). *Readings in social psychology.* New York: Henry Holt.

Thibaut, J. (1950). An experimental study of the cohesiveness of underprivileged groups. *Human Relations*, *3*, 251-278.

Thibaut, J., & Kelley, H.H. (1959). *The social psychology of groups*. New York: Wiley.

Triplett, N. (1898). The dynamogenic factors in pacemaking and competition. *Journal of American Psychology*, *9*, 507-533.

Zeigarnik, B. (1927). Das Behalten erledigter und unerledigter Handlungen. *Psychologische Forschung*, *9*, 1-85.

Zeigarnik, B. (1984). Kurt Lewin and Soviet Psychology. *Journal of Social Issues*, *40*, 181-192.

Zimbardo, P.G. (1969). *The cognitive control of motivation: The consequences of choice and dissonance*. Glenview, Ill.: Scott Foresman.